What the

BIBLE REALLY
TELLS US

What the
BIBLE REALLY
TELLS US

The Essential Guide to
BIBLICAL LITERACY

T. J. WRAY

ROWMAN & LITTLEFIELD PUBLISHERS, INC.
Lanham • Boulder • New York • Toronto • Plymouth, UK

Published by Rowman & Littlefield Publishers, Inc.
A wholly owned subsidiary of The Rowman & Littlefield Publishing Group, Inc.
4501 Forbes Boulevard, Suite 200, Lanham, Maryland 20706
http://www.rowmanlittlefield.com

Estover Road, Plymouth PL6 7PY, United Kingdom

Distributed by National Book Network

British Library Cataloguing in Publication Information Available

Library of Congress Cataloging-in-Publication Data
Wray, T. J.
  What the Bible really tells us : the essential guide to biblical literacy / T.J. Wray.
      p. cm.
  Includes index.
  ISBN 978-0-7425-6253-0 (cloth : alk. paper) —
  ISBN 978-1-4422-1293-0 (ebook)
  1. Bible—Criticism, interpretation, etc. I. Title.
BS511.3.W73 2011
220.6—dc22   2011011778

∞ ™ The paper used in this publication meets the minimum requirements of
American National Standard for Information Sciences—Permanence of Paper for
Printed Library Materials, ANSI/NISO Z39.48-1992.

Printed in the United States of America

For Denis
my *anam cara*,
with love

Contents

Tables

Acknowledgments

I would like to express my heartfelt appreciation to my wonderful family, especially my husband, Denis, and my children, Bob, Anne, and Jack, for their love and continued support. I am also immensely grateful for the many friends and colleagues who continue to encourage and affirm my work, especially Walter Burr, the man who started it all, Fr. Raymond Collins, and Dr. John Greeley. Thanks also to my agent, Rob McQuilkin; my editor, Sarah Stanton; and my production editor, Patricia Stevenson, for their patience, enthusiasm, and dedication to this important project. Finally, a big thank-you to my amazing students at Salve Regina University, whose curiosity and questions served as the inspiration behind this book.

Introduction

Always bear in mind that your own resolution to succeed is more important than any other.

—ABRAHAM LINCOLN

I magine this: Your best friend tells you that she has recently joined a club. Not only has *she* joined this club, but she also signed up her entire family for membership. This club requires weekly meetings and monetary donations, and members must follow a set of rules and regulations, many of which are challenging and difficult. The club leader, whom members are expected to support financially, inspires and guides the group so that the rules can be followed more diligently. In exchange for their support and commitment, members enjoy being part of a larger community who share similar values and beliefs grounded in a set of ancient writings that serve as the guiding moral compass for the club.

You might feel compelled to ask your friend a few questions about this club and its curious book of laws. "Where did this club originate? Who is its founder? Who wrote the guidebook for this club? What is the club's vision or mission? Who is the leader of the club and where does he or she get his or her authority?" Interestingly, your friend shrugs and answers each question the same way: "It's all in the book." Naturally, you assume that she has read and carefully studied "the book" at great length before undertaking such a huge commitment. So imagine how shocked you would be to learn that your friend has never actually taken the time to read the book at all.

Strange as this little scenario may seem, it nonetheless exemplifies the way in which many of us unquestioningly approach the Bible and our faith. Since most of us inherit the religion of our family, we end up simply going through the motions, performing rituals, honoring holy days, and reciting the prayers our parents taught to us as children. All admirable—if only we had an inkling as to what all of it really means.

Even though few Americans actually read the Bible, most still believe it to be a holy and authoritative book. A recent Gallup poll asked a group of over a thousand Americans to declare which of the following statements comes closest to describing their views about the Bible:

a. The Bible is the actual word of God and is to be taken literally, word for word.
b. The Bible is inspired by God and the work of human agents, but not everything in it is to be taken literally.
c. The Bible is a collection of ancient fables, history, and legends recorded by man.

Of those polled, 31 percent said they believe the Bible is the actual word of God and that it should be taken literally, while 47 percent said that the Bible, though inspired by God, should not always be taken literally. Only 19 percent stated that they believe the Bible is a collection of ancient fables, history, and legends recorded by humans. We can conclude, then, that the overwhelming majority of those polled at the very least take the Bible seriously.

While the results of this poll, and others like it, are not necessarily surprising, it presents us with an interesting paradox. If the Bible occupies such an important place in the lives of the majority of Americans, then we might logically assume that this vast majority has actually studied—or at least read—the Bible; but this seems *not* to be the case. Based on my many years teaching and talking to various religious (and nonreligious) groups about the Bible, I have come to believe that, for many, the Bible has become more of a *symbol* of faith—much like a cross or an icon—rather than inspired writings that have sustained generations through the joys and tragedies of life.

But how, you might ask, can someone profess belief in a Bible-based religion without first knowing and understanding what the Bible actually says? Good question. After all, most of us would not claim to be a Shakespearean scholar simply because we had a book of his sonnets or had read a few of his plays. We would feel too intimidated to engage in any kind of meaningful debate with a true Shakespearean scholar, recognizing our own lack of knowledge in this area. Instead, we would likely listen and learn; and hopefully, that scholar would have something to teach us about Shakespeare—who Shakespeare was, what he wrote, the history that informs his writings, and how his sonnets are meant to be read and his plays understood.

In the case of the Bible, however, the faithful and faithless alike often feel as if they are somehow automatically competent to discuss the Bible simply because they have a dusty copy of it on their bookshelf. And I am speaking from personal experience here. Oftentimes, when people find out what I teach, they waste no time trying to engage me in a discussion about such hot-button issues as abortion or homosexuality, invoking what they believe to be valid biblical precepts that they have likely garnered from television preachers, magazines, or the Internet. Few, if any, have ever studied the Bible in a serious way with a competent teacher.

Everyone is certainly entitled to express an opinion; however, when it comes to ancient texts like the Bible, many lack even the most basic skills of discernment. Because most people are not equipped to interpret the Bible for themselves, they rely on others to interpret it for them. Unfortunately, often the people entrusted with this task, including many members of the clergy, have had little or no formal training in biblical studies.

Now, more than ever, there is an urgent need to address the dangers of biblical illiteracy. In the post-9/11 world of suicide bombers, "satanic" regimes, and religious fanaticism, people have turned to the Bible with greater intensity looking for guidance, consolation, and answers as to why the world has become so fraught with peril and uncertainty. For the average person, however, thumbing through the pages of the Bible in search of such answers can prove to be a difficult task, because, quite frankly, most people do not know where to begin. In frustration, most abandon their efforts and instead rely on "those in the know" to provide answers to life's most vexing problems. There is a steady stable of televangelists, radio talk show hosts, and celebrities, as well as numerous homegrown Internet sites that purport to have the real truth. But most of these "resources" are filled with misinterpretations, misapplications, and downright distortions regarding what the Bible says and what it teaches.

While ignorance of Scripture is commonplace today, it is actually an age-old problem. Throughout history, the Bible has been used to defend such atrocities as the Crusades, the Spanish Inquisition, environmental exploitation, subjugation of women (including wife beating), and countless other acts of human barbarity, simply because someone in power interpreted a particular passage in the wrong way.

What the Bible Really Tells Us seeks to address the real and urgent problem of contemporary biblical illiteracy. As a seasoned professor of religious studies, each semester, I stand before a new crop of students, most of whom have never read a single page of the Bible. A few will become as captivated by the Bible as I was so many years ago (and continue to be) and will devote themselves to further study. But most are taking my class not because they are particularly interested in learning about the Bible, but because it is part of an academic requirement. I know, however, that once they begin to read and understand the Bible, including its complex history and various literary styles, they will come to appreciate its genius. Still, given my diverse audience, I must proceed with caution. One of my initial goals as their teacher is to help my students gain confidence in approaching the biblical text. To this end, I have developed a method of education without intimidation that enables students to navigate the Bible with relative ease in just a few classes. *What the Bible Really Tells Us* employs this tried-and-true method, which, very generally, begins by first addressing some of the causes of biblical illiteracy (the Problem), followed by a method that leads to biblical competency (the Solution).

This is not, however, a "how to read the Bible" book. There are plenty of those and most are pedantic, preachy, or mired in scholarly jargon that often seems to dismiss the primacy of the Bible for the millions of people who "take it very seriously." This book will certainly disappoint those readers for whom the Bible is beyond analysis, a divine document to be trusted and obeyed but never subjected to interpretation. Likewise, this book will also disappoint those who wish to see the Bible exposed as an antiquated and primitive text that has little bearing on modern life. The Bible cannot be relegated to either of these extreme views.

In this book, we will seek to understand the communications of the ancient Jewish and Christian communities whose struggles were so different from and so similar to our own. In order to understand their writings, we will pay close attention to the meaning of their words, the structures of their speech, and the circumstances of their lives. Beyond these philological and historical facets, however, great ambiguities remain.

Almost daily, someone will tell me that they would like to read the Bible but complain that it takes too much time or that the language of the Bible is too confusing. "I've tried to read the Bible at least a dozen times over the years," a student said recently, "but I've never gotten much past Genesis before just giving up. I can't seem to keep all those names and places and who begat who in my head."

My student is not alone. Chances are, if you picked up this book, then you have probably also tried and failed in your commitment to read the Bible. And it is little wonder so many people throw in the towel and simply give up after a few chapters. We are, after all, dealing with a vast and varied collection of ancient texts. Most of us, for example, might feel overwhelmed trying to decipher ancient Babylonian epics or ancient Greek poetry, so it stands to reason that the ancient Jewish and Christian writings that comprise the Bible might be a little intimidating to a lot of people.

I understand the trepidations and excuses because I hear them all the time from my students, friends, family, and colleagues. But I also know that gaining proficiency in reading the Bible is not rocket science. For the past twenty years, I have taught people of all ages how to read and understand the Bible in a relatively short period of time. You do not need a wall full of fancy degrees or an inordinate amount of time. What you do need is an interest, a bit of determination, a good deal of patience (especially at the beginning, when everything seems so new), and an attitude of openness to learning new things. I have arranged the chapters to ease you into the process. The first three chapters are designed to help you understand the problems of biblical illiteracy and to arm you with some basic tools to help you to better read and understand the Bible. The seven biblical themes that occupy chapters 4 through 10 will expose you to a variety of biblical texts and allow you to begin to use these tools.

In chapter 1, readers are invited to take the Sixty-Second Super-Easy Bible Quiz. This quiz requires you to answer five basic true/false questions about the Bible, followed by a detailed explanation of why a particular question is either true or false. Designed to help measure how much you already know—or do not know—about the Bible, this brief quiz serves as the first step in identifying the Problem.

Chapter 2 explores the roots of the Problem from a historical perspective so that you can begin to understand the causes of biblical illiteracy. Having established the likely causes of the Problem today, subsequent chapters constitute a methodology that works toward the Solution.

Intended as a reference chapter to which you may return time and time again, the Solution begins in chapter 3. This chapter will give you a crash course in Bible basics, including such things as the geography of the Ancient Near East (ANE), something about its history, and the authorship and arrangement of the various biblical texts. Once you have some basic understanding of the world of biblical antiquity, chapters 4 through 10 will explore seven important biblical themes: suffering; Heaven and hell; wealth and riches; sexuality and gender; law and justice; the environment; and, finally, prayer and worship. You will not only learn something of what the Bible has to say about these important issues but also understand the context in which the various texts we will consider are written.

In order to better facilitate learning, chapters dealing with the seven biblical themes will follow a predictable format that basically begins with a brief introduction, followed by several statements that reflect commonly held assumptions many people, but particularly my students, have about the biblical theme under consideration. In my university classroom, when I bring up a topic, such as money, sex, or the environment, I conduct a brief poll of sorts and ask students to tell me what they believe the Bible says about the topic. Over the years, their responses have become quite predictable. I have included three to five of these common assumptions in each of the seven thematic chapters. Although my students serve as my primary source in assembling the common assumptions, I have also taken into account the many workshops, presentations, and catechetical work I have done with people of all ages and from all backgrounds. In any case, each of these assumptions will be then explored in light of what the Bible actually says—or does not say—about it. For example, chapter 5, "Final Destinations: Heaven and Hell," examines what the Bible has to say about life after death. The most popular commonly held assumptions people have regarding our postmortem fate are as follows (remember that the respondents believe these assumptions come directly from the Bible):

1. The Bible describes Heaven and hell in great detail.
2. The Bible tells us that good people go to Heaven and bad people go to hell.
3. The Bible teaches us that Heaven is a place of repose, where we meet all of our dead relatives and enjoy the company of God for all eternity.
4. The Bible teaches us that hell is a place of unending torment, ruled by Satan.

We will explore these assumptions by turning to the Bible and examining what it has to say in light of what we know about the text or texts in question. This means that you are expected to read the Bible alongside this book—for this is the primary means by which you will gain both competence and confidence in understanding what the Bible really says. While I do not promote one translation of the Bible over another (currently, there are dozens of English translations available, from the King James Version to the Revised English Bible), I have chosen to use the New Oxford Annotated Bible (the New Revised Standard Version, or NRSV) and all citations, unless otherwise noted, come from that translation. Whichever translation you use, be certain that your translation is a study Bible. I will speak more about this in chapter 3, but for now, just know that study Bibles provide maps, commentaries, and footnotes that can be helpful for both the novice and the seasoned reader.

Chapters 4 and 5 will use a more general approach and explore key texts in the Bible that help to either support or negate the various assumptions. This initial approach is intended to bring the reader along slowly, but you will notice a shift in approach in chapters 6 through 10. In these chapters, I will assume that you are better able to engage the biblical text and, accordingly, I will use a more focused approach and offer commentary on each individual assumption. The shift is subtle, but I want to alert you to it at the outset. I will offer a brief reminder of the differences in approach in chapters 4 and 6.

It is important to note that our exploration of each theme is not meant to be an exhaustive endeavor; each of our topics could be (and have been) the subject of an entire book. Moreover, I know from experience that information overload is the quickest way for students to lose interest and fail. The idea here is to engage the Bible with topics that are of likely interest to most readers, and to illuminate the big picture, rather than providing a comprehensive treatment of each subject. You will note that I often return to key texts and characters—such as the Creation stories, the Exodus tale, and certain of Jesus' parables—not only because they are germane to the topic or theme but also as a way to probe the texts more deeply in a variety of contexts.

Regardless of theme or passage under consideration, you must pause and ask yourself three fundamental questions:

1. What does this passage have to say about God?
2. What does this passage have to say about me?
3. What does this passage have to say about others (community)?

These questions serve as the driving force behind every story, poem, prophecy, or parable in the Bible, and they are key in unlocking the profound lessons the biblical writers seek to impart to us. Try to keep these three questions in mind as we move forward.

In discussing each theme, I have tried to remain faithful to the thoughts, ideas, and intentions (as well as I discern them) of the biblical author or authors, something I hope you will also learn to do. This does not mean, however, that my interpretations are definitive (and yours will not be either). One of the many reasons the Bible has survived for over two millennia is because various individuals and groups have felt strengthened and nourished by a particular story due to the manner in which they understood it. Whether you read the Bible for pure enjoyment, intellectual curiosity, or to enliven your faith, my primary goal is to empower you to interpret the text accurately. I hope you will view this book as a starting point for further study. To that end, I have provided an extensive resources section at the end of this book.

There are several technical issues that are fundamentally important as we begin our journey together. The first has to do with the way in which I refer to the two main sections of the Bible, commonly called the "Old Testament" and the "New Testament." While I will refer to the second main section of the Bible by its common designation, the "New Testament," I prefer the term "Hebrew Bible" rather than "Old Testament"

when referring to the first main section of the Bible. While the terms "Old Testament" and "Hebrew Bible" are often used interchangeably, I feel the latter designation is not only more accurate but also more respectful of Judaism. (The Christian designation "Old Testament" carries a somewhat negative connotation for many because the adjective "old" implies something outdated and in need of replacement.)

The second issue has to do with the use of inclusive language, in particular, the way in which I refer to God (Yhwh). Although there are references to God in the Hebrew Bible that are feminine, the overwhelming majority of references reflect the patriarchal assumption at the time that God is male. I have tried to use inclusive language for God when possible and appropriate. There are times, however, when inclusive language makes reading difficult and confusing—and it deviates from the text and the author's intention. Often, the practice appears contrived and artificial to the point of making a mockery of the convention. To avoid both confusion and the appearance of political correctness for political correctness's sake, there will be times when I reluctantly resort to the traditional practice of assigning the male pronoun to God.

The third issue has to do with biblical citations. Sometimes, I will include certain passages and other times, I will simply offer a parenthetical citation with the book(s), chapter(s), and verse(s), as in (Genesis 1–3). In order to gain a fuller understanding of the commentary I provide, I encourage you to read all parenthetical citations. The various books of the Bible are usually abbreviated when a chapter includes verses, but spelled out when an entire chapter is cited. I will also sometimes list texts for you to examine and compare to a particular passage, using the common abbreviation "cf." (from the Latin word *confer*, meaning compare). For a list of all of the books in both the Hebrew Bible and the New Testament, including their abbreviations, please refer to tables 3.1 and 3.2 found in chapter 3.

Finally, in keeping with the conventions of modern historical and biblical scholarship, I will use BCE (Before the Common Era) instead of BC (Before Christ) and CE (Common Era) rather than AD (*Anno Domini*, Latin for "In the year of our Lord") when indicating specific dates.

At the beginning of each new semester, I hold up the Bible and say to my class: "This is a book that has changed the lives of millions of people. It has inspired, comforted, and sustained generations through the countless challenges of life. But, it has also been used as a way to justify hatred, war, and every imaginable social injustice under the sun, all in the name of God. It is my hope that by the end of the semester, you will be able to read and understand the Bible, to discuss it intelligently with others, and to recognize when others abuse it." This is also my hope for everyone who reads *What the Bible Really Tells Us*.

Take the Test

THE SIXTY-SECOND SUPER-EASY BIBLE QUIZ

The important thing is not to stop questioning. Curiosity has its own reason for existing.

—ALBERT EINSTEIN

There is nothing students hate more than the dreaded pop quiz. Having spent the better part of my life on the other side of the lectern, I also detested pop quizzes and now, as a professor, I generally do not give them to my students. I do, however, make one exception: At the start of each semester, I begin all of my Bible courses with the Sixty-Second Super-Easy Bible Quiz. This short, five-question, true-or-false quiz provides me with a quick and easy way to assess how much my students already know—or do not know—about the Bible. Students generally groan when, on the first day of class, I tell them that I am giving them a quiz, but when I reassure them that this quiz will not be collected or graded, there is a collective sigh of relief.

As I pass out the quiz, I instruct the class to answer each question with their first gut response; most finish in less than thirty seconds, and few find any of the questions the least bit challenging. In fact, I often overhear students commenting to their neighbors that if this quiz is any indication of the caliber of the course, then the class will surely be a "cakewalk."

After students complete the quiz, we review each question and discuss their responses, first with a general show of hands as I ask: Who thinks the question is true? Who thinks the question is false? I allow time for students to offer comments or rationales for why they believe an answer to a certain question is true or false. Then it is my turn. Within minutes, the illusions of a "cakewalk" class disappear like a plate of brownies in a frat house.

As a class, we open the Bible to the passage or passages that relate to the question under consideration and probe a bit deeper. For most, this is the first time they have ever taken the biblical text in hand and moved their eyes and fingers across the page. And, for the vast majority, it is also the first time they have ever entered into a serious conversation about the Bible. It is always an important moment, not only for my students but also for me, because I know that by the end of the term, there will be thirty more biblically literate people in the world.

It seems fitting, then, to begin this book with the same quiz that I use in my university classroom. My instructions for you are the same instructions I give to my own students: Answer the following true/false questions in under sixty seconds. Once you have answered all of the questions, turn the page to check your answers and read the commentary that follows each question. If you have a Bible handy, you might want to take it out so that you can read the relevant passages for yourself. Though I will include key verses in my explanations after each question, it will be good practice for you to begin to actually read the passages for yourself. Good luck!

The Sixty-Second Super-Easy Bible Quiz

Question One

True or False: Eve tempts Adam with an apple in the Garden of Eden.

Question Two

True or False: Moses is God's willing leader who frees the Israelites from Egyptian bondage.

Question Three

True or False: David is Israel's first king.

Question Four

True or False: Three Wise Men bring gifts to the baby Jesus in Bethlehem.

Question Five

True or False: Some of Jesus' Apostles (Matthew, Mark, Luke, and John) write the Gospel accounts of his life, death, and resurrection.

Finished? Turn the page and check your answers!

Question One: True or False—Eve tempts Adam with an apple in the Garden of Eden

The answer to question one is FALSE. If you answered this first question incorrectly, take heart; you are not alone. The majority of my students also fail to correctly answer this deceptively simple question, and they usually respond with incredulity when I tell them that the answer is, in fact, false. Some students seem genuinely confused and usually respond defensively: "How can the answer be *false*? Everyone knows that Eve is the temptress who lures Adam to eat the forbidden apple! In my Sunday school class, we were taught that Eve is responsible for the Fall!" In their protests, they often cling to their incorrect answer, rereading the question in search of some sort of trickery. Surely their Sunday school teachers, parents, and preachers cannot all be wrong! They demand proof, and so, together, we read the passage that deals with this question (Gen 3:1–6).

Before we engage the text, however, I alert the class to the fact that the story of Adam and Eve is really the second of *two* Creation narratives found in the first book of the Bible, Genesis, and that different authors write their version of events during different periods of time and for different audiences. The first Creation story (Gen 1–2:4)—the one in which God creates the Earth in six days and rests on the seventh (the Sabbath)—opens the Bible with its majestic prose, "In the beginning . . ." This particular version is written during the sixth century BCE, while the story of Adam and Eve (Gen 2:4–3:24) is written during the ninth century BCE. This means that the Adam and Eve story is actually the *earlier* version of the two Creation accounts. Curiously, even though the Adam and Eve story is the older of the two, it appears second in the canon (*canon* is from the Greek word meaning "rule" and refers to the official books of the Bible). Most students are surprised to learn that there are actually *two* completely different Creation stories that appear side by side in Genesis, and some ask why *both* traditions have been preserved. The simple answer is that both stories are well known and treasured during biblical antiquity and the biblical editors who compile the various texts to be included in the canon feel that both stories are of equal importance.

We often see this sort of thing in the Bible. For example, there are two conflicting traditions of the well-known story of Noah's Ark, again penned by two different authors—the same authors who also write the two Creation accounts. These authors are commonly known by the simple designations of "P" and "J." The writer known as P, which stands for "Priestly," is the author of the first Creation story. In the P version of the Noah tale, Noah is instructed by the LORD to bring a male and female pair of every animal aboard the ark (Gen 6:19; 7:8–9, 15), while the author known simply as "J," which stands for "Yahwist" (in German, *Jahwist*, thus the designation "J"), states that Noah should bring seven pairs of "clean" animals and one pair of "unclean" animals aboard the ark. The J author is also credited with writing the Adam and Eve story. Other differences in the Noah story include the fact that P refers to the LORD as *God* while J always calls the Deity *Yhwh*. In the P version, the rain and the gradual receding of the water lasts for a year, but in J's version, it rains for forty days and nights and the water recedes over forty days. Finally, P has Noah sending forth a dove from the ark, but in the J version, he sends a raven.

Despite these and many other differences in each version of the Noah tale, a later editor, sometimes called a "redactor," has woven both stories together into a single narrative. Most people have never read the text closely enough to discern this fact. Which brings us to yet another crucial point to keep in mind as we move forward: The Bible has been heavily edited.

But we are getting ahead of ourselves. Questions of canonization (the process by which certain books are either included or excluded from the Bible), authorship (who wrote—or who we think wrote—the different books found in the Bible), various translations of the Bible (the New Revised Standard Version, the King James, and the New American Bible, just to name a few), and other technical issues related to the Bible will be addressed in more detail later. For the moment, let us first return to the reasons why question one is false by examining the passage that supposedly contains the temptation scene in the Garden of Eden:

> Now the serpent was more crafty than any other wild animal that the LORD God had made. He said to the woman, "Did God say, 'You shall not eat from any tree in the garden'?" The woman said to the serpent, "We may eat of the fruit of the trees in the garden; but God said, 'You shall not eat of the fruit of the tree that is in the middle of the garden, nor shall you touch it, or you shall die.'" But the serpent said to the woman, "You will not die; for God knows that when you eat of it your eyes will be opened, and you will be like God, knowing good and evil." So when the woman saw that the tree was good for food, and that it was a delight to the eyes, and that the tree was to be desired to make one wise, she took of its fruit and ate; and she also gave some to her husband, who was with her, and he ate. (Gen 3:1–6)

A careful reading of Gen 3:1–6 yields several important facts: For starters, there is no mention of the *kind* of fruit that proves to be so irresistible to humans. Why, then, do we all seem to think that the fruit is an apple? Most scholars subscribe to one of two theories, the first of which has to do with translation. In the sixth century, a Latin translation of this passage erroneously renders the word "fruit" as "apple," reflecting the common belief that the forbidden fruit is indeed an apple, and thus perpetuating the misconception. But how does this common belief emerge in the first place? Some scholars trace this to a Latin pun on *malus* (apple) and *malum* (evil), thus connecting the fruit (and, by association, Eve) to something bad. The second theory is that apples are connected to knowledge and since the fruit comes from the tree of knowledge, it is generally assumed that it must be an apple. There are also sexual connotations associated with the fruit because, in Hebrew, the verb "to know" (as in "he knew her in the biblical sense") can also refer to sexual intercourse. This may explain why Eve is usually branded as a seductress.

Mindful of the fact that apples are not a typical Middle Eastern fruit (they do not grow well in this area of the world), Jewish sources cite the fruit as either grapes or possibly a fig. But all of this is merely conjecture, as the text simply reads "fruit." What we can say for certain, however, is that the author of this story is not interested in details such as the type of fruit—not because it does not matter—but because the overall lesson of the story has nothing to do with the *kind* of fruit. The focus of the story has to do with obedience and adherence to God's command to refrain from eating the fruit, something that the man and woman fail to do.

Another reason why this first quiz question is untrue has to do with the so-called temptation scene. The image of Eve luring her mate with an apple has been the subject of countless paintings, songs, poems, and even beer commercials, but as seductive as this image may be, it is nonetheless biblically inaccurate. Again, a close reading of the text shows that Adam is actually standing *alongside* Eve during her conversation with the snake, and even though he is perfectly aware of God's prohibition against eating the fruit, he does nothing to remind Eve of God's grave injunction: "You may freely eat of every tree of the garden; but of the tree of the knowledge of good and evil you shall not eat, for in the day that you eat of it you shall die" (Gen 2:16–17). Interestingly, Eve is not yet created when God issues this command to Adam; God does not create the woman until several verses later (Gen 2:21–22).

Of course, whether or not Eve is present when God makes it clear to Adam that certain trees are off-limits is somewhat immaterial. During her conversation with the snake, it is obvious that Eve understands that the fruit is forbidden. We can assume that perhaps Adam warns her about this or that God, at some point, tells Eve directly not to eat the fruit, though the story does not explicitly state either. By making these assumptions, however, we are alerted to the fact that people make assumptions about what the Bible says all of the time. When a particular story lacks certain details, as in the case with Eve and her knowledge of the forbidden fruit, there is a human tendency to fill in the cracks or to connect the dots, making the story say what we think it *ought* to say. This, of course, can lead to misunderstanding, and we run the risk of distorting the author's original intentions.

In many ways, the scene is a bit of a letdown. Eve simply looks at the fruit and thinks it will make her wise and that it appears to be tasty. She takes some of the fruit and gives some to her husband, and *both of them eat it*. Today, we might call this simple act "sharing." But that would miss the point of the story, for this is not a story about sharing. This is a story about obedience. If God says do not eat the fruit, then humans must obey; there is no room for quibbling or rationalizing one's actions. In the Bible, when God says no, God means *no*. This is an important lesson and one that reverberates throughout the Bible. And it is the central lesson of this particular story.

One final comment on quiz question number one: Students sometimes mark this question false (the correct answer), but for the wrong reason. That is, some students feel that this question is false because they believe that it is the Devil, in the guise of the snake, who tempts Adam and Eve to eat the fruit. While it is clear that both Adam and Eve are present during Eve's discussion with the snake—and it is equally clear that the snake is rather convincing—the notion that the snake is anything more than just a snake is a very common misconception. Nowhere in the story does it state—or imply—that the serpent is actually a demonic figure of any kind—and most certainly not the Devil or Satan of later (much later) Jewish and Christian lore. The anonymous author or authors of this story have no real under-standing of a satanic figure capable of undermining God's dictates. During this time period, God, and God alone, is the source of good and evil. God himself states this emphatically in the book of Isaiah:

> I am the LORD, and there is
> no other.
> I form light and create darkness,
> I make weal and create woe;
> I the LORD do all these things. (Is 45:6–7)

The idea of an evil being—Satan—who stands in opposition to God *does* eventually emerge in Jewish and Christian thought, but this idea takes centuries to materialize.

The snake, therefore, is simply one of God's creatures. Incidentally, it is the English poet, John Milton, who is the first to cast Satan in the role of the serpent in his classic *Paradise Lost* (1667). In Milton's poem, Satan is a highly developed figure who commands a legion of other demons. Milton's Satan slithers into the Garden of Eden, assumes the form of a snake, and lures Adam and Eve to sin. While this scenario is absent in the biblical account, it nonetheless serves as an excellent example of how certain writings outside the pages of holy writ can sometimes bleed into our religious narratives. Over time, the biblically illiterate masses come to accept Milton's work of fiction as part of their gospel truth, assuming that his epic poem comes from the pages of the Bible. Had the masses actually *read* the Bible, they would understand Milton's poem as a work of fiction and his characterization of Satan as the snake in Garden of Eden as part of Milton's genius imagination.

Of course, many of Milton's countrymen and women were illiterate, so this conflation of fact and fiction is somewhat understandable; but even today this sort of blending of stories continues. We often fail to check the facts and assume that if a preacher or teacher says something, it must be true. I hope that after reading this book, you will no longer simply accept the conventional wisdom or rely on hearsay but will instead feel confident in turning to the source, the Bible, to read and understand the story for yourself.

With this very brief explanation of question one, we now move ahead to question number two.

Question Two: True or False—Moses is God's willing leader who frees the Israelites from Egyptian bondage

The answer to question two is FALSE. Before we explore why this second quiz question is false, it seems prudent to say a few words about Moses, whose story begins in the second book of the Bible, Exodus, and continues through the rest of the Torah (the first five books of the Bible, also known as the Pentateuch, meaning "five scrolls" in Greek). Moses is a towering biblical figure, admired not only for his courage but also for his unique and efficacious relationship with the LORD. Though you may have never actually read the story of Moses in the Bible, you are probably more familiar with it than most Bible stories. Many of us have seen Hollywood's version of the Moses story, most notably the Cecile B. DeMille classic, *The Ten Commandments*, or perhaps the DreamWorks adaptation, *The Prince of Egypt*.

According to the biblical version of the story, Moses, the son of Hebrew slaves, is born during a very precarious time for the Children of Israel. Many years earlier, the Israelites migrate from their home in Canaan (roughly the same geographic area as modern Israel/Palestine) to Egypt in search of food during a famine. Mass migrations due to famines are quite common during this time, and archaeological evidence supports this aspect of the story. The Israelites end up settling in Egypt and, for reasons that are not clear, they are eventually enslaved under a ruthless unnamed Egyptian Pharaoh. Paranoid that the Hebrew men will someday rise up against him, Pharaoh begins a killing campaign. He commands the midwives, Shiphrah and Puah, to kill all the newborn baby boys that they deliver to the Hebrew slave women; the girls, however, may live. Pharaoh knows that it is men who make war, and it is best to cut off the tree before it has a chance to sprout. Pharaoh does not appear to be a very forward-thinking sort of leader, however, and apparently does not realize that in murdering all the Hebrew male infants, he will effectively eliminate much of his future slave labor force.

Thanks to the heroic efforts of several women, however, including the midwives, who bravely ignore Pharaoh's decree, and Moses' mother, Jochebed, who hides him from the authorities, Moses escapes death. Unable to conceal him any longer, Jochebed places Moses in a basket, and, under the watchful eye of his big sister, Miriam, sets him adrift down the Nile River. Jochebed's motivations for doing this are not revealed in the text, but her actions result in a huge ironic twist: Pharaoh's own daughter retrieves the basket and adopts Moses, raising him as an Egyptian prince right under the nose of her father!

After narrating these events, the Bible, in typical fast-forward fashion, presents us with a suddenly grown-up Moses. The initial portrait of the adult Moses, however, is not a very flattering one. Witnessing an Egyptian taskmaster beating a Hebrew slave, Moses kills the Egyptian and hides the body in the desert sand. Fearing prosecution, he runs away to a distant land. Thinking he has left his old life behind, he settles down with a wife, has a son, and works as a shepherd.

So far, Moses is not what we might expect of a hero. After all, he is a murderer and a coward who tries to run away from his past. But then—and now—wherever we go, our past is not far behind. Moses' bucolic life takes a sudden and dramatic turn when God appears to him in the flames of a bush that is on fire, but not consumed. God calls and commissions Moses to rescue his fellow Israelites from the shackles of Egyptian enslavement.

It is in the commissioning scene that we find the reason why question number two is false, for while the Bible does indeed credit Moses as the liberator of the Israelites from slavery, he is not exactly *willing*. When God calls, Moses expresses reluctance:

> Then Moses answered, "But suppose they do not believe me or listen to me, but say, 'The LORD did not appear to you.'" . . . But Moses said to the LORD, "O my LORD, I have never been eloquent, neither in the past nor even now that you have spoken to your servant; but I am slow of speech and slow of tongue." Then the LORD said to him, "Who gives speech to mortals? Who makes them mute or deaf, seeing or blind? Is it not I, the LORD? Now go, and I will be with your mouth and teach you what you are to speak." But he said, "O my LORD, please send someone else." (Exod 4:1, 10–13)

As we can see from this short passage, Moses would just as soon pass on the LORD's summons to liberate his own people from slavery. In fact, his litany of excuses is almost comical: He fears that the Israelites will not listen to him, complains that he is a poor speaker ("slow of speech and tongue" is actually the Bible's way of saying that Moses is a stutterer), and even goes so far as to suggest that perhaps the LORD should send someone else!

While all of this may seem confusing—for this flawed image of Moses is certainly not the Moses presented in movies or in Sunday school—displaying reluctance to God's call is actually a common biblical motif. Most of the prophets, in fact, respond in much the same way as Moses. Perhaps it is Moses' all-too-human failings and his initial reticence to answer God's call that is so appealing to the ancient author and audience. For, if God can take the likes of Moses—a murderer, coward, and ineloquent speaker—and transform him into a fearless leader, then there is hope for us as well. Maybe this is the reason why the story of Moses continues to intrigue and inspire us even today. I will have more to say about Moses in chapter 8, as he is a key player in the unfolding story of the people of Israel.

Questions number one and two are false, but what about question number three?

Question Three: True or False—David is Israel's first king

The answer to question three is also FALSE. In my university classroom, I usually begin our discussion of this question with another, more general question. I ask my students if they can name any of the dozens of kings mentioned in the Bible. More often than not, the only kings they are able to recall are King David and, occasionally, David's son and successor, King Solomon, the architect and builder of the great Temple in Jerusalem.

While David is certainly Israel's most *popular* king, the first king is a man named Saul. Although the better-known exploits of Israel's charismatic *second* king, David, a "man after the LORD's heart" (1 Sam 13:14), often eclipse Saul's story, King Saul's rapid rise to power and his tragic fall from the LORD's grace is one of the most heartrending stories in the Bible.

David is described as an ambitious, though somewhat corrupt, leader, while Saul is portrayed as a tall, handsome, unassuming young man (1 Sam 9:2) who has no interest in becoming king. But the influential prophet Samuel eventually persuades Saul to accept this honor. As a new monarch, King Saul has several successful initial exploits, including a stunning victory over one of Israel's archenemies, the Ammonites (1 Samuel 11). Saul's early successes, however, are short-lived. Perhaps it is his lack of maturity, poor counsel from those close to him, or the inevitable corruption that comes with power, but Saul and his kingship soon begin to unravel.

Through a series of foolish, heretical, and politically inept episodes, Saul slowly loses control—of his kingdom, his family, and ultimately his mind. Most disturbing of all, however, is the fact that God sends a "tormenting spirit" to harass poor Saul (1 Sam 16:14). And, in what modern psychologists might label as schizophrenia or some other profound mental disorder, this "tormenting spirit" causes Saul to behave erratically. Consumed with paranoia, Saul becomes deeply depressed and is plagued by strange voices and visions.

As Saul spirals downward, David is waiting in the wings, biding his time and growing in popularity among the people. Eventually, the citizenry (including Saul's own children) begin to fear Saul's violent outbursts and bizarre behavior and switch their alliances in favor of the politically savvy David. Sadly, Saul and his sons are killed in a battle against the Philistines (1 Sam 31:6) and their bodies are desecrated. This tragedy opens the door for David, who now ascends to the throne. Though he becomes a typical royal despot, the LORD nonetheless favors him, and David remains Israel's most powerful and memorable *second* king.

And so, the first three questions are all false. When I give this quiz to my class, students who have been confident in their first three answers and eagerly raise their hands when I ask, "How many of you think this question is true? How many of you think this question is false?" are now less confident. They wonder if perhaps all of the questions are false or if the first three questions are designed to trick them into answering false for the final two. They look nervously at their answer to question four, which seems to be the easiest question so far, and most students feel as if they have finally answered at least one question correctly. How did you respond?

Question Four: True or False—Three Wise Men bring gifts to the baby Jesus in Bethlehem

The answer to question four is FALSE. The delightful story of the mysterious visitors on a quest to find the baby Jesus is found only in Matthew's Gospel, the first of the four canonical Gospels in the New Testament. Although the Gospel of Matthew appears first in the canon, it is not the first Gospel written. That distinction goes to the Gospel of Mark, written in about 70 CE, followed by Luke in 85 CE, then Matthew, which dates to about 90 CE, and finally the Gospel of John, which is written in about 95 CE. Students sometimes question why the Gospels are arranged out of chronological sequence, and scholars have proposed various theories in this regard, but the simplest answer is that the Gospel of Matthew, particularly favored by early Christians, is placed first in the canon as a way to honor it and convey its special stature.

Only two of the four Gospels, Matthew and Luke, offer us an account of Jesus' birth, while Mark and John open with an adult Jesus. Though we tend to commingle both of the birth stories in Matthew and Luke, the so-called infancy narratives are actually quite different. Luke recounts the familiar story of the inn with no room and the shepherds in the field who receive an angelic visitation:

> In that region there were shepherds living in the fields, keeping watch over their flock by night. Then an angel of the Lord stood before them, and the glory of the Lord shone around them, and they were terrified. But the angel said to them, "Do not be afraid; for see—I am bringing you good news of great joy for all the people: to you is born this day in the city of David a Savior, who is the Messiah, the Lord." (Luke 2:8–11)

These and other details are absent in Matthew's version. According to Matthew, sometime after Jesus' birth, certain individuals come from the East to pay him homage. These individuals follow a bright star that they believe will lead them to the "King of the Jews." They first visit King Herod and inquire about the special child. Apparently, Herod's murderous reputation is unknown to the visitors, and, after they locate the baby Jesus, they must be warned in a dream not to reveal the child's whereabouts to Herod, as he had requested. Herod is prone to eliminate the competition; he will have no rival King of the Jews, even if that rival is an infant.

The magi leave Jerusalem and continue to follow the star until they encounter the infant, Jesus, in the town of Bethlehem. Our Christmas carols ("We Three Kings of Orient Are") and ceramic, gift-bearing figures under our Christmas trees tell us that the visitors are three wise men, but the exact number of the individuals who visit the Christ child is never actually mentioned in the text:

> In the time of King Herod, after Jesus was born in Bethlehem of Judea, wise men from the East came to Jerusalem, asking, "Where is the child who has been born king of the Jews? For we observed his star at its rising, and have come to pay him homage." When King Herod heard this, he was frightened, and all Jerusalem with him; and calling together all the chief priests and scribes of the people, he inquired of them where the Messiah was to be born. They told him, "In Bethlehem of Judea; for so it has been written by the prophet: 'And you, Bethlehem, in the land of Judah, are by no means least among the rulers of Judah; for from you shall come a ruler who is to shepherd my people Israel.'" Then Herod secretly called for the wise men and learned from them the exact time when the star had appeared. Then he sent them to Bethlehem, saying, "Go and search diligently for the child; and when you have found him, bring me word so that I may also go and pay him homage." When they had heard the king, they set out; and there, ahead of them, went the star that they had seen at its rising, until it stopped over the place where the child was. When they saw that the star had stopped, they were overwhelmed with joy. On entering the house, they saw the child with Mary his mother; and they knelt down and paid him homage. Then, opening their treasure chests, they offered him gifts of gold, frankincense, and myrrh. And having been warned in a dream not to return to Herod, they left for their own country by another road. (Matt 2:1–12)

Most scholars believe that the tradition of three visitors arises from the three gifts mentioned: gold, frankincense, and myrrh. But, again, the text does not state the number of gift-bearing individuals. The Greek word for the visitors (the New Testament is originally written in an ancient form of Greek) is *magi*. Often translated as wise men, sages, astrologers, or magicians, *magi* is a plural but entirely gender-neutral noun, so it specifies only that there is more than one visitor; the sex of the magi remains unclear. Hence, we may be talking about as few as a pair of visitors—or many visitors (male, female, or both); we simply do not know.

Quite often, when I discuss this fourth quiz question with my class, a student will cite the names of the three wise men—Gaspar (or sometimes

Caspar), Melchior, and Balthasar—as "proof" that the magi are three in number and male in gender. But, the fact is, nowhere in the Bible do these names appear. So, if the names do not appear in the Bible, why do we memorize them as children and immortalize them yearly at Christmastime? The names actually spring from a much later tradition, but not all Christians agree on the names.

The Eastern Church has various names for the magi; for example, Syrian Christians know them as Larvandad, Gushnasaph, and Hormisdas. In the West, however, they are known as Gaspar, Melchior, and Balthasar. Scholars cite an ancient, sixth-century Greek text as the original source for these three names, which, over time, have been absorbed into the Christian tradition surrounding Christmas.

Some may feel a sense of confusion or even disappointment when they realize that their precious childhood memories of the three wise men do not come directly from the pages of the Bible. But, this does not make the story any less important. Moreover, question number four serves as an excellent example of how the biblical text and tradition (cherished rituals or beliefs outside of Scripture) often coexist. Indeed, many of our prayers, holiday celebrations, and religious practices do not come from the pages of Scripture, but instead develop slowly over time, and can add to the rich tapestry of faith.

We have just one final question, which also deals with the New Testament.

Question Five: True or False—Several of Jesus' Apostles (Matthew, Mark, Luke, and John) write the Gospel accounts of his life, death, and resurrection

The answer to this final question is, once again, FALSE. While scholars continue to debate the authorship of the four canonical Gospels, to date, the identities of the authors who write the accounts of Jesus' life and times remain a mystery. The application of the four Evangelists' names—like the placement of the Gospels within the New Testament—comes from deeply held traditions within the early Church rather than from specific individuals named Matthew, Mark, Luke, and John.

The Gospels (from the Greek, meaning "good news") are essentially short stories that convey key events in the life of Jesus. They are not biographical in the modern sense, of course, as they lack the minutiae and detailed descriptions that contemporary audiences demand. The anonymous authors seek instead to focus on Jesus' oral teachings, miracles, and actions in light of their faith.

I will discuss the Gospels and the New Testament in more detail in the subsequent chapters, but very basically, three of the four Gospels (Matthew, Mark, and Luke) are so similar in content that scholars refer to them as the "Synoptic Gospels." *Synoptic* comes from the Greek, meaning "like view." Matthew, Mark, and Luke present Jesus' story in the same general order and all follow parallel courses of events that highlight Jesus' ministry.

The Gospel of John, however, is quite different. John's portrait of Jesus emphasizes Jesus' divine nature. Roughly 90 percent of the material in John is unique to John and not found in the Synoptic Gospels. For example, in John, Jesus moves back and forth between his home in the Galilee and Jerusalem, but in the Synoptics, Jesus travels to Jerusalem only once, during the final week of his life. And although Jesus' primary role in the Synoptics is that of exorcist, John does not record a single exorcism. These are only a few differences between the Gospels, but these differences, as we shall see, are significant in the development of Christianity and our understanding of Jesus.

Many people are surprised to learn that the four canonical Gospels are not the only gospels written. Early Christians produced many others, among them gospels purportedly written by those near and dear to Jesus, including some of the Apostles. For instance, according to some scholars, the Gospel of Thomas, unearthed in 1947 near Nag Hammadi, Egypt, is the work of Thomas, one of Jesus' Apostles. First written around the same time period as the Synoptic Gospels, the Gospel of Thomas contains 114 "Jesus sayings" and offers us unique insights into the early followers of Jesus. Other noncanonical gospels include the Gospel of Peter, the Infancy Gospel of James, and the Gospel of Mary Magdalene.

All this aside, if we return to the question of authorship of the four canonical Gospels, we can argue that questions concerning the true identity of the Evangelists are certainly intriguing, but for people of faith, the identity of the individuals who pen the tales of Jesus' life remains a secondary question. What matters most are the stories themselves and the timeless lessons they impart, not only for the earliest followers of Jesus but also for Christians today.

So, how did you do? If you are like most of my college students, chances are you probably did not answer more than one or two questions correctly, and most likely, none. On the other hand, some students actually do quite well. Many answer more than half of the questions correctly. But usually, when pressed, few of them are able to justify their answers. Most admit that they answered the question based on a hunch or some vague recollection from Sunday school.

But even if you answered all or most of the questions correctly, and you are able to explain your answers adequately, this book is still for you. The purpose of this book is not only to teach you something about the Bible but also to empower you by giving you the basic tools necessary to continue learning more about the Bible beyond the pages of this book. I now invite you to journey with me to explore the fascinating collection of ancient texts that for centuries has captivated the hearts and minds of millions: the Bible.

2

A Tree with Deep Roots

A Brief History of
Biblical Illiteracy

Difficulty is the excuse history never accepts.

—EDWARD R. MURROW

Why is it that we no longer read the Bible? And, for the precious
few who actually do read it, why is it that so many misunderstand or misinterpret its meaning? These are crucial and forma-
tive questions that will be addressed at the end of this chapter, but perhaps
the best way to begin our exploration of the origins of biblical illiteracy
is to first say a few words about the history of the Bible. I am not talking
here about "biblical history"—the Bible's particular chronology of events
that includes such things as the creation of the world; the giving of the
Law (or Torah); and, in the New Testament, the coming of Christ—which
sometimes differs from recorded history outside the pages of the Bible.
Rather, I mean the Bible's own "bibliohistory," which is a complex history
that spans over two thousand years. This bibliohistory cannot be fully
explored in a single chapter; I shall instead focus on key events and offer
a general overview of the factors that led us to our present state of biblical

illiteracy. What follows is my "best guess" assessment of the situation, as it is difficult to pinpoint the exact moment in time when people stopped reading the Bible. But I will offer this tease: It is a fairly recent phenomenon. We will start with the basics and then explore the Bible's slow and steady rise from a collection of oral traditions to sacred Scripture.

The word *Bible* is an English spelling of the Greek word *biblia*, which means "little books." The name itself reminds us that *the Bible*, now a single work contained between two covers, begins as a collection of individual books, or scrolls, written over a long period of time by different authors. The original texts (of which there are no surviving copies) were usually written on a paperlike material called papyrus (made from the papyrus plant). The pages were then wrapped around a short wooden pole to form a scroll. Unfortunately, papyrus is not a very durable material, so most ancient manuscripts have been lost in the sands of time.

The Bible is divided into two main sections. The first section (the larger of the two) is the Hebrew Bible (commonly called the "Old Testament" by Christians), and the second section (much smaller) is called the "New Testament," or the "Christian Testament." There are twenty-seven books in the New Testament and either thirty-nine (in Jewish and Protestant Bibles) or forty-six books (Catholic editions) in the Hebrew Bible (chapter 3 will explain these differences in more detail). There are many translations of the Bible currently in use, including the New Revised Standard Version (NRSV) (the version used for citing passages in this book), the King James Version (KJV), the New International Version (NIV), the Jerusalem Bible (JB), the New American Bible (NAB), and scores more.

The Bible begins as a collection of sacred scrolls written and edited over the course of a thousand years by the Jewish people. The canonization of the Hebrew Bible is completed sometime between 200 BCE and 200 CE. These sacred Scriptures are stored in temples and handled by scribes. Sometime during the first and second centuries of the Common Era, a group that would become known as Christians emerges, leading to two different, yet similar, Bibles. The early followers of the Jesus movement add four Gospels, the Acts of the Apostles, an apocalypse (the book of Revelation), and twenty-one letters (attributed to Paul, Peter, John, and others) to the original Jewish writings to form the Christian Bible. The New Testament, which exists in some form by around 200 CE, parallels the production of a Jewish sequel to the Hebrew Bible: the rabbinic writings on Jewish law and tradition known as the Mishnah and Talmud.

Before a single word of the Hebrew Bible is ever written, however, there is a rich and abiding oral tradition whereby the faithful regale friends and family members with the stories that are part of the religious and cultural heritage of God's Chosen People. Most of the oral traditions are eventually collected and written down so that they can be passed on to future generations. A similar oral tradition is present during the growing pains that mark the post-Easter community, as fledging house churches emerge during the aftermath of Jesus' death and resurrection. Early followers of the Jesus movement share stories of his life and miracles as they patiently await his return (the Parousia), which they believe will usher in a New Age for all humanity. When it becomes clear that Christ's return is not imminent, however, several of his followers put pen to papyrus and immortalize the key events in his life and the crucial aspects of his teachings. The canonical Gospels of Matthew, Mark, Luke, and John are the precious gems of their efforts.

In its early years, the Bible is read and revered in synagogues and churches and becomes the centerpiece of later traditions that develop in Judaism and Christianity. The faithful recite many of the stories from memory and take seriously the important lessons that lie at the heart of these stories. People are familiar with the biblical characters, and many parents even choose biblical names for their children, hoping, for example, that their son might inherit the Wisdom of Solomon or that their daughter might grow to be as courageous as Deborah. Although Judaism, for the most part, has always encouraged lively debate, thoughtful discussion, and critical analysis of the biblical text, for Christians the teachings and traditions of the Church (and for centuries, there is only one church—the Catholic Church) slowly take precedence. Over time, individual reading of the Bible is discouraged, and soon the faithful begin to rely on the Church for proper interpretation of the biblical text. It is unclear exactly when this shift occurs, but in the late fourth century, St. Jerome translates the Bible from Hebrew and Greek into Latin, then the common language of the people (hence the term Latin *Vulgate*). As we shall see, however, throughout history, the translation of the Bible into the *lingua franca* of the common person is often viewed with suspicion. It is not surprising, then, that Jerome's translation is not very popular during his own time.

Although there are some rival translations, the Latin Vulgate prevails and is eventually adopted as the "official Bible" of the Catholic Church, but by this time, Latin has become a dead language. Hence, by the Middle Ages (the period between the fall of the Roman Empire and the Renaissance), the official Bible of the Church is in an archaic language that the vast majority of the people do not understand. Worse still, most of the clergy know only a form of puppet-Latin, enough to say Mass, but not enough to actually read and understand the Bible. Thus, the interpretation of the sacred Scriptures becomes the domain of an exclusive few who can decipher Latin.

The Latin Vulgate carries the early Church through most of the Middle Ages and is never seriously challenged. But things are about to change. John Wycliffe (1328–1384), a theologian, philosopher, and priest at Oxford University, is the first to translate the Bible into English. Wycliffe's earliest readers are likely his students and colleagues—the so-called educated elite. Soon, however, others outside the hallowed halls of academia are also interested in reading the Bible in English. This apparently rankles some in the Church, who shrilly warn of the dangers of "private interpretation"—a valid concern, but surely not the only concern. With the Bible and its interpretation securely resting in the holy hands of a select few, order and control can be maintained. There is no telling what might happen if an average parishioner got his hands on an English version he could actually read!

Accordingly, copies of Wycliffe's English Bibles are considered a form of heterodoxy and eventually outlawed; anyone found with an English Bible is subject to torture and execution. For many, the desire to read the Bible in their native language is worth the risk, however, and Wycliffe Bibles continue to be copied and distributed throughout England.

In 1382, Wycliffe's teachings are formally condemned as heretical, and he is forced to leave his post at Oxford. Retiring in the tiny town of Lutterworth, he resumes his duties as the rector of St. Mary's Church. But he continues to promote the importance of a readable Bible in the vernacular of the people and rails against the Church for its steadfast refusal to acknowledge any Bible other than the Vulgate. He dies two years later and is buried in his parish cemetery. Forty-four years after his death, under papal decree, his body is exhumed and burned, a grotesque and barbaric sentence imposed upon traitors to the Church.

If this action is meant to discourage others from following in Wycliffe's footsteps, it fails miserably. Indeed, Wycliffe's movement has many adherents, and change is in the air. Called Lollards (from a Dutch word that means "mumble"), Wycliffe's disciples are viewed by some as religious fanatics who insist on a Bible-based faith; any traditions not found in the Bible, such as the sacrament of penance and the veneration of saints, are eschewed. Labeled as heretics, Lollards are arrested and many are tortured and executed, but this violent persecution does little to stem the tide of change, for the proverbial genie is already out of the bottle and there is no going back.

Martin Luther (1483–1546), a priest and theologian, denounces many of the practices of the Roman Catholic Church—ninety-five, to be exact—and in 1517, he nails his list of grievances to the church door in Wittenberg, Germany, setting into motion the wheels of the Protestant

Reformation. Like the Lollards, he takes issue with nonbiblical Church teachings, including papal authority and that nasty practice of selling indulgences in order to free the souls of the dearly departed from the shackles of purgatory (which is, even in the Church's opinion, abusive; *indulgence* is simply a term used to indicate the remission of temporal punishment for sins that had been forgiven).

Luther's List sets off a firestorm of religious change, the effects of which are still being felt today. But, insofar as the Bible is concerned, Luther agrees that it should be available for the masses and written in the vernacular of the people. He translates the Bible into German for his countrymen, and other reformers, particularly in England, set out to do the same. While the faithful in northern Europe seem willing to accept this change, this is not the case in England, where the crusty guardians of the faith still insist that the Vulgate is the only permissible translation. The wave of reform, however, creates a steady stream of courageous men and women who risk everything in order to have a Bible that even a boy behind the plough can read. One such maverick is the pious and intellectually gifted William Tyndale (1494–1536). Fluent in Greek and Hebrew, Tyndale is committed to translating the Bible into common English and at first attempts to gain approval for his work through the proper channels. He approaches his local bishop, a fellow intellectual, Cuthbert Tunstall, in hopes of gaining his support. Tunstall, however, is not one to break ranks with the prevailing political opinions of the Church and apparently suspects strains of Protestantism in Tyndale's request. Tunstall refuses to endorse Tyndale's efforts to create an English version of the Bible, and Tyndale is forced to relocate to the more Reformation-friendly Germany to continue his work.

Despite several setbacks, Tyndale publishes his first translation of the New Testament in 1526 and sets his sights on translating the Pentateuch (Torah). Tyndale Bibles are beautifully illustrated and pocket-sized (there are several surviving copies, one of which is on display in the British Library in London). Their compact size allows them to be easily smuggled into England where they sell like hotcakes on the black market. Some shipments are confiscated and burned, and those caught with a copy are subject to imprisonment and even death. As his illegal Bibles flow into England, Tyndale continues his work, translating the Hebrew Bible, but he must be wary of those who seek to silence his seditious pen, for the old guard in England has spies. In 1535, one of those spies catches up with Tyndale in Antwerp. Tyndale is arrested, convicted of heresy, imprisoned, and then executed a year later. In a sad irony, within two years of Tyndale's death, Protestantism sweeps through England, King Henry VIII declares himself the head of the Church of England, and English Bibles, now legal, grace every pulpit and pew in Britain.

What happens between the sixteenth century, when people literally risk their lives in order to read the Bible in plain English, and the twenty-first century, when, despite the fact that there are dozens of English (and every other conceivable language) translations readily available, people do not seem inclined to read the Bible at all? As a college professor, I know that it is not just the Bible that people skip reading; teachers have a difficult time getting students to read anything bound between two covers. But the problem of biblical illiteracy begins long before the present web-surfing, text-messaging, Facebooking, instant-gratification generation that confounds professors and parents today.

During the seventeenth and eighteenth centuries, the seeds of the Scientific Revolution (sown centuries earlier with geniuses like Leonardo da Vinci and Copernicus) begin to sprout. People in Europe, and eventually America, begin to look at life from a different perspective, questioning previously held truths, searching for empirical evidence to support theories, and positing new ideas about life and the universe. Great minds, such as Galileo (1564–1642) and Isaac Newton (1643–1727), transform the way in which we understand the universe. Galileo's improvements with regard to the telescope allow him to peer into the heavens and to confirm the earlier theories of Copernicus (1473–1543), which hold that the sun, not the Earth, is at the center of the universe. Newton, of course, is remembered for his laws of gravity and motion, which are now standards in nearly all high school textbooks, but are nothing short of revolutionary for Newton's time.

Scottish anthropologist Sir James George Frazer (1854–1941) observes that human beings pass through three phases of development in which they attempt to control nature: first through magic, then through religion, and finally through science. Although each new phase always retains vestiges of the previous iteration, much of the world moves in the direction of science in search of answers to the big questions (and the small ones, too) in life.

Despite the growing interest in rational thinking and science, however, up until the late 1800s, the Bible is still widely read and respected as an authoritative source for living a good and moral life. American presidents, including Abraham Lincoln and Woodrow Wilson, quote from the Bible without offending anyone; writers, like Herman Melville and Nathaniel Hawthorne, allude to the Bible and people understand their references; musicians William Billings and later John Knowles Paine set the Psalms to music and people actually know that what they are singing comes from sacred Scripture.

A seismic shift in biblical literacy occurs in 1859 when a British scientist, Charles Darwin, publishes his landmark book, *Origin of Species*. Darwin's work centers on the concept that differences in species occur over a period of time due to something he calls natural selection, or the process by which certain favorable traits are passed on to future generations and unfavorable traits are essentially "bred out," which can even result in new species. This concept is at the center of evolutionary biology and is widely—though certainly not universally—accepted today. Unlike many of the major players in the Scientific Revolution, however, Darwin does not write in the scholarly jargon of a scientist, preferring instead to write a book that will be accessible and readable for the general public. He apparently succeeds admirably, for his book becomes enormously popular and causes quite a stir.

Though Darwin certainly is not the first to explore evolutionary theory, his book allows the average reader to enter into the scientific debate concerning the origins of life. For many, Darwin's ideas are revolutionary and compelling and help to illuminate the existential question humans have asked through the ages: Why am I here? Darwin inspires other scientists, such as Mary and Louis Leakey, to search for evidence of our earliest ancestors. Soon, evolutionary theory finds its way into the vernacular of the people and into textbooks, and it is generally regarded today as fact rather than theory (despite the fact that Darwin himself clearly states that natural selection is indeed just a *theory*).

But not everyone agrees. Some view Darwin's work—and others who follow in his footsteps—with suspicion and even contempt. They feel that evolution contradicts certain biblical truths—namely, that all humans descend from the first couple, Adam and Eve. Those who study Darwin and his life rightfully point out that he never intends to undermine religion or to dismiss the Bible; in fact, he is quite mindful of religious sensibilities. But in the years following Darwin's initial work, a tug-of-war begins to develop between the so-called evolutionists (or those who believe in a common origin of humankind that evolves from primates) and traditionalists, who insist that a literal reading of the biblical Creation accounts can be the only source of truth for believers. This either-or kind of thinking has resulted in pitched debates, fevered arguments, and an ever-growing chasm between the two extremes.

The Bible has been the unfortunate casualty in this divide, read and cast to the side as fanciful mythology by the liberalists; revered and clutched to the chest as the only source of truth by the traditionalists. The vast majority of people, however, fall somewhere in between these two camps. This middle group—the majority—represents those who have likely never read or studied the Bible in any real sense; they simply go though the motions of their faith tradition (or not) and wonder what all the fuss is about. Some in this middle group may have explored the Bible and evolution and have come to view them as complementary rather than contradictory; that is, one can maintain God as the Creator without ignoring the God-given gifts of science and reason.

The growing acceptance of evolutionary theory is hugely important in our quest to try to understand how and why people stop reading the Bible, and though it does not completely explain the current problem of biblical illiteracy, it does serve as a signpost, pointing us in the right direction. The Scientific Revolution paves the way for the next major stop on our journey, the Industrial Revolution of the eighteenth and nineteenth centuries. Begun in Britain, the Industrial Revolution heralds changes in agriculture, manufacturing, mining, and nearly every other form of industry. This movement toward the development and implementation of machine-based labor has far-reaching social, cultural, and economic consequences throughout Europe and North America. The middle class experiences a population boom and factories soon begin dotting the landscape, causing a shift away from a rural lifestyle to a more urban one. People now have a wider variety of job choices and greater chances for advancement in the workplace. Travel is made easier due to improvements in the steam engine, railroad system, and roads. New discoveries in medicine result in a decrease of the infant mortality rate, an increase in life expectancy, and a whole new arsenal of drugs used to combat and prevent illness.

As the fuel from the Industrial Revolution moves us headlong into the twentieth century, a new field of medicine is born: psychology. Thanks to the pioneering work of Sigmund Freud (considered the father of modern psychology) and others who follow in his footsteps (though many will diverge from his well-worn path), we gain startling new insights into the human mind and a whole new vocabulary designed to tell us why we do the things we do. An atheist, Freud's initial view of religion is somewhat dismissive; he sees religious beliefs as little more than a quivering heap of infantile needs or wish fulfillments rooted in fantasies and driven by guilt. His later writings, however, seem to indicate an interest in exploring religions through a historical and psychological lens, testing out his own theories as a way to explain religious phenomena. Although he continues to view religious faith as something akin to mass delusion, he also feels that the task of the psychologically mature individual is, in a sense, to "grow out of" their childish religious beliefs. If all of this sounds a little clinical and depressing, we must remember that Freud, himself, is not a very happy individual, and, whether or not we agree with him (he has enjoyed many detractors, far too numerous to mention), his work greatly influences the way in which many people view religion and, by extension, the Bible. Freud's work has since been expanded, dismissed, refined, and defined by countless others who seek to understand and help alleviate psychological suffering. Moreover, his work spawns a new and exciting discipline, aptly called the psychology of religion, the courses of which are quite popular on college campuses.

As the twentieth century roars ahead, life becomes faster-paced and many people begin to experience greater economic stability, which leads to an increased consumption of goods and services. In short, people begin to collect things—clothing, furniture, appliances, and assorted gadgetry. Collecting "stuff" becomes (and still is) almost a religion itself. (Interestingly, psychology has a term for pathologically collecting and holding on to things: hoarding.) The common side effect of the acquisition of material goods, however, is that all our "stuff" requires looking after. We work long hours to afford a nice home in which we may store our many possessions and, consequently, we use our "leisure time" not for leisure, but to sort, inventory, and maintain all our things. Storage facilities are now popular because our homes can no longer contain all of our stuff. Weekends are spent changing the oil in our cars, mowing the lawn, dusting the knick-knacks that line our shelves, defragmenting our computers, and, of course, going from place to place, buying more stuff.

The by-product of all this is a sort of self-imposed isolation. Most of us rarely know the people who live next door to us, and we are too busy to try to get to know them. People cannot seem to take a walk, ride a bike, or sit on a park bench without being connected to an iPod, which effectively sends a "leave me alone" message to others. We watch movies on our laptops instead of at the movie theater with other people, and we eat dinner in front of the television, instead of around the dinner table with the people we most love. Our children are so overbooked with parent-arranged activities that they are unable to organize a neighborhood game of kickball on their own—but they probably do not even know most of the other kids in their neighborhood anyway. In the past, families would live under the same roof and work toward common goals, not only due to sharing a common living space and loving bonds but also through having less stuff and fewer outside commitments. "Family time" has now become a staged event or an orchestrated outing that parents feel compelled to arrange and children feel forced to attend. The so-called breakdown of the American family is not just about the staggering divorce rate; families may live under the same roof, but they circulate in isolated orbits, each member chasing after his or her version of what it means to be successful in this competitive, technologically driven world.

All of this does not leave much time for the cultivation of a religious or spiritual life, much less reading the Bible. It is no wonder that church attendance in the United States and Western Europe has experienced a steady and unprecedented decline; who has the time?

I am not saying that all technology is bad—for I am writing these very words on my trusty laptop. But when we combine the effects of technology with the other factors mentioned briefly in this chapter—ecclesial squabbles over such things as translating the Bible into the vernacular of the people; the rise in rational thinking; scientific breakthroughs, including the field of psychology; and the leaps in industry that led to a complete upheaval in the social, cultural, and economic life of citizens—we can see why it is that we no longer read or understand the Bible.

Some might be inclined to shrug their shoulders and ask, "So what? Why does it matter if we don't read (or understand) the Bible?" Of course, the most obvious reason to read the Bible is to strengthen, renew, and sustain our faith. Religious faith aside, the Bible is the foundational text for Western religious thought and has influenced nearly every aspect of Western civilization, including art, music, literature, philosophy, education, science, law, and government. This means that biblical illiteracy is a problem that extends beyond the scope of religion and connotes a more extensive lack of knowledge.

College professors have a bird's-eye view of this problem and struggle to modify their classes in order to compensate. But the end result, which is surely the case in my own discipline of religious/biblical studies, is that teachers must spend a significant amount of time engaged in remedial work before actually teaching the objectives of the course. This means that we must first teach what we once took for granted as common knowledge—that our students have some awareness and basic understanding of key biblical stories, truths, and ideas. Imagine, for example, the challenges an art professor might face when presenting Italian Renaissance art, or an English professor's frustration in teaching John Milton's *Paradise Lost*, both of which center on biblical characters and themes, to a group of students who know nothing about the Bible.

But biblical illiteracy extends far beyond the classroom. It infiltrates the courtroom (most laws in the United States are founded on biblical principles), the boardroom (most precepts regarding business ethics are biblically based), and even the bedroom (our concept of love and fidelity are firmly rooted in biblical teachings). Simply put, knowledge of the Bible is a critical part of our overall education. If you agree, at least in principle, then the next logical question is this: Where do we go from here?

You have already taken the first step in choosing to read this book. Step number two is equally important: purchase (or borrow from the library) a Bible. While there are many fine English translations of the Bible, as mentioned in the introduction, I have chosen to use *The New Oxford Annotated Bible* (with Apocrypha) in writing this book. This particular Bible is based on the *New Revised Standard Version* translation and has scholarly commentary about each section, detailed footnotes, maps, and other helpful study materials intended to appeal to a diverse audience. You are free, of course, to consult your particular favorite version of the Bible, but I do suggest that you use a "study Bible" (study Bibles come in many different versions). You should read your Bible alongside *What the Bible Really Tells Us*, as this will enable you to gain a fuller understanding of the passages we will discuss. Using your Bible early on and often will help you to become familiar with the way the Bible is arranged. You might also consider investing in Bible tabs, small tags that affix to the various books of the Bible, which makes locating and moving between biblical books quick and easy. You can purchase these cheaply from most booksellers or on Amazon, or you can make your own Bible tabs (many of my students do this using Post-it® notes).

The third step is to try, as best you can, to remain open to the process of learning. This does not mean that you should put aside your particular faith perspective or that you should suddenly adopt a new one. But resistance to new ideas and different ways of looking at things are roadblocks to learning. Of course, you do not have to agree with everything in this book; on the contrary, the most important thing I hope to teach you is to think critically for yourself. This is sometimes difficult to do when it comes to the Bible because, traditionally, it has often been subjected to territorial guardianship, caught in a game of one-upmanship between the faithful and the skeptical; the traditionalist and the scholar; the pious and impious. Yet the there is no exclusive ownership, for the Bible belongs to all of us.

There are those, of course, who insist that we must read the Bible from a particular perspective—usually *their* perspective—but the vast libraries of commentary, both Jewish and Christian, reflecting every conceivable point of view, point to a different reality. This reality allows for diverse opinions to coexist and cautions us to avoid narrow-mindedness, for there is ample room for everyone.

The style of interpretation pursued in this book is to treat the Bible like any other piece of literature. That is, with measures of sympathy and suspicion, with curiosity about its authors and their times, with full appreciation of what we can learn from the collateral fields of biblical studies, including history, archaeology, anthropology, and philology. This book is written primarily with Christians and Jews in mind, as well as those with other or no religious affiliations who simply wish to learn more about the Bible. I am fully aware that some readers, both conservative and liberal, may experience the occasional discomfort that comes from the fear that their beliefs are being challenged, but I also know that true learning happens when we are asked to step out of our comfort zone to explore other perspectives, and this is exactly what I hope you will do. Let us now explore some basic facts regarding the Bible that will serve as the framework for subsequent chapters.

3

Bible Basics

IT'S NOT ROCKET SCIENCE!

*The Bible grows more beautiful as we grow in our
understanding of it.*

—JOHANN WOLFGANG VON GOETHE

At the close of the previous chapter, we observed that the Bible has
influenced nearly every corner of Western civilization. It impacts
the moral and ethical precepts of contemporary democracies,
anchoring fields as diverse as law, politics, medicine, education, and business. The Bible's remarkable stories, memorable characters, and eternal
truths are immortalized in countless paintings, stories, songs, poetry, and
film. And, of course, the Bible is the centerpiece of Judeo-Christian religious faith, ritual, and worship. Indeed, no education, formal or otherwise,
is complete without some basic understanding of the Bible.

Each semester when I scan the roster of new names, I know that the
job ahead of me is a daunting one because I must essentially begin from
scratch. Experience teaches me, however, that I must bring students along
slowly; too much information too soon will not only discourage them but
also confirm the common misconception that the Bible is indecipherable
for the average person. And so, before we actually start to *read* the Bible, I

spend several classes laying the foundation for our journey. This important background information, or what I call the "Bible Basics," includes lessons about the history and geography of the Ancient Near East (ANE), the authorship and various translations of the Bible in use today, and lessons that center on the nature of God in the Bible. Along with this very basic information, I also speak briefly about the so-called "tools of the trade" biblical scholars use when working with the Bible, tools that my students (and readers of this book) will soon utilize with relative ease.

On the very first day of class, I encourage students to practice flipping through the various books of the Bible in order to familiarize themselves with the names of the books and the placement of these books within the canon. I want them to grow accustomed to handling the Bible, and I urge them to jot down notes in their Bibles—during class discussions and when they are conducting research on their own—for future reference. As we begin, I also encourage you to do these things as well.

In this chapter, I will present a condensed version of what I do in my own classroom. Do not feel as if you must read and remember everything in this chapter; instead, consider it a reference chapter, to which you may return often as you make your way through the rest of this book. The clearly delineated subject heads will enable you to easily navigate the information. The list of resources at the end of this book will be helpful as you begin to make your way through the chapters and assist you in further study. And so we begin our investigation with a brief exploration of the world of the Ancient Near East, the cradle of civilization that gave birth to the Bible.

The Lay of the Land: The Ancient Near East

The geographical, historical, cultural, economic, and political world of the Ancient Near East serves as the backdrop for the Bible. While this world will be explored in greater detail as we investigate the seven biblical themes in chapters 4 through 10, it is important to have some basic understanding of the "setting" of the Bible. If you have a study Bible with maps (the maps are usually located in the back of study Bibles), you may wish to review the various maps in conjunction with this section. The geographical location of the ANE begins in Egypt, and includes Israel, Syria, Arabia, modern-day Iraq, Iran, Turkey, Lebanon, Jordan, and the fringe areas beyond these borders.

Various tribes and ethnic groups are scattered throughout this region, largely along the arc of the Fertile Crescent, the broad semicircle that stretches from the Nile to the Tigris and Euphrates rivers. The largest of these ethnic groups, of which the people of Israel are a part, are the Semites. The geographical location of Israel is both a blessing and a curse. Its location is part of a larger trade route, which facilitates the transmission of stories and ideas from other lands (there are numerous references to other cultures and foreign religious practices in the Bible), but this location also makes Israel vulnerable to attacks—not only from the powerful northern empires of Assyria and, later, Babylonia but also from the south (Egypt) and even from beyond its shores—such as the marauding warriors known as the "sea peoples" from the eastern Mediterranean.

The Bible usually speaks of nations other than Israel in very unflattering terms. This is because Israel is frequently at odds with these other nations and the biblical authors tend to demonize their enemies. Israel's confrontations with the great empires of Egypt, Assyria, Babylonia, Persia, Greece, and Rome result in occupation and near destruction. But in addition to these big bullies, there are local troublemakers, including the Philistines, Edomites, Ammonites, Moabites, and others who share common borders with Israel.

When the Bible talks about Israel, however, it can be confusing, because at different periods of time "Israel" can refer to only the northern part of the nation, while other times it includes the north and the south. Similarly, the southern part of this area is often referred to as Judah or, during the Roman period, Judea. We are talking about the same landmass, but war and politics often changes the name of this geographical location. To confuse matters even more, "Israel" is also an alternate name for the biblical patriarch, Jacob.

If you have not yet done so, take a few moments to examine the maps of the Ancient Near East and of Israel and its local neighbors in your study Bible. Having a basic lay of the land will enable you to visualize the various places and peoples mentioned in the Bible. If you do not have a study Bible, you can view some excellent biblical maps online (see, for example, www.bible-history.com/maps/).

A Brief History of Biblical Times

When we discuss "biblical history," we are usually referring to the historical setting according to the biblical authors, which may not reflect our modern understanding of history. For example, the Creation story in Gen 1–2:4 (briefly mentioned in chapter 1) says that God creates the world and the various forms of life (including humans) in a single week. Modern science, on the other hand, presents a more gradual creation history, beginning with the creation of the Earth roughly 4.5 billion years ago and the first human somewhere around 2.2–1.6 million years ago. Another difference between the view of history expressed in the Bible and our contemporary view is that sometimes a biblical story may have begun as an oral tradition. Since the account or accounts—for often there are competing versions of the same story—are not written down until many years after the purported event, it is nearly impossible to be confident about the exact details of the story. Of course, the biblical writers are not particularly interested in relating the sort of history found in our modern textbooks, for theirs is a religious history that looks at life through a particular lens of faith.

The subject of "biblical history" versus "secular history" is a topic of ongoing debate, and scholars on all sides continue to argue fiercely and persuasively for one date or another regarding the composition of the various books of the Bible. No one, of course, can claim to be *the* authoritative source when it comes to dating ancient manuscripts. And, despite the scientific advances in fields such as archaeology, the truth is there is still a great deal we simply do not know about the world of the ANE and the Bible.

What we do know for certain is that the Bible relates several pivotal events that apparently shape the consciousness and religious perspectives of the people known as Israel. Very briefly, these pivotal events begin with the creation of the world and humankind, as narrated in the first three chapters of Genesis. As part of the so-called "Primeval History" (or beginning of history) that spans the first eleven chapters of Genesis, this history also includes the stories of Cain and Abel (Gen 4:1–16), the story of the flood (Genesis 6–9), and the Tower of Babel (Gen 11:1–9). But the most important event in the Primeval History is the story of Creation, which expresses Israel's particular worldview. This worldview holds that God is the author of life, creator of everything, both human and nonhuman, and that the world and all of creation is good.

It is somewhat surprising, then, that the first story narrated after the creation of the world puts this basic worldview to the test. The story of Cain and his brother Abel follows the story of the expulsion of their parents, Adam and Eve, from the paradise of Eden (Gen 3:23–24) and represents the darker side of humankind. A mere four chapters into the book of Genesis, Cain kills his brother Abel, and we have the uneasy sense that things are getting off on the wrong foot. In the next few chapters, chaos and mayhem continue to escalate until God decides that a do-over is in order. So, God sends a cataclysmic flood that destroys the Earth and all that is in it, sparing only the righteous Noah, his family, and certain select animals.

The Primeval History is more or less a rushed prelude to the Big Story, the tale that the ancient authors are most eager to tell: the story of Abraham. The call of Abraham from his home in southern Mesopotamia to the land of Canaan, where he enters into a covenant with God with the divine promises of descendants and the land, is the second major event in the Bible (Gen 12:1–3). Although Abraham receives the promise of a long-awaited son (Gen 21:1–3), it is not until the book of Joshua that the people of Israel gain a relatively secure dwelling place in the Promised Land. A mere two generations after Abraham, his grandson Jacob will, along with his sons and their families, leave this famine-stricken Promised Land for Egypt.

The early portion of the book of Exodus details this period when Jacob's descendants live in Egypt. Moses liberates the Israelites from slavery and leads them on a forty-year trek back to Canaan. Along the way, at the pilgrimage site of Mount Sinai, Moses receives the Torah, the religious-legal code that binds the people of Israel to its God. Following the death of Moses, Joshua, his successor, leads the people into the Promised Land. So now we have the creation of the world, a community ethic, and the Israelites living in the Promised Land. This seems like the end of the story—but the tale is only just beginning.

Little Israel grows up and becomes a nation in its own right. And, wanting to be like other nations, Israel demands from God a king, the greatest of whom is David, proclaimed in the Bible as God's unrivaled favorite against whom all future kings are measured. The rise and fall of the monarchy (1–2 Samuel and 1–2 Kings) and the parade of mostly despicable kings is followed by the eventual loss of the land—first to the Assyrians, who attack the Northern Kingdom of Israel, with its capital of Samaria in 721 BCE—and then to the Babylonians, who invade Judah to the south and capture its capital, Jerusalem, in 587 BCE.

Both of these events are narrated in some detail in the Bible, but it is the Babylonian invasion under King Nebuchadnezzar (and the subsequent exile of the Israelites to Babylonia) that is considered perhaps the most pivotal event in the Hebrew Bible. In fact, when we speak of the two general time periods in the Hebrew Bible, we generally refer to them as either "preexilic" or "postexilic." Although the Jewish exiles, under an edict of liberation from the Persian king, Cyrus, eventually return to the Promised Land, their problems are far from over.

Roughly two hundred years of rather benign Persian rule is followed by the Greek Period (332–63 BCE). Hellenistic culture is introduced and flourishes in many parts of the ANE, including much of Israel. Following the death of Alexander the Great, Judah is ruled by the despised

Antiochus IV, a Syrian, whose violent persecutions of pious Jews is described in grisly detail in the two books of Maccabees, found in the Apocrypha (Catholic versions of the Bible include these books in the Bible proper). This persecution results in a revolt and a brief period of Jewish self-rule (142–63 BCE).

In 63 BCE, Pompey and his Roman soldiers conquer Judea, absorbing it as part of the Roman Empire for the next 130 years. Jesus of Nazareth lives and dies under Roman rule. Eventually, the Jews rebel against the Romans, and, sadly, this rebellion results in the devastation of the Promised Land in 70 CE.

This very brief description of the highlights of biblical history is intended as an overview for you as you make your way through the rest of this book. I have provided a brief, easy-to-read timeline, "Brief History of Biblical Times," for your perusal (see table 3.1). Try to get into the habit of referring to this timeline as often as possible so that you can begin to get an overall sense of the historical placement of various books of the Bible. Learning a bit about the history and geography of the Bible will enable you to begin to see a chronology emerge. This will give you a clearer picture of the events narrated, and you will start to make connections between events, characters, and certain themes.

The Authorship of the Bible

Several books of the Bible announce their primary author in their opening lines (Micah: "the word of the LORD that came to Micah"; Galatians: "Paul . . . to the churches of Galatia"). Others do not (Genesis: "In the beginning, when God created the heavens and the earth"; the Gospel of John: "In the beginning was the Word"). The titles given to biblical books, such as 1 Samuel and the Gospel According to Mark, often suggest authors, but these titles are actually appended to the books after their composition. In fact, in the books of Samuel and the Gospel of Mark, there is no indication that they are written by the prophet or saint with whom the book has come to be associated, and the truth is that we do not know who wrote them.

The pious have always considered the contents of the Bible as inspired by God, but just how this all transpires is a bit of a mystery. Inquiring minds, however, have demanded and produced a set of traditions about the authorship of various books in the Bible. According to tradition, Moses writes the first five books of the Bible (the Pentateuch or Torah), David writes most of the Psalms, Solomon authors Proverbs and Ecclesiastes, and Paul pens the Epistles. Historians, however, are not satisfied with these

Table 3.1. Timeline: Brief History of Biblical Times

Recorded Hebrew Scriptures History

10,000 BCE (?)	Primeval Period: Gen 1–11 (Adam and Eve through Babel)
1850–1270 BCE	Patriarchal Period, Gen 12–50 (Abraham through Joseph in Egypt)
1270–1130 BCE	Exodus/Wandering/Settlement Period, Exodus to Conquest Period (Joshua)
1130–1020 BCE	Period of the Judges
1000–587 BCE	Period of the Monarchy
920 BCE	Divided Monarchy—Judah to the south, Israel to the north
721 BCE	The fall of Israel to Sargon II of Assyria
587 BCE	The fall of Judah to Nebuchadnezzar of Babylonia
587–538 BCE	Exilic Period
539 BCE	Cyrus of Persia conquers Babylon
538 BCE	Edict of Cyrus; exiles free to return
538–332 BCE	Persian Period
332–63 BCE	Greek Period

Early New Testament Period

63 BCE	Roman Period begins
40–4 BCE	King Herod
6 BCE(?)–30 CE	Jesus of Nazareth
50–63 CE	Paul's Letters
70 CE	Destruction of the second temple
70–95 CE	Gospels written
90 CE	Jewish canon
350 CE	Christian canon

answers, and a vast scholarly enterprise, with many competing theories, has been devoted to naming "the real authors" of Scripture.

Most of the books themselves do not directly name their authors, and an unbiased reading makes some of the traditional authors suspicious. For example, does Moses really write the account of his own death in Deut 34:5? Does Paul write certain letters generations after his death? In an attempt to answer such questions, scholars have developed an alphabet-soup roster of hypothetical authors such as J, E, D, P, Dtr, and Q to refer to the actual authors of biblical books. Two of these authors, J and P, are discussed briefly in my explanation of question one on the Sixty-Second Super-Easy Bible Quiz (True or False? "Eve tempts Adam with an apple

in the Garden of Eden"). As I mentioned in chapter 1, there are two Creation stories written by two different authors—whom scholars call "P"
and "J"—and they write for different audiences at different periods of
time. We will delve into this in more detail in future chapters, but in addition to P and J, scholars have discerned at least two other sources for the
material found in the Torah—E and D—thus, the four letters are commonly referred to as JEDP, or the "four-source documentary hypothesis."
This means that if this hypothesis is correct (and remember, a hypothesis
is just a fancy word for a theory or an educated guess), then the Torah or
Pentateuch is compiled from a variety of sources, which might also include
oral traditions.

The two earliest writers are J and E. Recall that J, or the Yahwist,
refers to God as Yhwh. The E source, on the other hand, consistently
refers to God as *Elohim*, the more generic term for God, thus the designation "E." The J source is largely an epic narrative that traces the emer-
gence of Israel as a nation and is likely written during the ninth century
BCE. Most scholars think that J lives in Judah, since his concerns reflect
Jerusalem and the monarchy (typical southern concerns). Material from E
originates in the north and is written around the eighth century BCE. This
earlier source seems more concerned with largely northern issues, such as
the covenant and the conquest of the land.

The Deuteronomist, or D, source reflects concepts found in the book
of Deuteronomy—specifically, obedience to God and covenantal loyalty—
and is probably written during the sixth century BCE. Finally, the Priestly
(P) source, containing the first Creation account in Genesis, is concerned
with priestly functions and religious laws, and P's stickler-for-the-rules
writing style reflects this. Most scholars date P to the fifth century BCE
or later.

Of course, this is a very brief description of the four-source documentary hypothesis, but the most important thing to understand is that these
four versions are woven together by a later redactor or redactors into its
present form. As scholars continue to debate the authorship of various
books of the Bible, many have even abandoned the JEDP theory altogether.
I mention it here only as an example of how we have come to understand
the piecing together of different stories into a cohesive narrative by the
biblical redactor(s)—and because you will likely encounter references to
JEDP in future readings.

Other ascriptions of authorship are designed to give the writing the
air of antiquity and authority. The older and more revered the author,
the better. The impulse to firmly associate texts with respected elders as a
way of expressing their significance has guided the traditions that link the

biblical books with the greatest names of biblical history; thus the Torah is referred to as the "Five Books of Moses" and the Psalms are ascribed to David. This is a common convention in antiquity, and we see this practice at work in more modern history. For instance, scores of towns in New England (and elsewhere) display plaques on various buildings that claim "George Washington slept (or ate, or visited) here." However tenuous the connection between a certain place and the first president of the United States may be, such connections make the places seem more important.

Scholars and traditionalists often clash over such issues as authorship, but sometimes they actually agree: It seems that Paul *did* write Romans and Amos *did* speak many of the oracles contained in the book that bears his name. As I mentioned in chapter 2, however, the jigsaw puzzle of who writes what when and for whom is an interesting academic exercise, but actually has little bearing on the faith life of believers who hold the Bible so dear. The scholarly debate and endless quibbling over authorship, to some, is like arguing over whether a fine wine tastes better in a crystal glass or a plastic cup; it is the wine that matters, not the glass or cup.

The Bibles

Although the term *Bible* is commonly used to refer to the Jewish and Christian Scriptures, the truth is that there is more than one Bible. The Jewish Bible is quite different in many ways from the Christian Bible, and even among Christians, there are differing versions still. I am not talking here about the differences among translations of the Bible, but substantial differences in the content and the sequence of books of the Bible. All Bibles derive from the Jewish Bible, which comes into existence over the course of roughly a thousand years, and grows incrementally over time. Scholars cannot say with any certainty when the earliest Hebrew religious teachings, songs, prayers, ritual protocols, and stories are written, but by around 500 BCE, it is safe to say that there exists a set of scrolls known as the *Torah*. Within another couple of centuries, the Prophets section (in Hebrew *Nevi'im*) coalesces into something approximating the prophetic books we know today. A final section, the Writings (or *Ketuvim*), anchored by the Psalms, emerges in the final centuries before the Common Era. The terms *Torah*, *Nevi'im*, and *Ketuvim*, and the resulting acronym *TaNaK*, are often used by Jews to refer to their Scriptures.

Around the turn of the Common Era, the Bible is still more or less a collection of scrolls, written largely in Hebrew. Portions of two scrolls, Daniel and Ezra, are written in Aramaic, the language of the Persian Empire, and the spoken language of Jesus.

The most important intellectual centers of Jewish life in the final centuries before the Common Era are in Babylon and Jerusalem. The version of the Jewish Bible, written in Hebrew and Aramaic, is called the Masoretic Text (MT), in honor of the Masoretes ("transmitters"), the class of scribes who, over centuries, preserve the Hebrew Bible and ensure its safe passage from the ancient world into our own.

The Egyptian city of Alexandria is another important center of Jewish learning in the ancient world. Between 300 and 100 BCE, the Jewish community in Alexandria translates its collection of scriptural scrolls into Greek. This edition of the Bible, Jewish in origin but later adopted by Greek-speaking Christians, is called the Septuagint, from the Latin for *seventy* (often abbreviated with the Roman numerals LXX), after a tradition that seventy-two Jewish scribes, working in isolation for seventy-two days, providentially emerge from their labors with identical versions of the scrolls on which they are working.

The most germane feature of this Greek version of the Jewish Bible is that it is *not* identical to the Masoretic Text, which becomes the standard among Jews. The Septuagint contains extra material that Protestants refer to as the Apocrypha (which means "hidden" or "esoteric"). The Apocrypha has a stable set of contents, and some Christian Bibles include it between the Hebrew Bible and the New Testament. While both Protestants and Catholics agree on the same twenty-seven books of the New Testament, Catholic versions of the Hebrew Bible include seven more books (usually found in the Apocrypha in Protestant Bibles) than the thirty-nine books found in the Protestant and Jewish versions. These extra books are as follows: Tobit, Judith, 1–2 Maccabees, Wisdom of Solomon, Sirach, and Baruch. Catholic Bibles also have additional chapters and verses in the books of Daniel and Esther.

In general, Christian Bibles are different from the Jewish Bible in the sequence of texts (see table 3.2). The early Christians begin with the contents of the Hebrew Bible and then add their own sacred documents. As already mentioned, the three-part Jewish Bible, the TaNaK, consists of the *Torah*, *Nevi'im*, and *Ketuvim*: Law, Prophets, and Writings. The sequence of the Torah is the same in both Jewish and Christian Bibles: Genesis, Exodus, Leviticus, Numbers, and Deuteronomy. The contents of the second and third sections of the Jewish Bible, the *Nevi'im* and *Ketuvim*, the Prophets and Writings, are also preserved in the Christian Bible, but their order has been rearranged. The most important changes relate to the Prophets.

The second section of the Jewish Bible, the Prophets, or *Nevi'im*, contains two different sets of materials, traditionally known as the Former Prophets and the Latter Prophets. The Former Prophets, so-called because

Table 3.2. The Order of the Hebrew Bible Canon
(with Abbreviations)

Jewish Bible	Protestant Bible	Catholic Bible
Genesis (Gen)	Genesis (Gen)	Genesis (Gen)
Exodus (Exod)	Exodus (Exod)	Exodus (Exod)
Leviticus (Lev)	Leviticus (Lev)	Leviticus (Lev)
Numbers (Num)	Numbers (Num)	Numbers (Num)
Deuteronomy (Deut)	Deuteronomy (Deut)	Deuteronomy (Deut)
Joshua (Josh)	Joshua (Josh)	Joshua (Josh)
Judges (Judg)	Judges (Judg)	Judges (Judg)
1–2 Samuel (1–2 Sam)	Ruth (Ruth)	Ruth (Ruth)
1–2 Kings (1–2 Kgs)	1–2 Samuel (1–2 Sam)	1–2 Samuel (1–2 Sam)
Isaiah (Is)	1–2 Kings (1–2 Kgs)	1–2 Kings (1–2 Kgs)
Jeremiah (Jer)	1–2 Chronicles (1–2 Chron)	1–2 Chronicles (1–2 Chron)
Ezekiel (Ezek)	Ezra (Ezra)	Ezra (Ezra)
Hosea (Hos)	Nehemiah (Neh)	Nehemiah (Neh)
Joel (Joel)	Esther (Esth)	Tobit (Tobit)
Amos (Amos)	Job (Job)	Judith (Jud)
Obadiah (Obad)	Psalms (Ps)	Esther (Esth)
Jonah (Jon)	Proverbs (Prov)	1–2 Maccabees (1–2 Macc)
Micah (Mic)	Ecclesiastes (Eccl)	Job (Job)
Nahum (Nah)	Song of Solomon (Song)	Psalms (Ps)
Habakkuk (Hab)	Isaiah (Is)	Proverbs (Prov)
Zephaniah (Zeph)	Jeremiah (Jer)	Ecclesiastes (Eccl)
Haggai (Hag)	Lamentations (Lam)	Song of Songs (Song)
Zechariah (Zech)	Ezekiel (Ezek)	Wisdom (Wis)
Malachi (Mal)	Daniel (Dan)	Sirach (Sir)
Psalms (Ps)	Hosea (Hos)	Isaiah (Is)
Proverbs (Prov)	Joel (Joel)	Jeremiah (Jer)
Job (Job)	Amos (Amos)	Lamentations (Lam)
Song of Solomon (Song)	Obadiah (Obad)	Baruch (Bar)
Ruth (Ruth)	Jonah (Jon)	Ezekiel (Ezek)
Lamentations (Lam)	Micah (Mic)	Daniel (Dan)
Ecclesiastes (Eccl)	Nahum (Nah)	Hosea (Hos)
Esther (Esth)	Habakkuk (Hab)	Joel (Joel)
Daniel (Dan)	Zephaniah (Zeph)	Amos (Amos)
Ezra-Nehemiah (Ezra-Neh)	Haggai (Hag)	Obadiah (Obad)
1–2 Chronicles (1–2 Chron)	Zechariah (Zech)	Jonah (Jon)
	Malachi (Mal)	Micah (Mic)
		Nahum (Nah)
		Habakkuk (Hab)
		Zephaniah (Zeph)
		Haggai (Hag)
		Zechariah (Zech)
		Malachi (Mal)

they tell stories about an earlier era, include Joshua, Judges, 1–2 Samuel, and 1–2 Kings. The Latter Prophets consist of the Major Prophets (Isaiah, Jeremiah, and Ezekiel—Christians also include Daniel) and the Minor Prophets (Hosea, Joel, Amos, Obadiah, Jonah, Micah, Nahum, Habakkuk, Zephaniah, Haggai, Zechariah, and Malachi). It should be noted that the so-called Minor Prophets are not any less important than the Major Prophets, as "major versus minor" are meant only to refer to the length of each book (or scroll).

It is within the Prophets section that Jewish and Christian Bibles, identical in content, offer different sequences. In Jewish Bibles, the Former Prophets follow the Torah and the Latter Prophets follow the Former Prophets. In the Christian version of the Hebrew Bible, the Former Prophets, just like in Jewish Bibles, come immediately after the final book of the Torah, Deuteronomy; the Latter Prophets, however, are excised and moved to the end. Most scholars think this move reflects the early Christian Church's understanding that the Gospels, the first section of the New Testament, represent the fulfillment of the hopes of the Latter Prophets. Another difference between the sequencing of books in the Jewish and Christian writings is that the book of Lamentations, traditionally associated with the prophet Jeremiah, immediately follows the book that bears his name in Christian Bibles.

The order of the books of the *Ketuvim*, the Writings, also differs in Jewish and Christian Bibles. The sequence of books in Jewish Bibles roughly reflects the chronological order in which the various scrolls emerge and are accepted as sacred: the Torah by 500 BCE; the Prophets by, roughly, around 300 BCE; and the Writings by 100 BCE. The order of the *Ketuvim* in the Christian version of the Hebrew Bible has its own chronology. For example, books among the Writings that are historical in nature (such as Ruth, 1 and 2 Chronicles, Ezra, Nehemiah, and Esther) have been inserted among the Former Prophets, which have the same kind of chronological narrative.

The other most significant difference between the Jewish and Christian Writings, however, has to do with the book of Daniel. In Jewish tradition, Daniel is one of the Writings. This is because it is written relatively late in the centuries before the Common Era, long after the contents of the Law and Prophets are in circulation. But in Christian Bibles, Daniel is in the prophetic section, between Ezekiel and Hosea, which reflects the Christian recognition of Daniel as one of the Major Prophets.

The ending of each version of the Hebrew Bible is also different. The book of 2 Chronicles marks the conclusion of the Jewish Bible with a call for Jewish exiles in Babylon to return home to Jerusalem.

Thus says King Cyrus of Persia: The LORD, the God of heaven, has given me all the kingdoms of the earth, and he has charged me to build him a house at Jerusalem, which is in Judah. Whoever is among you of all his people, may the LORD his God be with him! Let him go up. (2 Chron 36:23)

By contrast, the Christian version ends with the prophet Malachi and mention of the return of Elijah, who is considered the forerunner of the Messiah: "Lo, I will send you the prophet Elijah for the great and ter-rible day of the LORD comes" (Mal 4:5). This Christian exit makes for a smooth segue into the New Testament, which begins with Matthew's Gospel. Christian readers move from Elijah to John the Baptist, from the LORD to Jesus. Which brings us to the chief difference between the Jewish and Christian Bibles: the New Testament.

The New Testament

As I mentioned in chapter 1, the New Testament is a collection of four independent accounts of Jesus' life (the Gospels), an idealized version of community life in the early years following Jesus' death (the Acts of the Apostles), twenty-one epistles (letters attributed to Paul, Peter, John, and others), and an apocalypse (the book of Revelation) (see table 3.3). Just as with the Hebrew Bible, the authorship of these texts is a debated issue. Christian tradition assigns as author of each book one of Jesus' original disciples or a renowned figure in the early Church, but no one knows for certain who wrote much of the material. What we do know for certain is that the earliest Christian writer is a man named Paul.

Though most people typically cite Jesus as the founder of Christian-ity, the fact remains that Jesus is born and dies a religious Jew. He never intends to found a new religion; rather, Jesus seeks to rectify some of the problems within Judaism. All of his actions point to this truth, and Jesus himself says as much (Matt 5:17). Jesus is more of a religious reformer, and it is really Paul, the Jewish missionary to the Gentiles, who is respon-sible for the spread of Christianity beyond the shores of ancient Israel. Although thirteen letters in the New Testament are ascribed to him, it is likely that only seven are from his hand: Romans, 1 Corinthians, 2 Cor-inthians, Galatians, Philippians, 1 Thessalonians, and Philemon. Because the other six letters differ in style and reflect the concerns of a later time in Christian history, most scholars agree that these are written in Paul's name by his followers sometime after his death. The earliest of the seven authentic Pauline Epistles is 1 Thessalonians, written in about 50 CE,

Table 3.3. The New Testament (with Abbreviations)

The Gospels	Other "Pauline" Letters
Matthew (Matt)	2 Thessalonians (2 Thess)
Mark (Mark)	Colossians (Col)
Luke (Luke)	1–2 Timothy (1–2 Tim)
John (John)	Titus (Titus)
	Ephesians (Eph)
Acts of the Apostles (Acts)	
	Other Apostolic Letters
Authentic Pauline Epistles	Hebrews (Heb)
Romans (Rom)	James (Jam)
1–2 Corinthians (1–2 Cor)	1 Peter (1 Pet)
Galatians (Gal)	2 Peter (2 Pet)
Philippians (Phil)	1, 2, 3, John (1, 2, 3 Jn)
1 Thessalonians (1 Thess)	Jude (Jude)
Philemon (Phlm)	
	Revelation (Rev)

which makes it the oldest complete Christian document, older even than the Gospels.

Saul, who is known in the Hellenistic world as Paul, is born in Tarsus, located in modern Turkey, in about 5 CE, which makes him a contemporary of Jesus. He studies under Gamaliel, one of the greatest Jewish teachers, and becomes a Pharisee (Acts 23:6–8; 26:4–5; Phil 3:5). A former persecutor of early Christians, Saul/Paul is transformed by a visionary encounter with the risen Jesus (Gal 1:11–17; Acts 9:1–9; 22:3–11; 26:12–19; cf. 1 Cor 15:8). Following his conversion experience, by all accounts, Paul seems to have been a tireless missionary, committed to spreading the Good News about Jesus. Paul's letters are designed to address specific problems and issues within the early Christian communities he founded, mostly in Asia Minor. He encounters some staunch opposition, both from some of the remaining Jerusalem Apostles as well as from outside factions who disagree with some of his teachings. Paul's theology has a profound impact on the emerging Christian Church and serves as a biblical linchpin for the Protestant Reformation.

The Gospels tell the story of Jesus of Nazareth through the eyes of the four authors (or *Evangelists*): Matthew, Mark, Luke, and John. As I mentioned in chapter 1, written between 70 and 95 CE, the Gospels take the form of biographical descriptions of Jesus' life; they cannot, however, be compared to modern biographies. The Gospels can best be described as *theological* stories about Jesus from a faith perspective. For example, other than the brief stories of Jesus' birth in Matthew and Luke—and one short scene of Jesus as an older child, being left behind in Jerusalem during a family pilgrimage (Luke 2:42–51)—there are no stories of Jesus' childhood or his life before we meet him in the Gospels as an adult.

Modern readers often wonder: Where was he all those years? What did he look like? Was he married? The Gospels are silent on such details because these questions are relatively unimportant in the story the Evangelists wished to tell. To them, the most important part of Jesus' life begins with his ministry. Incidentally, such stories about Jesus' early life and family become the subject of noncanonical, apocryphal gospels written within a century of the official Gospels. In 1947, the Dead Sea Scrolls, a collection of Jewish documents found in the Judean Desert, and the Nag Hammadi library, a collection of ancient books (or *codices*) found near Luxor in Egypt that preserve noncanonical Christian writings, were unearthed. These texts from ancient Jewish and Christian sects testify to the rich diversity of legends and doctrines among early Jews and Christians. One does not need to be a scholar to read and appreciate these texts, however; they are available in a variety of translations at any major book retailer.

The first three canonical Gospels, Matthew, Mark, and Luke, contain similar stories that generally follow the same order. As mentioned in chapter 1, because they are so alike, they are often called the *Synoptic Gospels* (synoptic is from the Greek, meaning "like view"). Biblical scholar Raymond F. Collins terms them "look-alike Gospels" and this is perhaps the best way to think about Matthew, Mark, and Luke. The Synoptic Gospels not only share a similar chronology of events in Jesus' life, but they also share many of the same themes or concerns, including the emphasis on Jesus as teacher, worker of miracles, and exorcist. In the Synoptic Gospels, Jesus proclaims the Kingdom of God is at hand, and he reaches out to the poor and disenfranchised.

The fourth Gospel, the Gospel of John, however, is quite different, both in the way in which Jesus is presented and in its theology. The Gospel of John is more verbose, more patently symbolic, and more philosophic than the Synoptic Gospels, which have a relatively straightforward narrative style. Still, regarding the major aspects of Jesus' life, all four Gospels agree: The Roman authorities condemn and crucify Jesus; he is buried, and he rises from the dead.

Acts of the Apostles, the book that follows the Gospel of John in the canon, is the second of two volumes written by the anonymous author of the Gospel of Luke. Acts chronicles, in ideal fashion, the adventures of the early Christian community following the resurrection of Jesus. The adventures begin in Jerusalem and end in Rome with Paul carrying the Good News to the heart of the Roman Empire. The spread of Christianity, the work of the Holy Spirit, the relationship between Judaism and Christianity, and the nonviolent nature of the Christian movement are among the central themes of Acts. Most scholars agree that Acts is written sometime between 80 and 85 CE.

A man named John (not the author of the fourth Gospel), a Christian exiled to the island of Patmos (Rev 1:1, 4, 9; 22:8), is the author of the final book of the New Testament, Revelation (not *Revelations*!). An excellent example of apocalyptic literature—a popular style of writing during this period—Revelation employs highly symbolic language to describe the "end time." The last book admitted into the Christian canon, Revelation describes a series of strange, symbolic visions and cosmic battles between the forces of good (led by Christ) and evil (led by Satan). The book of Revelation is the most misunderstood, misapplied, and, some might argue, the most "dangerous" book in the Bible. Over the centuries, including recent history, those who fail to recognize the symbolism and literary style inherent in this ancient text have used it for propaganda purposes and to quite simply frighten people. I will discuss this more in future chapters, but, for now, it is important to understand that apocalyptic literature is a literature of crisis, written to address concerns during the author's lifetime, not ours. It is wrong, however, to assume that modern readers cannot find hope and meaning in the book of Revelation (for they can and surely do), but we must recognize the author's audience and remain faithful to his intentions.

Armed with this very basic understanding of the Hebrew Bible and New Testament, it seems prudent to say a few words about the center of it all: God.

God in the Bible

The Bible, at its base, is really a story about God. Scholars and sages, rabbis and priests, the faithful and the skeptical, all have their opinions about God—who God is and what God wants from us. But what does the *Bible* tell us about God? We cannot make generalizations about the God of the Bible—for God, like the evolution of the Bible itself, changes over time. The biblical God is complicated, inscrutable, and mercurial. And this truth is just as apparent to the ancients as it is to us. Recall, for example, that it is God, the frenetic artist, who creates all forms of life in the first two chapters of Genesis, only to then destroy his flawed masterpiece in a catastrophic flood a few chapters later. This same God, in the Exodus tale, inflicts unimaginable horror on the Egyptians in the form of deadly plagues, but then parts the sea so the Israelites (his undisputed favored ones, at least in this story) can cross dry-shod to escape Pharaoh's pursuing army. And it is God who dictates the ruinous destruction of Jerusalem and the exaggerated punishment of the Exile—but then, in an about-face, offers the hope of restoration to the demoralized exiles as they prepare to return to the Promised Land.

Though some, quite rightly, rationalize that the elusive nature of the biblical God is evidence of God's grandeur, one thing is for certain: The God of the Bible is an enigma, impossible to pin down, and full of surprises. And, of all the characters in the Bible, God is perhaps the most tragic. Time and time again, God lays down the rules for humans to follow, and humans promise that they will be faithful; yet, time and time again, the rules are broken and God's punishment follows. This unfortunate cycle repeats itself throughout the Bible, and one cannot help but wonder why God does not simply give up on us.

The two most common names for God in the Hebrew Bible are *Elohim* and *Yhwh*. Elohim can mean either "God" or "gods," depending on the context. Yhwh, the special name of the deity who makes a covenant with the people of Israel, is usually pronounced "Yahweh," though no one is certain that this is indeed the correct pronunciation. God reveals his name to Moses when he calls upon Moses to demand that Pharaoh release the Hebrews from Egyptian slavery. Moses is unsure that the slaves will follow him, so he asks God, "If I come to the Israelites and say to them, 'The God of your ancestors has sent me to you,' and they ask me, 'What is his name?' what shall I say to them?" God says to Moses, "I am Who I am" (Exod 3:13–15). What does God mean by this expression? Karen Armstrong, the author of *The History of God*, believes that "I am Who I am" is a Hebrew idiomatic expression used to denote deliberate vagueness. In other words, God will be whomever and whatever God chooses to be.

The Hebrew words might also mean "I will be who I will be" or "I cause to be what I cause to be." This phrase "I cause to be what I cause to be" (in other words, "I make everything happen," as clear a statement of monotheism as you will find) gets formulated as a single word in Hebrew: Yhwh. Over time, God's name is considered too sacred to enunciate, so, instead, the Hebrew word *adonay*, "my Lord," is used. The Hebrew word *Yhwh* is translated in English Bibles as "the LORD," and the latter word is often doubly marked as special in printed Bibles by rendering it in an initial capital and small capitals.

The three great monotheistic religions—Judaism, Christianity, and Islam—all profess belief in one God, and we tend to assume that monotheism happens all at once. But the Bible itself indicates that this is not the case. There are numerous references in the Bible to gods other than The One. Indeed, at least initially, the LORD of the Universe faces some hefty competition; Yhwh is not always alone in the hearts and minds of the people. Rival gods and goddesses (Baal, Astarte, Molech, and many more) of neighboring peoples often prove irresistible to the Israelites, which results in the LORD's punishment and in condemnation by the biblical authors.

> The Israelites again did what was evil in the sight of the LORD, worshiping the Baals and the Astartes, the gods of Aram, the gods of Sidon, the gods of Moab, the gods of the Ammonites, the gods of the Philistines. Thus they abandoned the LORD and did not worship him. (Judg 10:6)

> [B]ecause of all the evil of the people of Israel and the people of Judah that they did to provoke me to anger . . . . They set up their abominations in the house that bears my name, and defiled it. They built the high places of Baal in the valley of the son of Hinnom, to offer up their sons and daughters to Molech. (Jer 32:32–35)

> You shall tear down their altars, break their pillars, and cut down their sacred poles (for you shall worship no other god, because the LORD, whose name is Jealous, is a jealous God). (Exod 34:13–14)

Over time, largely thanks to the prophetic movement in Israel, God secures his place as The One and Only. With the triumph of monotheism, God mellows, and, toward the end of the Hebrew Bible, God's graciousness and love for his Chosen People is emphasized.

In the New Testament, this love and concern is most manifest in Jesus, whom Christians believe to be the incarnation (God made flesh) of The One. According to Christians, human experience allows people to encounter God in the tangible daily tasks of living a life in Christ, and also in more transcendent ways, for this new life offers the promise of redemption and salvation for humankind.

As we move through the various themes in chapters 4 through 10, it is important to understand that different writers at different time periods understand God in different ways. The same can be said of us today. If you were with fifty other passengers on a bus in any major city in the United States and each passenger was asked to describe God, chances are, you would receive fifty different descriptions. If those fifty people were to discuss their opinions about God, I can guarantee that more than a few arguments would ensue. This is because our life experiences help to shape our understanding of God. The biblical authors also have their own experiences of God. As we enter into their stories, we may encounter a variety of images of God, many of which seem to contradict each other. While this may initially confuse some readers, if you keep in mind the fact that the author is trying to explain his or her understanding of God, you will be able to appreciate the important lessons or truths the writer is trying to convey. Over time, you will probably come to appreciate this varied portrait of God, perhaps viewing it as an intricate mosaic that speaks to you in a variety of different ways, depending upon your circumstances.

Working through the Bible: Tools of the Trade

In order to begin to read and understand the Bible, you will first have to master a few tricks of the trade. None of these skills are particularly difficult, and my own students—even those who struggle at first—gain competency in using these tools in a relatively short period of time. The first and most important tool is something you already have: curiosity. Every scholar expresses intellectual curiosity about a particular book or passage in the Bible, and this drives him or her to find answers to certain questions. You would not be reading this book if you were not at least curious about the Bible.

The second tool of the trade is to use a good translation of the Bible. I already discussed the fact that there are many different translations available today, but I neglected to mention the fact that many of these translations are, in a word, terrible. Any serious student of the Bible must use a reputable translation, and preferably a study Bible. Remember that study Bibles offer helpful commentary and footnotes along with the biblical text. They are essentially the Bible, but with notes. Although you may be partial to your particular translation of the Bible, if you are serious about learning, then you might want to invest in a study Bible or at least check one out of your local library. As far as which study Bible is best, I recommend the *Catholic Study Bible*, which uses the New American Bible translation, for Catholics; for Jews, the *Jewish Study Bible* is a good choice. Protestants might consider the New Revised Standard Version as found in one of two excellent study Bible versions: the *New Oxford Annotated Bible* or the *New Interpreters' Study Bible*. I have included full citations of these Bibles in the resources section.

The third important tool in biblical studies is exegesis (from the Greek, meaning "to lead out of"). Simply put, exegesis is the process of trying to figure out the original meaning of a particular text through careful analysis and interpretation. Though there are different approaches, all exegesis has to do with examining the historical context of the text in order to ascertain the author's meaning. It is not as difficult as it sounds, however, because biblical scholars have already done most of the work for you. There are shelves of biblical commentaries at your disposal, written by a variety of experts in related fields. These fields include history, geography, Ancient Near Eastern languages, gender studies, anthropology, linguistics, philology, theology, archaeology, and more.

Your initial task is to find a good biblical commentary that takes into account these diverse fields. I recommend the *New Jerome Biblical Commentary*, a standard in biblical studies. It is affordable, if you decide to purchase it, but it is also available at most public libraries. The *New Jerome Biblical Commentary* will be an enormous help to you as you gain competency in reading the Bible. Filled with introductory material, commentary on every single passage in the Bible, charts, and maps, it will quickly become an indispensable tool for you. I have included the full citations of several excellent biblical commentaries, including the *New Jerome Biblical Commentary*, in the resources section for your perusal.

You may think that you can read and interpret the Bible for yourself and may wonder why you need a commentary at all. Well, you probably can read and interpret a given passage for yourself, but more often than not, most people tend to insert modern ideas into ancient texts, thus making the text say something that author or authors never intended it to say. For example, question one on the Sixty-Second Super-Easy Bible Quiz has to do with Adam, Eve, and the snake in the Garden of Eden. I said in my commentary about this question that some students assume that the snake in the Garden is the Devil. This is an excellent example of making the text say something that the author does not intend. The J writer (the purported author) has no concept of Satan or any other evil being opposed to God. The idea of Satan takes many years to develop, and inserting modern notions of Satan into the story changes its meaning.

A good biblical commentary will alert you to the historical context of the story as well as the literary genre of the passage, both of which will help you to understand the purpose behind the story, parable, or poem. Once you have a solid understanding of the text, you can begin to think about its relevance today. This is referred to as *hermeneutics*, a fancy word that has a very down-to-earth meaning. Essentially, you want to understand the original meaning of the text and then glean contemporary applications. Most of the time, people simply skip the exegetical part, either due to ignorance or laziness, and jump to the hermeneutical part. But this can lead to distortions—reading into the text false meanings. The best hermeneutics are grounded in solid exegesis. Remember that.

As we deal with the seven themes that comprise the next seven chapters, you will notice that I often cite or directly quote from select passages to help elucidate a particular point (I have already begun this practice in a somewhat abbreviated fashion in chapters 1 through 3). You should consider reading these passages and perhaps the material surrounding them, first from your study Bible, carefully reviewing all footnotes connected to particular verses. Once you have done this, turn next to your biblical commentary and explore the scholarly opinion regarding the verses under consideration. This is time consuming, especially at the beginning, but it will help you in a variety of ways. Perhaps most important, it will enable you to grow accustomed to the process of reading and interpreting; this is the first skill all scholars must learn. The information in your study Bible and commentary will also help you to understand such key elements as context, historical setting, authorship (if known), and any connections the passage might have to other parts of the Bible.

It is important to remember that I will be treating specific *themes*, such as Heaven and hell, which I have arranged *topically* in this book. However, the Bible—and your commentary—is *not* arranged topically. You cannot open your commentary and find a specific chapter on Heaven any more than you can crack open the Bible and find everything it says about Heaven in one convenient place. The Bible itself is, for the most part, arranged chronologically, using a historical framework, though there are books and passages that certainly fall out of this general historical order. Your commentary is arranged sequentially, following the general layout of the Bible, something you will come to greatly appreciate. I have chosen to use a thematic approach because it is more interesting and it also allows the reader to examine a wide variety of biblical texts in a single chapter. All of this helps to build both knowledge and competency in reading the Bible in the most efficient way possible. Indeed, one of my goals is to have you flipping around the Bible like a pro by the end of the second theme!

Important Resources Outside of the Bible

In addition to a solid biblical commentary, there are many other resources that can help you to better understand the Bible. Scholars and laypeople alike have generated a vast array of articles, books, websites, blogs, and countless other written materials that can help shed light on nearly every aspect of the Bible. A good Bible concordance (a massive text that alphabetically lists biblical words and where they can be found in the Bible) can also serve as an indispensable tool. The most popular biblical concordance is the *New Strong's Expanded Exhaustive Concordance of the Bible*, listed in the resources section of this book.

Another important resource is the archaeological record. During the past 150 years, archaeologists have unearthed vast treasure troves of artifacts that assist us in better understanding the world of the Bible. Various towns and cities have been meticulously excavated, some for generations, and have yielded their secrets. More than any other time in history, we are now better able to reconstruct many of the events in the Bible. This discipline, often termed "biblical archaeology," is more appropriately "Ancient Near Eastern archaeology," as much of what has been discovered exceeds the scope of the biblical narrative. The inclusion of material remains helps many of the stories in the Bible to come alive and, as a professor, there is nothing more thrilling for me then to walk with my students through the excavated ruins of places they have read about in the Bible. Incorporating the archaeological record into biblical studies has become part and parcel of most Bible college courses and there is even a new version of the Bible—the *NIV Archaeological Study Bible: An Illustrated Walk through Biblical History and Culture,* published by Zondervan—that includes photographs and descriptions of various sites associated with stories in the Bible.

In addition to books, commentaries, concordances, and material remains, there are certain historical texts that enable us to imagine what life was like during biblical antiquity. For instance, the Jewish historian Flavius Josephus (37–100 CE) describes the Jewish revolt against the Romans (66–70 CE) in his *The Jewish War.* Josephus' *Antiquities of the Jews* is a twenty-volume work that traces the history of the world according to the Jews, using the Bible as the definitive source for the first ten volumes. Other ancient texts, such as the aforementioned Dead Sea Scrolls and Nag Hammadi documents, are among hundreds that have been uncovered and translated into English.

Moving Forward

Beginning any new enterprise is always a bit overwhelming at first. If you have carefully read this chapter, you might be feeling as if you have your work cut out for you. My students often express similar sentiments after the first week or so of class. I understand their apprehension, and suspect that some readers of this book share them. When I respond to my students' concerns, I ask them to trust me and remain open-minded. I urge them to put away their preconceived notions about the Bible and to simply listen, read, and learn. I also reassure them that the information presented in the first few weeks of class will become clearer as we begin to directly engage the Bible. And so I ask these things of you, too, as we move forward to discuss our first theme: the Problem of Pain.

The Problem of Pain

Why Do We Suffer?

Think occasionally of the suffering of which you spare yourself the sight.

—ALBERT SCHWEITZER

W hy is the world such a mess? Why do good and decent people die every day from debilitating and painful illnesses? Why are so many of the world's children condemned to lives of poverty and pain? Why are there earthquakes, hurricanes, mudslides, and other natural disasters that destroy villages, homes, and lives? After watching the evening news, which daily brings us up close and personal to the varieties of human suffering, we cannot help but ask such questions. Crime, disease, and violence, although they may appear to be the hallmark of our age, are nothing new. We are simply better informed. We know that pain and suffering occur in every corner of the world, and all we have to do is to log on to our computer or switch on our cable television to learn about the latest epidemic, terrorist attack, or tsunami that has caused mass suffering and death.

The foundational question concerning the reason(s) why we suffer has plagued humanity since the dawn of time. In fact, it is *the* central question with which most of us wrestle today. While many attractive and thoughtful responses to the question of suffering have been put forth by prophets, mystics, theologians, philosophers, clergy, and countless others who have felt the ripple effect of pain in one of its many guises, none are completely satisfying. More often than not, we push back from the table still hungry. The failure to adequately address this perplexing issue is often cited as the reason behind the mass exodus of (mostly) young people from the religious institutions in which they are reared.

Though less informed about world events, people living in biblical times experience much of what we experience today: illness, grief, heartbreak, war, hunger, poverty, and natural disasters, and they, too, wonder why humankind is apparently destined to suffer. The Problem of Pain enters the human story as described in the Bible in the second chapter of Genesis. The story begins well enough: The LORD creates an idyllic paradise for Adam and Eve; there is no sickness, no hunger, and no death. Peace and harmony reign, and all is right between humans and God. But then, in Eden as in life, the other shoe drops. In the very next chapter, everything changes when a single choice unleashes a cyclone of consequences that affect the lives of all future generations, forever polluting the paradise that is Eden.

According to the story, Adam and Eve willfully disobey God's injunction that prohibits eating a particular fruit. No reason is given for this injunction, and no reason is necessary; when God issues a command, humans must comply or suffer the consequences. The motif of the forbidden thing is an age-old one, told in countless tales by nearly every culture in the world, and it speaks to our human inclination to want the very thing that we cannot have—in this case, the fruit. But the story is about much more than wanting something that we cannot have. The story of Adam and Eve (Genesis 3) and their disobedience is the biblical explanation of how pain and suffering first enter the world. The author of the story makes it clear that we suffer when we choose to disobey God's commands.

Though the point may be well taken, the story offers us an incomplete rationale for human misery. We are familiar with the suffering that results from our own poor choices—as in the case of Adam and Eve—but what about the suffering that comes from sources beyond our control, like childhood cancers, earthquakes, paralyzing accidents, and random shootings?

When I address the question of pain in my college classroom, I usually begin by asking the following question: Why do *you think* we suffer? I encourage students to consider this for a moment and to write down their responses. I then invite them to share what they believe to be the root cause of suffering with the rest of the class. I encourage you, too, to pause for a moment and reflect upon this question and, if possible, to write down what you feel is the reason(s) why we suffer.

Over the years, I have carefully listened to the litany of responses put forth by thousands of students concerning what they perceive to be the cause of human misery. What follows is a short list of the most popular answers to this question in no particular order:

1. Suffering is a form of punishment for sin.
2. What goes around comes around—we get what we deserve.
3. Everything happens for a reason, including suffering.
4. We suffer in order to learn something; it is, in a sense, a test.
5. Suffering is random; it just happens.

I have observed that most students have very little trouble coming up with a rationale to explain suffering and that this rationale is very much part of their worldview. In fact, they often state their beliefs regarding the Problem of Pain with great authority. This is, for the most part, because many of them are between the ages of eighteen and twenty-two—well before the age when we typically experience our share of aches and pains, the loss of loved ones, bitter disappointments, and shattered dreams. It is all well and good to formulate a pat answer regarding the source of suffering if you have never really been affected by it—when it is merely a theoretical abstraction. Though most of my students, thankfully, have not yet experienced real suffering firsthand, there are some who have. Several years ago, I had a bright and unusually mature sophomore student named Amanda, whose mother had recently died of cancer. Since I conduct this exercise at the beginning of the semester, I had no way of knowing that Amanda had just lost her mother. After several students shared their responses regarding suffering, I asked Amanda for her thoughts. She shook her head and said simply, "I don't know why innocent people suffer in this world. I guess there are some things that I will never understand and suffering is one of them." Not surprisingly, Amanda's answer to the question of suffering came from her personal journey of grief and loss. But her response is actually quite "biblical," as we shall soon see.

Recall that in the introduction to this book, I mentioned that I would begin by using a more general approach in this chapter and in the next. That is, we will explore key texts in the Bible that help to either support or negate our commonly held assumptions. Our focus, therefore, will be a bit narrow in scope. In chapters 6 through 10, however, I will assume a greater competency on your part and will therefore offer commentary that is more specific to each individual assumption, but broader. We will, in a sense, cast a wider net as your comfort level in using the Bible increases. Let us now turn to our subject at hand, pain and suffering.

In exploring suffering, we turn first to the book of Job in the Hebrew Bible, considered by many to be the Bible's most comprehensive response to the Problem of Pain. Next, we will examine the way in which the great prophets account for suffering, including the book of Daniel, an apocalyptic text whose rationale for human misery influences first-century thinkers, including Jesus.

In the New Testament, we shall explore what Jesus and Paul have to say about suffering and conclude with another apocalyptic text, the final book in the New Testament, the book of Revelation. Although I will offer a brief summary of the texts under consideration, as always, I recommend that you read them on your own, with the aid of your commentary. I also encourage you to take notes and pose questions that you might want to explore for yourself at some future date. Begin to look for connections between the texts and make note of the meaning behind the words. Try to avoid reading your own personal biases into the texts and, instead, allow the text to speak to you. Read the biblical passages I cite for you slowly and be sure to examine all of the footnotes in your study Bible. When a particular town, city, or region is mentioned in the text, turn to the maps in the back of your study Bible (or Google the place!) and try to locate it. Students and scholars read the Bible in this proactive way, and now is the time for you to use these tried-and-true methods of probing the biblical text.

The Suffering of Job

The book of Job is the quintessential tale of undeserved suffering. Job is a good and pious man whose unprovoked suffering moves the reader, both ancient and modern, to ask the eternal question, "If God truly loves us, how can God allow us to suffer?" This initial question leads to others: "Why did God create a world in which we suffer in the first place? Why do bad people often flourish and innocent people sometimes suffer? Is God testing me? Why does God rescue some, but not all?" and many more. Theologians often refer to these theological conundrums as the problems of *theodicy*; that is, how can we reconcile a God that is all-knowing, all-loving, and all-powerful (attributes typically associated with God) to a world riddled with heartache, despair, and death?

The theodicy question is at the heart of the book of Job, for despite his faithfulness to the LORD, Job suffers unimaginable losses. First, Job is divested of his wealth and livelihood; next, his ten children all die in a freak storm on the same day; and finally, Job suffers serious health problems that render him incapacitated. A man described as "blameless and upright, one who feared the LORD and turned away from evil" (Job 1:1), Job is a good person who certainly does not deserve such personal devastation. Centuries of devout Christians and Jews have turned to Job in times of personal crisis, not so much for answers (the reason for Job's suffering—or suffering in general—is never fully explained in the story) but for comfort. We find consolation in Job's pain because it speaks to our own pain and our innate sense of the unfairness of it all.

Scholars do not know for certain when the book of Job is written. Most imagine that it is written after the Exile, between 530 and 400 BCE, as a way of dealing with the question of whether God treats Israel justly by sending its people into exile in the first place. Such a question cannot be addressed directly, for at this time, it is considered a sacrilege. Instead, the author of Job gives us a hypothetical story about a legendary character who suffers unjustly.

The book of Job is well known, even among those who have never taken the time to read it, not only because it deals with the theodicy question, but also because it features another interesting character: Satan. Actually, that's satan with a lowercase *s*, or, more appropriately, *hassatan*, in Hebrew. Though most modern biblical translations incorrectly render the Hebrew *hassatan* "Satan" in English, it is important to note that this character is not the Devil, as we know him today, but merely a member of the Divine Court of the LORD. Throughout the Bible, God is frequently mentioned in the context of royalty—a heavenly King, on a throne, surrounded by angelic creatures. This heavenly entourage, called the *benay elohim* (sons of God) in Hebrew, is modeled after the attendants of earthly kings. *Hassatan* in Job is merely a member of this throng of adoring footmen who are part of God's royal entourage and who do the LORD's bidding. In Hebrew, the *ha* part of *hassatan* is a definite article—"the" in English—and *satan* is variously translated to mean "adversary," "troublemaker," or "obstructer." Thus, *hassatan* denotes this character's particular *function* in the story and should not be understood as a proper noun. Still, Job features the most developed and sustained appearance of the cosmic troublemaker, *hassatan*, who is Satan's direct biblical ancestor. *Hassatan's* role in Job is to test the integrity of this righteous man in order to discern the mettle of Job's faith.

The action in the story shifts between the earthly realm and God's heavenly abode; *hassatan* moves with ease between both spheres, causing strife and creating mayhem. We first meet *hassatan* at a gathering of the Heavenly Council: "One day the heavenly beings came to present themselves before the LORD and Satan [*hassatan*] also came among them" (Job

1:6). "Where have you come from?" (Job 1:7), God asks *hassatan*, and he replies, "From going to and fro on the earth, and from walking up and down on it" (Job 1:7). God then engages in a bit of bragging about Job's piety and wonders if *hassatan* observed Job's fidelity during his earthly roving activities: "Have you considered my servant, Job? There is no one like him on earth, a blameless and upright man who fears God and turns away from evil" (Job 1:8). "Fear of God" in the Hebrew sense does not mean that Job is afraid of God; rather, it denotes awe, loyalty, and respect for God. *Hassatan* assumes Job's piety is less than heroic and is grounded in some sort of ulterior motive. After all, it is easy to love and worship God if one has a charmed life and is abundantly blessed by good fortune, like Job. *Hassatan's* subsequent rhetorical question goes straight to the heart of the matter: "Does Job fear God for nothing?" (Job 1:9). As far as *hassatan* is concerned, Job's piety is the result of Job's good fortune: "Have you not put a fence around him and his house and all that he has on every side? You have blessed the work of his hands, and his possessions have increased in the land" (Job 1:10).

The word "fence" reminds us that Job and his family, his wealth, and his good health enjoy God's special protection. Job's world is safe and his "fences" secure—that is, until the Troublemaker, *hassatan*, offers a challenge to God to remove those fences, to see what Job is made of behind all that insulation: "But stretch out your hand now and touch all that he has, and he will curse you to your face" (Job 1:11). God considers the challenge and allows *hassatan* to inflict unimaginable misery on Job to test his devotion, but God has one proviso— *hassatan* is not allowed to harm Job physically, at least not yet (Job 1:12). Before we go any further, it is important for the reader to understand that *hassatan* has no power to act on his own; his ability to cause trouble for Job comes only from the LORD. This disquieting fact—that *God* is behind Job's systematic ruination—is often overlooked in a cursory reading of the story.

Hassatan wastes no time ruining Job's life. First, Job's livestock are stolen by raiders; next, Job's herds and field hands are incinerated in a brush fire; then Job's camels and stable hands are lost to a marauding band; finally, unspeakably, Job's ten children, assembled for a family occasion, die in a tornado (Job 1:13–19). Job's reaction reflects the grief customs of his day: he tears his garment, shaves his head, falls to the ground, and affirms God's sovereignty (Job 1:20–21). "Naked I came from my mother's womb, and naked shall I return there; the LORD gave, and the LORD has taken away; blessed be the name of the LORD" (Job 1:22). Job passes the first test, yet we cannot help but observe that, so far, God does not look very good in the story, and things only get worse.

The second test follows the same pattern. At another gathering of the *benay elohim*, God again boasts, "Have you considered my servant Job? There is no one like him on earth, a blameless and upright man who fears God and turns away from evil" (Job 2:3; 1:8). The repetition serves to heighten the tension between God and the Adversary, and we wince at the fact that God's victory is at Job's expense.

Ironically, God blames *hassatan* for Job's reversal of fortune—"He [Job] still persists in his integrity, although you [*hassatan*] incited me against him, to destroy him for no reason" (Job 2:3)—but careful readers know full well that it is *God* who provokes *hassatan* to consider Job in the first place, and it is *God* who grants *hassatan* permission to dismantle the structures of this righteous man's life. In round one, God places limits on what *hassatan* may do to Job (he cannot physically harm him). *Hassatan*, however, views this restriction as the reason behind God's victory: "Skin for skin! All that people have they will give to save their lives. But stretch out your hand now and touch his bone and his flesh, and he will curse you to your face" (Job 2:4–5). In the Troublemaker's opinion, Job's piety is only skin deep; the point God scores in round one is only because God places limits on *hassatan*. The Adversary now challenges God to withdraw his initial proviso and to allow *hassatan* to physically hurt Job. God is so certain of Job's faithfulness that he relents and permits *hassatan* to inflict physical pain upon Job, but the LORD has a new condition: The Adversary may hurt Job and make him sick, but he may not take Job's life (Job 2:6).

The Troublemaker once again departs the heavenly realm and, returning to Job's earthly home (cf. Job 1:12 and 2:2), wastes no time adding to Job's misery by inflicting "loathsome sores on Job from the sole of his foot to the crown of his head" (Job 2:7). The image of the once robust Job is pathetic as he sits in an ash pit, scraping his boils with a potsherd (Job 2:8). Despite *hassatan*'s actions, however, Job passes the second test with flying colors: "In all this Job did not sin with his lips" (Job 2:10). With Job's ruination complete and his piety an established fact, God wins the second and final round, and *hassatan* drops out of the story.

The rest of the book includes over thirty chapters of anguished conversation in which Job's three "friends," Eliphaz, Bildad, and Zophar, assert that, despite Job's protests of innocence, Job's suffering must be the result of sin. Even Job's wife thinks he must be guilty (Job 2:9). The normally patient and pious Job soon rages against the prevailing wisdom that we somehow get what we deserve, and he challenges God to offer an explanation for Job's pain. In response to Job's challenge, God makes a dramatic appearance in a whirlwind and spends three chapters (Job 38–40) reminding Job of the wonders and mysteries of creation, effectively giving a non-answer to the question "Why?" on the lips of the multitudes of suffering Jobs from the beginning of time.

Armed with the basics of the story, let us now return to our short list—the common suppositions most of my students offer for human suffering—to see how they square with Job's plight. We must first recall that throughout the text, Job maintains his innocence, even though his friends and wife insist that Job must be guilty or else God would not punish him to such a degree. The reader, of course, knows that Job is punished *not* because he sins, but as part of a wager between God and *hassatan*; hence, suppositions one and two—suffering is the result of sin and we get what we deserve—do not apply in Job's case. In biblical times, however, many people subscribe to this sort of thinking, and in a very real sense, the book of Job is a protest of sorts against what is then the prevailing wisdom that humans must pay a price for sin, and what goes around comes around.

The book of Job is part of a category or genre of writing known as the Wisdom literature of the Bible, which also includes the Psalms, Proverbs, and Ecclesiastes (all part of the *Ketuvim*, or Writings, discussed in chapter 2). The Wisdom tradition in ancient Israel reflects a particular worldview and style of writing that emphasizes the good life. The way humans achieve this ideal life is through hard work, self-control, appropriate speech, fear of God, and proper behavior. Certain biblical characters, like the wise patriarch Joseph (Genesis 37–50), embody these characteristics and therefore serve as models for the rest of us. The Wisdom tradition navigates the thorny issues of good and evil by basically focusing on the acquisition of virtues, which produce proper conduct and lead to success in life. Most Wisdom writings are instructive, relating teachings either from a teacher to student or father to son.

The Wisdom tradition makes it all sound so easy—behave in a certain way and good things will come to you. This sort of thinking, however, comes up short when we encounter a sufferer like Job, who does all the right things but still experiences undeserved pain. The author of the book of Job questions the veracity of "Wisdom thinking" and essentially turns it inside out. Aside from challenging the then-traditional worldview, one of the reasons why Job is considered a literary masterpiece is because we side with Job (and, ostensibly, the author), perhaps because we cannot help but see a bit of ourselves in Job's misery. Anyone who has felt singled out by misfortune, anyone who has seemingly followed all the rules but still encounters more than his or her share of suffering, and anyone who has witnessed the affliction of a good and decent person is moved by the unfairness of Job's situation.

Suppositions four and five—that everything happens for a reason or that suffering is simply random—also do not apply in Job's case, for it is clear that Job's misery is orchestrated by the LORD for reasons that make little or no sense to us. That Job does not instigate his own misery but is instead the victim of God's bet with an underling in his heavenly entourage makes Job's troubles even more difficult to bear. There is no denying the fact, however, that Job is tested—supposition number three—and that he passes the test. Despite his misfortunes, he remains faithful to the LORD. The testing of Job has led others to believe that perhaps they, too, are being tested. Suffering souls in search of reasons behind their pain often claim that there is no other plausible explanation. This is another reason why we feel a certain kinship with Job.

In sum, while the book of Job is undoubtedly an important and inspirational text in a number of ways, it fails to address the root cause of suffering. At best, the author merely points out the fallacies of the Wisdom tradition without offering a satisfying explanation for undeserved pain. The story of Job may not offer us a definitive answer regarding the reason why good people suffer, but in the deafening silence of Job's unanswered question, many suffering people who feel the sting of life's unfairness find hope in this righteous man's steadfast loyalty to an unfathomable, unforthcoming, and unknowable God.

Pain and the Prophets

If we cannot find a satisfying answer to the Problem of Pain in Job, where can we find it? Some turn to Israel's prophets for answers. The prophets act as spokespersons for God, and though the majority of prophets are male, there are some female prophets. For example, Miriam, the sister of Moses (Exod 15:20–21; Numbers 12), and the judge, Deborah (Judges 4–5). In the Hebrew Bible, there are basically two types of prophets: writing and non-writing prophets. The writing prophets have books named after them, and they—or sometimes a scribe—write down their messages from God. As I mentioned in chapter 3, some of these books are larger than others: Isaiah, Jeremiah, Ezekiel, and Daniel. These prophets, because of their larger books, are commonly referred to as the Major Prophets, while twelve others—Hosea, Joel, Amos, Obadiah, Jonah, Micah, Nahum, Habbakuk, Zephaniah, Haggai, Zechariah, and Malachi—are called Minor Prophets. Examples of the so-called non-writing prophets include figures such as Nathan (2 Samuel), Elijah, and Elisha (1–2 Kings).

The prophets transform the way in which ancient Jews—and later, Christians and Muslims—understand suffering. Simply put, the prophets view suffering as a natural consequence of failing to follow God's commands. The prophets make it clear that the God of Israel does not look the other way when humans transgress; no one is allowed to sneak away from the scene of a crime without being held accountable:

> Ah, you who call evil good
> and good evil,
> who put darkness for light
> and light for darkness,
> who put bitter for sweet
> and sweet for bitter!
> Ah, you who are wise in your
> own eyes,
> and shrewd in your own sight!
> Ah, you who are heroes in
> drinking wine
> and valiant at mixing drink,
> who acquit the guilty for a bribe,
> and deprive the innocent of their
> rights!
> Therefore as the tongue of fire
> devours the stubble,
> and as dry grass sinks down in
> the flame,
> so their root will become rotten,
> and their blossom go up like
> dust;
> for they have rejected the
> instruction of the LORD
> of hosts,
> and have despised the word of
> the Holy One of Israel. (Is 5:20–24)

God's punishments take many forms, ranging from droughts and famines to the terrifying devastation of foreign invaders who act as the LORD's lightning rod of reform. Israel must repent and return to the LORD or suffer grave consequences:

> Therefore the anger of the LORD
> was kindled against his
> people,

and he stretched out his hand
against them and struck
them;
the mountains quaked,
and their corpses were like refuse
in the streets.
For all this his anger has not
turned away,
and his hand is stretched
out still.
He will raise a signal for a nation
far away,
and whistle for a people at the
ends of the earth . . .
their arrows are sharp,
all their bows bent. (Is 5:25–26, 28)

Classical prophetic thought is nothing short of genius, for it helps to explain the unexplainable: Why are the poor crushed under the feet of the rich? Why do those in power abuse the trust of the people? How can disasters, like plagues and famines be allowed to claim the lives of God's Chosen People? The answer to all of these questions—and many more—is simple, at least as far as the prophets are concerned: The people fail to live up to their side of the covenant when they do not keep the LORD's commandments, and God has no choice but to punish the transgressors. The prophets make it clear that this is not a God with whom one trifles; the fine print must be read before entering into an agreement with such a demanding deity, and, more often than not, Israel signs without reading.

Many modern readers find this demanding point of view sobering and inflexible. Is there no wiggle room that takes into account foolish mistakes and human stupidity? What about God's love, mercy, and forgiveness? To these questions, the prophets likely respond that God *is* kind and merciful, but that God also has limits:

The LORD, the LORD,
a God merciful and gracious,
slow to anger,
and abounding in steadfast love
and faithfulness,
keeping steadfast love for the
thousandth generation,

forgiving iniquity and
transgression and sin,
yet by no means clearing the
guilty,
but visiting the iniquity of
the parents
upon the children
and the children's children
to the third and the fourth
generation. (Exod 34:6–7)

From the prophetic point of view, God insists that the guilty remain liable, sometimes for generations, which might explain the ancient obsession with genealogies. Barrenness, for instance, is viewed as a particularly harsh form of chastisement from God. If a couple cannot conceive a child, they will likely search for reasons as to why God is punishing them. They might first examine their own actions, trying to recall ways in which they might have offended the LORD. If they come up empty, they then review their family histories until they can point the finger at some distant relative who transgresses. Perhaps it is a great-grandfather's marital infidelity or a long-dead uncle's secret worship of idols that is to blame. Somebody, at some point in history, does something to move God to curse the barren couple.

To make matters worse, God's laws and expectations are often unclear and almost designed for human failure. Like a riddle that cannot be solved, the odds seem to be stacked against the Children of Israel from the get-go, as God seems to suggest:

Moreover, I gave them statutes that were not good and ordinances by which they could not live. I defiled them through their very gifts, in their offering up all their firstborn, in order that I might horrify them, so they might know I am the LORD. (Ezek 20:25–26)

The logical question on the lips of all believers is this: Who can stand? It appears that the answer is: no one. Just when we are ready to throw in the towel, however, hope glimmers darkly. For once the LORD exacts punishment, there is the promise of restoration:

Do not fear, for I have redeemed
you;
I have called you by name, you

are mine.
When you pass though the
waters, I will be with you;
and through the rivers, they
shall not overwhelm you;
when you walk through fire you
shall not be burned,
and the flame shall not
consume you . . .
Because you are precious in
my sight,
and honored, and I love you. (Is 43:1–2, 4)

If all of this seems confusing, that's because it *is* confusing. There are two main reasons why the prophetic explanations for pain and suffering are so difficult to understand. First, the notion that God *inflicts suffering* as a form of punishment is hard for modern readers to comprehend. We like to think of God as gracious and forgiving, but this is only one side of the prophets' notion of God. The prophetic worldview understands God's castigations and blessings as God's prerogatives (Is 45:6–7).

This points us in the direction of a second and arguably more complex issue: How can we turn to God in our suffering if God is, in fact, the architect of our present misery? If God is the instigator of our pain, why does God have any interest in alleviating it? Questions like these present an even bigger problem, for they hit at the heart of monotheism itself. The subject of monotheism is a complicated one, but it is at the center of the prophetic understanding of suffering, and we must therefore take a few moments to contemplate the biblical notion of belief in a single God.

The foundation of Jewish, Christian, and Islamic faith is belief in one God. Abraham is considered to be the founder of Judaism and is credited with bringing monotheism to the Jewish people. As I mentioned in chapter 3, the Jewish God, Yhwh, encounters some fierce competition from the assortment of gods and goddess worshipped by Israel's neighbors, and the Bible contains a multitude of references to deities other than Yhwh. It is safe to say that although the people of Israel eventually come to worship the One God, monotheism is a hard sell. Even after they enter into a covenant with the God of the Universe, Israel grudgingly acknowledges that other peoples have their own gods. This truth is implied in the First Commandment: "You shall have no other gods before me" (Exod 20:3). It is noteworthy that this Commandment does not say that no other gods exist; it states only that Yhwh is the exclusive God of Israel. Another example of this sort of thinking (called henotheism, or the worship of a single god without denying the existence of other gods) is found in the book of Judges, where we read that the Israelites had "abandoned the LORD, the God of their ancestors, who had brought them out of the land of Egypt," and "followed other gods, from among the gods of the peoples who were all around them" (Judg 2:12). The simplest reading of texts such as these (and there are many more) is that perhaps some Israelites hold that while Yhwh is the God of Israel, he is not the *only* god. Eventually, however, this sort of thinking is replaced with a strict form of monotheism. This is due, in large part, to the success of the prophetic movement, which insists that the gods and goddesses of other nations are nothing but bogus fabrications.

> For I [Yhwh] am God, and there is no
> other;
> I am God, and there is no one
> like me. (Is 46:9)

The triumph of monotheism appears to have been a slow evolution and cannot be dated confidently before the period of the Babylonian Exile in the mid-sixth century BCE. But how does monotheism figure into the question of suffering? Before the adoption of monotheism, the misfortunes suffered in life are often blamed on other gods or evil forces. In a monotheistic system, however, God alone is responsible. This, of course, brings us back to the beginning of the chapter and the question of theodicy and Job's untenable situation. In what appears to be a huge irony, Job finds himself in the unenviable position of asking God to rescue him, when it is, in fact, God who places Job in peril in the first place.

But how do the prophets compare to our short list of reasons why we suffer? Let us take a moment to review this list and to see how it squares with the prophetic understanding of the Problem of Pain:

1. Suffering is a form of punishment for sin.
2. What goes around comes around—we get what we deserve.
3. Everything happens for a reason, including suffering.
4. We suffer in order to learn something; it is, in a sense, a test.
5. Suffering is random; it just happens.

In the prophetic view, God alone is responsible for the joys and sorrows in life. Our pain is the result of God's reprimand and directly connected to sin, so supposition number one that regards sin as a form of punishment reflects the prophets' position. But this is problematic for us today. While we can certainly understand suffering that we bring upon ourselves (if I drink too much wine, I get a headache; if I drive too fast, I might get into an accident and hurt myself or others), but what about the sort of suffering that enters our lives and has absolutely nothing to do with our actions? The death of a loved one, debilitating illnesses, a bad economy, a cheating spouse, or the betrayal of a friend—how do the prophets explain these forms of human misfortune? The short answer is that they do not fully explain all forms of human suffering. The prophets focus largely on the failure of the people as a nation to uphold the covenant and do not, for the most part, address the scores of individual miseries that temper our happiness and cause strife. Their explanation for suffering is more or less a way to address the loss of land, foreign occupation, and exile, things we would view today as "political" or "national" concerns.

This nationalistic attitude toward suffering certainly negates reason number five, which insists that suffering is random, but it does find legs in the other four assertions. For instance, common assumption number two ("What goes around comes around—we get what we deserve") reflects the prophetic notion that Israel is punished because of her idolatrous behavior. The people are warned over and over to remain faithful to the One God, yet they are forever chasing after the more lenient and attractive gods of their neighbors. Israel's leaders—those who should know better—practice social injustice, abusing the rights of the people (Judg 10:6; Jer 32:32–35; Exod 34:13–14; Is 5:20–27). Ignoring these incessant prohibitions results in the LORD's reprimand in the form of exile from the Promised Land. The people, then, according to the prophets, get exactly what they deserve. If we look at assumption number three ("Everything happens for a reason, including suffering"), we find that it also reflects this view. There is no question as to why God must punish his Chosen Ones, for they know the rules and yet they choose to transgress. The reason for their castigation and loss of the land is to purge them of their insatiable desire for foreign gods. Similarly, supposition number four ("We suffer in order to learn something; it is, in a sense, a test") is also in line with prophetic thought. God challenges his people to live in accordance with certain laws. All challenges—then and now—are, at their core, tests of physical, mental, or emotional endurance. Moreover, God has a history of testing people— including Adam and Eve, Job, and the collective nation known as Israel. Most of those tested fail miserably and are punished with exile (Adam and Eve are thrown out of the Garden of Eden, and the Israelites are sent into exile). Job, of course, passes God's tests. He loses everything and never fully understands why. Though the prophets do not address Job's plight directly, they do resonate with the prevailing wisdom of Job's time that asserts that we somehow get what we deserve.

While the prophetic spin on suffering may find resonance with the people of biblical antiquity, modern readers often squirm under the weight of the notion that God is both the cause of and the remedy for our pain, or that God punishes or tests us. Even worse is the idea that we somehow get what we deserve or that everything happens for a reason. Anyone who has ever visited a sick child in the hospital, stood by a person unjustly accused, or read about the countless atrocities committed against humanity in the name of religion must doubt the truth of such suppositions. Ultimately, for many, understanding God in these terms is as unsatisfying as the non-answer given to Job's plaintive question, "Why?" This leads us to conclude that although the prophets offer their reasons for the suffering of the people as a whole—the failure of the nation to uphold the covenant—they fail to address suffering on a case-by-case basis. Perhaps they are as mystified by the suffering of innocent individuals as we are.

Suffering in the Book of Daniel

The mystery of a good man who suffers (Job) and the retributive justice for a recalcitrant nation (the prophetic understanding) have one thing in common: God is the mind behind it all. But somewhere in between the innocent sufferer and the disobedient sinner lies another explanation for pain. The Bible's apocalyptic books—both in the Hebrew Bible and the New Testament—offer an alternative rationale for the cause of human misery. According to the apocalyptic view, suffering emanates from evil forces at work in the world. Over time, these evil forces eventually coalesce into one formidable adversary, known as Satan.

Before we discuss the apocalyptic understanding of suffering, it seems prudent to say a few more words about apocalyptic literature in general. Jewish and Christian apocalyptic writing is a literary genre that grows out of a period of political unrest, religious factionalism, foreign domination, and tremendous social change. There are several apocalyptic books in the Bible, but the largest body of apocalyptic writings can be found in the Jewish Intertestamental literature, written during the roughly three-hundred- to four-hundred-year gap between the Hebrew Bible and New Testament (200 BCE–200 CE). The sheer quantity of writings during the Intertestamental Period attests to the popularity of this type of genre. I have already mentioned the Dead Sea scrolls, from Qumran in Israel—home of the Essenes, an ancient Jewish monastic order—and the Nag Hammadi documents from the Nile Valley (both discovered in 1947) as examples of two vast libraries that come to us from the Intertestamental Period, but there are hundreds more.

Oppressive parties and ideological rivals in apocalyptic literature are "revealed" (the basic meaning of the Greek word *apocalypsis* is "revelation") to be agents of cosmic forces working behind the scenes in order to destroy the righteous and conquer the world. As a genre, apocalyptic literature is distinct and fantastic. Replete with terrifying visions, loathsome beasts, frightening demons, and dramatic end-time scenarios, the overarching message is that good will triumph over evil. When we study apocalyptic literature in the classroom, I work with students and help them to first "decode" the symbols in the stories before reading the text. This is because apocalyptic literature tends to confound modern readers who are unfamiliar with this style of writing. Once they understand the symbols, however, reading is both enjoyable and easy.

In the book of Daniel, written in about 164 BCE, we find an excellent example of apocalyptic thought. Daniel 7–12 contains visionary tales that are typical in apocalyptic writings, including densely coded messages, gruesome beasts, and bizarre visions. For example, in Daniel 7, the prophet Daniel has a dream in which four hybrid beasts emerge out of the sea, some with multiple heads, horns, and wings. The beasts are examples of the sort of symbolism common to apocalyptic writing that must be deciphered before one can understand the meaning of the text. Though it appears that the meaning is clear to readers during the time when the book of Daniel is written, contemporary readers are often baffled by such terrifying images. In this book, the beasts represent four earthly kingdoms, all enemies of Israel, and their petty tyrants. The king of Babylon is featured as a lion with eagle's wings; the king of the Medes is represented as a bear with tusks; the Persian king as a four-headed winged leopard; and, finally, the Greek leader is a dragon with ten horns. After the beasts emerge, God (called the "Ancient One" in Daniel) appears in his heavenly throne room surrounded by a celestial throng, reminiscent of God's abode and adoring footmen in the prologue of Job. God destroys the ten-horned dragon, symbolic of the oppressive Greek ruler, Antiochus Epiphanes, whom the author clearly despises. Dominion is returned to the faithful Jews, symbolized as the "human being" coming with the clouds. Some argue that the "human being" is the archangel, Michael, who represents the faithful, while others identify this figure as the Messiah.

> And as I watched, the beast was put to death, and its body destroyed and
> given over to be burned with fire . . .
> I saw one like a human being

coming with the clouds
of heaven.
And he came to the Ancient One
and was presented before him.
To him was given dominion
and glory. (Dan 7:11, 13–14)

This strange vision reflects the suffering of the Jewish people under Greek rule and the author's hope that God will destroy the oppressors and restore Israel, with God alone as the sovereign ruler. In Daniel, the faithful suffer because of evil forces (for example, the Greek despot, Antiochus Epiphanes), but the author believes that eventually, good will triumph over evil. One cannot help but notice that a dualistic system begins to take shape in Daniel and apocalyptic writings in general. From this dualism, ever so slowly, a dark and frightening figure begins to emerge whom later generations will call Satan. In Daniel, however, no such figure exists, but the notion of external, evil forces apart from God *does* exist, and these malignant forces help to shape the author's understanding of suffering.

With our short list in mind, how does the apocalyptic book of Daniel figure into the Problem of Pain? Here, again, is our short list of commonly held assumptions regarding the reasons why good people suffer:

1. Suffering is a form of punishment for sin.
2. What goes around comes around—we get what we deserve.
3. Everything happens for a reason, including suffering.
4. We suffer in order to learn something; it is, in a sense, a test.
5. Suffering is random; it just happens.

The apocalyptic view asserts that there is an evil force at work in the world that opposes the will of God. Suffering, then, is not a form of punishment (commonly held assumption number one), nor is it a test (assumption number four) or a random occurrence (assumption number five). According to the apocalyptic writers, suffering does not mean that we deserve our pain, nor is it proof that what goes around comes around (commonly held assumptions two and three), which means that our short list finds no credence in Daniel. But why?

In the apocalyptic paradigm, suffering comes from a wholly malevolent source—ranging from corrupt earthly rulers, sometimes depicted as gruesome monsters to one familiar face in the crowd, Satan (whom we will discuss in more detail in the next chapter). God is no longer both the purveyor of pain and source of relief from it, as in the case of Job and the prophets. Instead, the apocalyptic view leaves God free to stand squarely on the side of the sufferer. This image of a more genteel God is far more appealing than the unpredictable Deity who delivers joy and pain in equal measures in much of the Hebrew Bible.

When students read these stories, they often wonder why God changes so much. Perhaps the best way to account for God's rather startling metamorphosis is look at it from a different perspective. That is, it is more likely that over time, as their level of theological sophistication increases, it is *the people* who change in their understanding of God. In any case, it is the notion of an oppositional force or cosmic corruptor that captures the imaginations of countless writers during the Intertestamental Period and, by the first century (the time of Jesus and Paul), this dualistic thinking becomes quite popular. Let us now turn our attention to the New Testament to see what it has to say about suffering.

Suffering and the New Testament: Jesus and Paul

Like the book of Daniel in the Hebrew Bible, the New Testament also has its share of apocalyptic writings, and Jesus and Paul are certainly apocalyptic thinkers. Jesus speaks repeatedly about the imminent arrival of the Kingdom of God, which to him is an earthly reality. Most people today assume that the Kingdom of God means Heaven, but this is not the case. For Jesus, the Kingdom is closely tied to his apocalyptic view of the end of days, which he believes is on the horizon and will usher in a new world order. This idea of a harmonious, transformed world (the Kingdom) that will replace the evil and corrupt present age is central to apocalyptic thought. Of course, some scholars rightly assert that it may have been the Gospel writers who are the apocalyptic thinkers and that they merely insert their thoughts about the end of days into some of Jesus' teachings. While we can never be 100 percent certain that the words we read in the Gospels are Jesus' exact words, I think we can assume that they are fairly close. And, if this is the case, Jesus clearly believes that the end is near. God's reign will inaugurate a new beginning, and the Jewish people will at last be free of foreign occupation (in this case, the Romans) so that the fruits of justice can flourish.

The birth pangs of the Kingdom, however, will involve a long and painful labor wrought with many trials and tribulations: "For nation will rise against nation, and kingdom against kingdom; there will be earthquakes in various places; there will be famines" (Mark 13:8). Jesus' message to his followers is, on the one hand, stark and frightening, but to those who endure the inevitable suffering that comes with the upheaval of the present age, there will be many rewards. He frames these rewards in terms of role reversals and gives meaning to the plight of the poor, the hungry, the bereaved, and the disenfranchised. They may be in the throes of suffering during the present iniquitous age, but in the Kingdom to come, it is the downtrodden who will prevail and the oppressors who will suffer:

> Then he looked up at his disciples and said:
> "Blessed are you who are poor,
> for yours is the kingdom of
> God. Blessed are you who are
> hungry now,
> for you will be filled. Blessed are you who weep now,
> for you will laugh.
> Blessed are you when people hate you, and when they exclude you,
>   revile you, and defame you on account of the Son of Man.
>   Rejoice in that day and leap for joy, for surely your reward
>   is great in heaven; for that is what their ancestors did to the
>   prophets.
> But woe to you who are rich,
> for you have received your
> consolation.
> Woe to you who are full now,
> for you will be hungry. Woe to you who are laughing
> now, for you will mourn and weep.
> Woe to you when all speak well of you, for that is what their ances-
>   tors did to the false prophets." (Luke 6:20–26)

These reversals indicate that there is a redemptive aspect to suffering. Jesus is the one who acts as Redeemer in his own salvific death, a concept that will become an important part of Christian faith. As the epitome of an innocent sufferer, Jesus endures the pain of the cross, and future generations of sufferers feel the kinship of their Redeemer as they endure the pain of illness, heartache, and grief.

Jesus also transforms the way suffering is traditionally understood. Most people during the first century believe that suffering is a form of punishment or that God is testing them. Jesus seems to indicate that neither is the case. In fact, his healing ministry demonstrates that he does not view illness or death as punishments but as occasions to reveal God's love. Indeed, for Jesus, the antidote to pain and suffering is love.

> As he walked along, he saw a man blind from birth. His disciples
> asked him, "Rabbi, who sinned, this man or his parents, that he

was born blind?" Jesus answered, "Neither this man nor his parents sinned; he was born blind so that God's works might be revealed in him." (John 9:1–3)

Moreover, Jesus challenges his followers to try to ease the suffering of others—even one's enemies—in his name. Suffering, then, takes on a moral imperative for the followers of Jesus, who are to carry on his healing ministry of love. Helping a neighbor, friend, or loved one who is suffering is profoundly connected to Christ's suffering.

> When the Son of Man comes in his glory, and all the angels with him, then he will sit on the throne of his glory. All the nations will be gathered before him, and he will separate people one from another as a shepherd separates the sheep from the goats, and he will put the sheep at his right hand and the goats at the left. Then the king will say to those at his right hand, "Come, you that are blessed by my Father, inherit the kingdom prepared for you from the foundation of the world; for I was hungry and you gave me food, I was thirsty and you gave me something to drink, I was a stranger and you welcomed me, I was naked and you gave me clothing, I was sick and you took care of me, I was in prison and you visited me." Then the righteous will answer him, "Lord, when was it that we saw you hungry and gave you food, or thirsty and gave you something to drink? And when was it that we saw you a stranger and welcomed you, or naked and gave you clothing? And when was it that we saw you sick or in prison and visited you?" And the king will answer them, "Truly I tell you, just as you did it to one of the least of these who are members of my family, you did it to me." (Matt 25:31–40)

Jesus not only teaches us about the redemptive value of suffering—and the call for us to work in love to help alleviate it—but he also fights beside us against the root cause suffering. Remember that in the apocalyptic worldview, evil forces disrupt and destroy lives. In the Gospels, these forces are embodied in Satan, the archnemesis of Jesus. In the New Testament, Satan is not the cosmic lackey featured in the book of Job. Now he is a fully developed being who blatantly challenges Jesus' authority and even infiltrates the ranks of those close to Jesus. Satan is not, however, allowed to simply move about in the world unopposed. Indeed, Jesus, the hero of the New Testament, steps forward to confront the villain at every turn. Although the Devil may have a few tricks up his sleeve, the authors of the New Testament make it clear that Satan is no match for God's Chosen

One. Time and time again, hero and villain engage in a struggle for universal supremacy—a struggle that ends with Satan's final banishment in the book of Revelation.

Returning to our short list, we find that none of the so-called rationales for human suffering enter into the mind-set of Jesus and many of his contemporaries.

1. Suffering is a form of punishment for sin.
2. What goes around comes around—we get what we deserve.
3. Everything happens for a reason, including suffering.
4. We suffer in order to learn something; it is, in a sense, a test.
5. Suffering is random; it just happens.

Jesus does not view suffering as a punishment or a test; it is not random or something we deserve; nor is it something we have brought upon ourselves. Suffering is the result of pervasive moral evil, whether in the form of brutal Roman tyranny, corrupt religious institutions, or Satan. Suffering, however, is a temporary condition and can be made less difficult through the compassion of others. Followers of Jesus are called to work in his name to ease suffering through acts of faith, hope, charity, selflessness, caring, and most of all, love. Ultimately, the sufferers of the present age will reap rewards in the end when the Kingdom of God ushers in the New Age.

Paul believes that his generation is standing on the threshold of this New Age, which is set into motion by Jesus' death and resurrection. It has, in a sense, already begun, which may account for the sense of urgency that pervades Paul's letters. Written between 50 and 64 CE, even before the earliest written Gospels, these letters are generally addressed to the fledgling churches founded by Paul during his missionary journeys (mainly in Asia Minor and Greece). A former persecutor of the followers of Jesus (Gal 1:13–15), Paul experiences a powerful conversion (Acts 9; cf. 1 Cor 15:7–8 and Gal 1:11–17) and embarks on an aggressive missionary campaign that transforms Christianity from a sect within Judaism to a universal religion.

We must be ever mindful of Paul's Jewish roots, however, as his Jewish background informs much of his thinking. Paul is a Pharisee (Acts 23:6–8; 26:4–5; Phil 3:5), which means he has training in the Hebrew Scriptures and strictly adheres to the teachings therein. Like the Hebrew prophets, Paul understands suffering as a form of punishment for sin, but he also shares the apocalyptic notion that suffering is the result of evil forces at work in the world. According to Paul, the redemptive death of Christ is the remedy for suffering. If there is a price to be paid for the sins of humanity (and the Pharisee in Paul believes that there is), then Jesus pays it for all of us. Like Jesus, Paul views suffering as a temporary condition. Followers of Jesus will be persecuted, but the end-time is looming in the distance, and soon Jesus will return and the righteous will experience liberation from the pain and misery of this world.

> You know what time it is, how it is now the moment for you to wake from sleep. For salvation is nearer to us now than when we became believers; the night is far gone, the day is near. Let us then lay aside the works of darkness and put on the armor of light. (Rom 13:11–12)

We now, once again, review our short list of common assumptions regarding why we suffer and compare it to Paul's thinking.

1. Suffering is a form of punishment for sin.
2. What goes around comes around—we get what we deserve.
3. Everything happens for a reason, including suffering.
4. We suffer in order to learn something; it is, in a sense, a test.
5. Suffering is random; it just happens.

It is clear that Paul's teachings agree with supposition one, which suggests suffering can be a form of God's punishment for sin (Rom 1:18). Because of his personal afflictions, including beatings, unjust imprisonment, illness, harassment from his many detractors, shipwrecks, and even division within the ranks of the churches he founded (2 Cor 11:23–28), we might even say that Paul would agree that suffering is oftentimes a test (supposition four). There is nothing to indicate that Paul believes suffering is something we deserve or that everything happens for a reason (suppositions two and three), and he certainly gives no indication that he thinks the Problem of Pain is simply random (supposition five). Nonetheless, Paul understands suffering, having endured his fair share of it, but for Paul— and for Jesus—suffering is something that must be endured while awaiting the arrival of the Kingdom: "For the present form of this world is passing away" (1 Cor 7:31). In this way, Paul's message can be viewed as quite hopeful, for he fervently believes that soon, Jesus will return and believers will experience lasting relief from all forms of suffering.

Suffering in Revelation

If the present age is truly passing away, what might the Parousia (the Second Coming of Christ) look like? This event appears in full Technicolor in the visions of a righteous sufferer, John of Patmos, in the book of Revelation. The apocalyptic book of Revelation, like the book of Daniel, contains many fantastic and terrifying visions that depict cosmic battles between the forces of good and evil; in Revelation, the combatants are God and Satan. Here we find the best example of apocalyptic writing in the New Testament and, in many ways, Revelation typifies Jewish-Christian apocalyptic writing in general (e.g., Daniel 7–12; Zechariah 7–14; Ezekiel 1–9; 26–27; 39–48).

I discussed apocalyptic literature earlier in this chapter and briefly in chapter 3, but it seems prudent to offer a few words of caution regarding the book of Revelation because it is one of the most problematic books in the Bible. I use the word *problematic* here because, in the hands of someone who does not understand ancient Jewish and Christian apocalyptic writing, Revelation can be misunderstood, misinterpreted, and downright harmful. There is no better argument for the importance of biblical literacy than the misuse and abuse of the book of Revelation. Witness cult leaders like David Koresh and Jim Jones, megalomaniacal preachers who see themselves as living in the end of days and who use the book of Revelation to terrify their followers into submission. As with any ancient text, particularly an apocalyptic book, we must proceed with equal measures of respect and caution.

Here is what the book of Revelation is not: It is not to be read literally. Like Daniel 7–12, Revelation employs a then-popular literary style that uses symbolic language to impart certain political, social, and religious truths, according to the author's point of view. The ancient author and his audience know that what they are reading is a stylized form of writing, in much the same way that if I hear hip-hop music on my radio, I know that it is a popular form of music, unique to the present generation (and will likely be misunderstood by generations two thousand years from now).

Revelation is not a prediction of the end of the world for contemporary readers—though many misguided individuals have tried to make it that. The authors can no more envision a world like ours any more than we can know what life is like on Mars. But why is it that so many modern readers assume a contemporary application? If you commit yourself to actually reading the text (along with your commentary, of course!), you will encounter a densely coded narrative, riddled with chaos, corruption, bloody battles, and death. It is not difficult to see similarities and to draw connections to our own mixed-up and dangerous world, and many people do just that. They read Revelation and feel that the end-time must be near because the world is such a terrible mess. As I write this, my own country is engaged in two wars, several nations are on the brink of economic collapse, and genocide in Darfur has claimed over four hundred thousand lives.

Let me be clear here: I am not saying that we cannot resonate with the terrifying scenarios in the book of Revelation and see contemporary connections, for the world then and now is a dangerous place. What I am asserting—and this is the opinion of the vast majority of biblical scholars—is that the author is writing about his fears and the crisis at hand for Christians in various parts of the Roman Empire toward the end of the first century. He writes down his dizzying series of visions while in exile (apparently for preaching the Christian message) on the island of Patmos (Rev 1:1, 4, 9; 22:8). But what is the situation that evokes such fear, urgency, and unsettling visions? Addressed to persecuted churches in Asia Minor (Revelation 2–3), Revelation is probably written between 81 and 96 CE, during the reign of the Roman emperor Domitian. It is common practice during this time for the emperor to be deified, and it is the civic duty of all citizens of the empire to publicly acknowledge the emperor as a god. This consists of little more than a public affirmation that is likely more fluff than substance. Indeed, few citizens actually believe the emperor is divine, and while they might publicly worship him, most still venerate their own household gods.

The persecutions in Revelation center on the refusal of Christians to publicly worship the emperor. Although there does not seem to be evidence that emperor veneration is ever strictly enforced in the Roman Empire, this does not preclude the possibility that, locally, it might have been. Hence, the refusal of Christians to engage in emperor worship, and the fear of repercussions that will likely follow this refusal, is the context in which Revelation is written. Since our primary focus in this chapter centers on suffering, understanding the context of Revelation is important, as it helps us to appreciate what the text teaches us about the Problem of Pain.

The book of Revelation begins with visions and messages directed to the seven churches of Asia Minor (Revelation 1–3), followed by visions that describe the present tribulation as the prelude to the end time (Revelation 4–18), and concludes with visions depicting God's triumphant victory over the forces of evil (Revelation 12–22). Like Daniel, in Revelation an evil force is at work behind the scenes, disrupting lives and leading Christians astray. The mastermind behind all this chaos is Satan, the King of Pain. Satan and his band of demonic thugs are no match for God, however. As a war in Heaven breaks out between the forces of good and the forces of evil, we find echoes of the angelic figure in Daniel. In Revelation, the forces of good are led by the patron saint of Israel, Michael (cf. Dan 7:11–13; 10:13, 21; 12:1), and his angelic troops march against the evil forces led by Satan and his demonic cohorts:

And war broke out in heaven; Michael and his angels fought against the dragon. The dragon and his angels fought back, but they were defeated, and there was no longer any place for them in heaven. The great dragon was thrown down, that ancient serpent, who is called the Devil and Satan, the deceiver of the whole world—he was thrown down to the earth, and his angels were thrown down with him. (Rev 12:7–9)

Satan's legion is vast, "as numerous as the sands of the sea" (Rev 20:8). But, despite their numbers, Satan and his army are quickly defeated:

And fire came down from heaven and consumed them. And the devil who had deceived them was thrown into the lake of fire and sulfur, where the beast and the false prophet were, and they will be tormented day and night forever and ever. (Rev 20:9–10)

The victory belongs to God alone, who, in one final and decisive action, brings about the end of Satan and his agents. Once Satan and his minion are defeated, the dead are resurrected (Rev 20:11–15) and a new age begins (Revelation 21). This New Age ushers in a change in cosmic order marked by hopefulness and peace. John's moving description of Heaven includes a vision of God, seated on a throne (Rev 21:1–3), and speaks about life in the New Age:

See, the home of God is
among mortals.
He will dwell with them;
they will be his peoples,
and God himself will be
with them;
he will wipe every tear from
their eyes.
Death will be no more;
mourning and crying and pain
will be no more,
for the first things have
passed away. (Rev 21:3–4)

What can be said of the book of Revelation in light of our short list?

1. Suffering is a form of punishment for sin.
2. What goes around comes around—we get what we deserve.
3. Everything happens for a reason, including suffering.

4. We suffer in order to learn something; it is, in a sense, a test.
5. Suffering is random; it just happens.

Like the apocalyptic book of Daniel, the author of Revelation would probably reject our short list out of hand. John of Patmos would disagree that suffering is a form of punishment or that everything happens for a reason. He would also eschew the notion that suffering is evidence that we get what we deserve or that it is a test or simply random. The author of Revelation views suffering as the result of an evil force that must be subdued. Following a battle of cosmic proportions, Satan will ultimately be defeated and God's Kingdom will reign. Hence, despite its gruesome and horrific scenarios, Revelation is ultimately a book that reassures the righteous sufferer that God is on their side and that goodness will prevail.

Conclusions

In our investigation of the Hebrew Bible's three main rationales for the Problem of Pain, we looked at the book of Job and the prophets, including the book of Daniel, and compared what they had to say to our short list that posits the causes of suffering from a modern perspective.

Some of the rationales on our short list clearly have roots in the Hebrew Bible; others do not. In general, we can say that the book of Job teaches us that even the most righteous among us are destined to suffer and that humans are not privy to the reasons why. Piety and faithfulness do not insulate us from the pain of sudden misfortune. The book of Job suggests that it is our task is to accept our fate and to place our unquestioning trust in God.

The prophets view suffering and blessings as the LORD's prerogatives, and the only way to avoid suffering is to obey God's commands. Obedience brings blessings; disobedience brings punishment. Theirs is a cut-and-dried nationalistic theology; Israel must keep the covenant or pay the consequences. Contemporary audiences often find this austere theology as challenging and as difficult as understanding Job's plight.

Finally, the apocalyptic view, as conveyed in the book of Daniel, understands the cause of suffering in terms of a cosmic force that acts in opposition to God. This represents a radical about-face in the traditional monotheistic model that views God as the sole proprietor of pleasure and pain. Apocalyptic writing, in a sense, frees God from the messy tangle of wires attached to a single, divine detonator and instead blames the sudden explosion of human misery on sinister forces. It is this new and, some might say, more palatable God who emerges in the New Testament—a

God who fights for the oppressed and downtrodden and who wants an end to the Problem of Pain as much as we do.

In the New Testament, the book of Revelation, another apocalyptic text, understands suffering as emanating from the malicious machinations of Satan, the Prince of Demons and archenemy of Christ. The situation, though dire, is nontheless temporary; through Christ, Satan and his legions are destroyed, once and for all. Jesus and Paul are apocalyptic thinkers who share a vision of the New Age that is to come. Jesus calls this New Age the Kingdom, and he envisions a world free of evil and suffering.

Paul shares Jesus' vision and sees the inauguration of the Kingdom as already under way, initiated by Jesus' saving death on the cross. Though the prophetic idea of suffering as punishment for sin finds little support in the New Testament, we do find such a position in the writings of Paul. Paul agrees with the prophetic notion of suffering, and he also agrees with Jesus—who views suffering as a necessary antecedent to the arrival of the Kingdom. Paul might share the prophets' belief that suffering is punishment for sin, but he also sees Jesus' death as atonement for all humanity. Paul's message, then, is a hopeful one.

In the introduction to this chapter, I noted that my students typically assert one (or more) of the following reasons to explain human misery. Let us take one final glance at our short list.

1. Suffering is a form punishment for sin.
2. What goes around comes around—we get what we deserve.
3. We suffer in order to learn something; it is, in a sense, a test.
4. Everything happens for a reason, including suffering.
5. Suffering is random; it just happens.

We looked at this list to see how it squares with what the Bible has to say about suffering. While it is easy to find the biblical roots from which our short list germinates, we note that despite the fact that the Bible has much to say about suffering, it nonetheless falls short of fully explaining the Problem of Pain. This leads us to conclude that maybe the response of my student Amanda, whom we met at the opening of this chapter, had it right all along. Recall that Amanda, who at a young age suffered the loss of her mother, was at a loss to explain the reason why good people suffer. The mystery of undeserved pain is indeed bewildering, and we cannot help but cast our eyes to the heavens and ask Job's question: "Why?" Given that there are no wholly satisfying answers, the challenge of the faithful reader seems to be the same challenge presented to Job: Perhaps we must simply learn to live with the question.

Final Destinations

HEAVEN AND HELL

The mind is its own place, and in itself
Can make a heaven of hell, a hell of heaven.

—JOHN MILTON

If you walked into a room of a hundred people who represented a cross-section of Americans and asked them what they believe the Bible teaches about Heaven and hell, you would likely come up with the following short list:

1. The Bible describes Heaven and hell in great detail.
2. The Bible tells us that good people go to Heaven and bad people go to hell.
3. The Bible teaches us that Heaven is a place of repose, where the deceased reunite with dead relatives and enjoy the company of God for all eternity.
4. The Bible teaches us that hell is a place of unending torment, ruled by Satan.

In this chapter, we shall consider these commonly held beliefs and explore what the Bible has to say—or does not say—about our final destination. We will follow the format used in chapter 4, probing key texts relating to Heaven and hell in a general way, searching for ways in which they either affirm or negate our four common assumptions.

Whenever I speak about Heaven and hell in class, I first show an image of Michelangelo's *The Last Judgment*, which graces the altar wall of the Sistine Chapel in Rome. Michelangelo's masterpiece features a detailed depiction of the Second Coming of Christ, replete with the righteous being taken into Heaven and the not-so-lucky wicked souls tumbling headlong into the horrors of hell. I have had the opportunity to view this fresco many times—once twenty minutes before the chapel officially opened. No matter how many times I see it, I find I am most captivated by the expressions on the faces of both the saved and the damned. In their respective beatific or tortured faces, one can glimpse the euphoria of Heaven and the hopelessness of hell. Michelangelo spent four years (from 1537 to 1541) creating a fresco that spoke to the faithful of his day, the vast majority of whom accepted Heaven and hell as literal realities.

Today, particularly in North American and Western Europe, there are diverse opinions concerning our final postmortem destinations. For believers, Heaven and hell are lofty and loathsome realities. But even among the most devout, there are widely divergent opinions about heavenly and hellish landscapes; what happens there; who goes where; and just what we do or, as the case may be, what is done to us there.

While Heaven and hell are established facts for many, there are those who contend that Heaven and hell are pure fantasy, part of the leftover trappings of a primitive belief system used by the Church to keep the faithful in the pews. For those who hold this view, Heaven is the proverbial dangling carrot, touted as the ultimate reward for the obediently pious, and hell is the frightening threat that helps to regulate the behavior of the unruly, impious, and nonconformist.

In between these two extremes exists a more moderate position comprised of those who understand Heaven and hell as states of being, rather than literal places that occupy the cosmic countryside. Some in this middle group may be at a loss to describe what these "states of being" are like, and others may simply sigh, preferring to leave their ultimate fate in the capable hands of their Creator. Most of my experience has come from those in this middle group—since the majority of my students identify themselves as moderates when it comes to Heaven and hell. I have observed, however, that some in this middle group often bite their lips and worry, not so much about the realities of Heaven and hell, but about a bigger question—*the* question, in fact—that has plagued the lot of humanity throughout the ages, regardless of their religious persuasion. And that question is this: What happens to us after we die? The concepts of Heaven and hell are uniquely tied to this fundamental concern because, when it comes down it, either we go on or we do not. If we do not go on, then we will never know it. But if we do go on, where is it that we go? Well, traditionally, there are two options, and since I am more of a tell-me-the-bad-news-first kind of person, we will begin with least appealing option: hell.

Going to Hell

In my class at the university, as a starting point for our discussion of hell, I usually begin by asking students the question: What are you afraid of? I ask this question because fear is really at the center of what hell is all about. Everything about hell induces fear in humans: fire; torture; separation from those we love; separation from God; and, perhaps most frightening of all, the dreaded concierge of hell, the Devil. But, because hell is all about fear, it is important that students understand their own fears before we embark on a meaningful discussion of hell. In class, I ask them to make a list of their top five fears. I now invite you to take a moment and make a short list of your own fears, either on paper or in your head.

Most of my students fear the same things we all fear: The loss of a loved one, illness, public speaking (psychologists tell us this particular fear ranks first on the long list of human fears), rejection, failure, and death. After generating and discussing student responses to the question of fear, the class generally agrees that death—either our own or that of someone we love—should top the list (as opposed to public speaking!). When we discuss the reasons why we are so afraid of death, some cite feelings that accompany the loss of someone they love and the pain associated with grief. When they discuss their own demise, they voice concerns surrounding the actual type of death (dying from a protracted disease and being murdered are most worrisome) and the ensuing aftermath of sorrow their loved ones will have to experience. Obviously, this is a rather sober discussion, and for most, it is the first time they have actually shared their private fears in such a public way. This preliminary exploration of our own fears is critical, however, if we are to truly understand what the Bible tells us about hell.

After a general discussion about fear, I next ask students to jot down what they know about hell and where they acquired this information. I emphasize to them that they do not have to believe everything they include on their list, as the purpose of this exercise is to simply figure out where they received their information. I urge you to pause for a moment and to also make a list of things you have learned about hell and from whom.

While few of my students admit that they believe in hell (in fact, most do not), they nonetheless describe it using an unsavory but well-known scenario: Hell is a place of fire and pain. Interestingly, however, most students insist that if there is a hell, only the most hardened criminals are sent there. "You have to be *really bad* to go to hell" is a typical response. When I ask, "How bad?" murderers, child molesters, and rapists are the leading contenders. "What about thieves and liars?" I ask, and most agree that those crimes seem not to warrant such a harsh punishment. And when I ask them where they got all of this information, they rarely give what we might think would be the standard response (that is, "in church" or "in Sunday school") but instead sheepishly cite a particular film (or in some cases, a video game) as their primary source. Aside from the fact that I deal largely with what some theologians and sociologists call an "unchurched generation," it is striking that they often have such graphic descriptions of a place they have never really thought much about in religious terms.

Slightly older folks (and some younger, too) have a different experience. Hell is discussed at home and is part of the theological equation that includes God, the Devil, and their respective abodes. The older generation might also point the finger at Sunday school teachers, clergy, or the cadre of stern-faced nuns from the 1950s as their primary sources of hellish information. Curiously absent as a source of information about hell in nearly all of these responses—young or old—is the Bible. Our task, then, is to find out what the Bible has to say about hell and to see if it finds resonance with the commonly held assumptions mentioned at the outset:

1. The Bible describes Heaven and hell in great detail.
2. The Bible tells us that good people go to Heaven and bad people go to hell.
3. The Bible teaches us that Heaven is a place of repose, where the deceased reunite with dead relatives and enjoy the company of God for all eternity.
4. The Bible teaches us that hell is a place of unending torment, ruled by Satan.

The most important thing to know about hell is that it changes over the course of centuries. Throughout hell's complex evolution, however, two essential facts remain: Believers (then and now) understand hell to be the last stop on the bus for unrepentant sinners and the Devil's dwelling place. Before we examine what the Hebrew Bible has to say about hell, we must first address the concept of an afterlife in ancient Israel.

Perhaps the best way to summarize the prevailing wisdom regarding the afterlife in ancient Israel is to quote from the book of Ecclesiastes:

> Vanity of vanities, says the
> Teacher,
> vanity of vanities! All is vanity!
> What do people gain from all
> the toil
> at which they toil under the
> sun?
> A generation goes, and a
> generation comes,
> but the earth remains forever.
> The sun rises and the sun
> goes down . . .
> What has been is what will be,
> and what has been done is what
> will be done;
> there is nothing new
> under the sun. (Eccl 1:2–5, 9)

Written in about 200 BCE, the author of Ecclesiastes—who identifies himself only as a "son of David" and king of Israel (Eccl 1:1, 12)—reflects the view held by most in ancient Israel, and as dismal as it may seem, their view does not envision or expect a life beyond the one they are currently living.

> For the fate of humans and the fate of animals is the same; as one dies, so dies the other. . . . All go to one place; all are from the dust, and all turn to dust again. Who knows whether the human spirit goes upward and the spirit of animals goes downward to the earth? (Eccl 3:19–21)

Though the idea that death is *the end* predominates much of the Hebrew Bible, there are some later texts, such as the book of Daniel (164 BCE), discussed in chapter 4, that demonstrate a belief in the resurrection of the body and even some type of eternal judgment: "Many of those who sleep in the dust of the earth shall awake, some to everlasting life, and some to shame and everlasting contempt" (Dan 12:2). Other relatively late texts also reflect this shift from a single life on this Earth to the possibility of a life beyond death. Written between 104 and 63 BCE, 2 Maccabees (found in the Apocrypha in Protestant Bibles but included in the Bible proper in the Catholic version of the Hebrew Bible) not only espouses a belief in the resurrection of the dead (2 Maccabees 7; 12:43-45) but also advocates prayer for the deceased (2 Macc 12:39–42). Certainly by the first century and the time of Jesus, belief in both the resurrection of the dead and judgment are commonplace, even as the final destinations (Heaven and hell) are only just beginning to develop. As we trace the evolution of hell, first in the Hebrew Bible and then in the New Testament, we will stop along the way to examine various outside influences on the Judeo-Christian version of hell.

Most ancient cultures, including the religious traditions of Israel's neighbors, have their own versions of hell and of evil beings who live in dark, foreboding netherworlds. We will look at a sampling of these later. But the Hebrew Bible does not describe such a place or such a being. Although the Hebrew Bible *does* mention a dark, creepy underworld called *Sheol* (in some English versions of the Bible inaccurately rendered as "hell"), this place is not fully developed and is not the same locale as hell. In fact, ancient Israel has no tradition of an after-death existence as such. The general consensus is that the dead linger for a time in *Sheol* before simply disappearing. Some scholars believe *Sheol* has its origins in Canaanite mythology, while others cite ancient rabbinic sources that hold that the spirit of the dead hovers close by for a year before disappearing. The story of the Witch of Endor and her dramatic encounter with King Saul (1 Samuel 28) is a little-known biblical tale that seems to support this idea.

In chapter 1, I briefly mentioned King Saul, who is plagued by a "tormenting spirit" sent by God as punishment for Saul's sins (1 Sam 15:26; 16:14). At the end of Saul's story, he stands alone, mired in his own insanity. But he is still the king, and kings in those days are first and foremost military figures. Saul must defend the people against their dreaded enemies, the Philistines, who are poised to attack. Saul turns to the LORD for guidance, but the LORD does not respond (1 Sam 28:6).

In desperation, he engages the services of a medium, the Witch of Endor, so that he can seek the counsel of the deceased prophet, Samuel. Surely, Samuel will know how to advise him. Before we go any further, we must note two important facts. First, the very act of consulting mediums is forbidden in Israel (Lev 19:31; 20:6, 27); and second, it is Saul himself who drives the mediums and magicians from the land (1 Sam 28:3), going so far as to issue the death penalty for anyone found guilty of engaging in sorcery (1 Sam 28:9–10). It is ironic, then, that Saul should violate his own decree and seek the help of the Witch.

The king disguises himself and travels by night to the little town of Endor to consult the Witch (1 Sam 28:8). Saul asks her to conjure up the spirit of Samuel, reassuring her that no harm will come to her even though technically she is breaking the law. The Witch is successful, and the cranky spirit of Samuel appears. The conversation between Saul and the ghost is a sobering one. Samuel informs the king that he and his sons will die the next day in battle (1 Sam 28:19), a terrible prophecy that comes utterly to fruition (1 Sam 31:6). Among other things, the story of Saul and the Witch of Endor seems to lend credence to the idea that the Israelites believe that the deceased linger in *Sheol* for a time—which is why Samuel is available for the witch's summons. But I must emphasize that this sort of limbo state is not fully understood and, again, *Sheol* certainly is not the same place as hell, at least not yet.

During what scholars refer to as the Second Temple Period (roughly 539 BCE to 70 CE), Jewish thinkers, bothered by the theodicy problem, begin to ponder the possibility of a system of reward and punishment that occurs not in this life but the next. While the exclusive abode of Yhwh is gradually refashioned to become the resting place for the righteous (though this idea takes many years to evolve, and I will say more about that later), what about the fate of sinners? Over time, associations between a smoldering garbage dump outside Jerusalem called Gehenna ("Valley of Hinnom") and the eerie pit of *Sheol* morph together and becomes a sort of early type of hell. Gehenna is actually the perfect hellish locale, as it is both a burning refuse heap and a place where the illicit religious practice of child sacrifice is carried out during the Iron Age (ca. 1200–550 BCE). This wholly real, geographic place becomes symbolically associated with the destination where the unrighteous are judged in the afterlife (Matt 10:28; 23:33).

The idea of "hell" does not appear in the Bible until the New Testament. The actual word, however, never appears. *Hell* is a Germanic word, the name of an underworld goddess (Hel). The New Testament uses the terms "Gehenna" and "Hades" to refer to the places we know as hell, though some versions of the Bible inaccurately translate both words to "hell." For this reason, when discussing the concept "hell" in the Synoptic Gospels, I will sometimes use the New American Bible (NAB) in my citations, rather than the New Revised Standard Version (NRSV) used throughout most of this book. In some cases, the NAB comes closer to the original Greek than the NRSV. When using any version other than the NRSV, I will make specific note of it following the citation.

Paul (writing about 50–64 CE) does not mention hell at all, though he does have plenty to say about the fate of sinners. Paul constructs a frightening laundry list of offences that will exclude one from the Kingdom of God:

> Now the works of the flesh are obvious: fornication, impurity, licentiousness, idolatry, sorcery, enmities, strife, jealousy, anger, quarrels, dissensions, factions, envy, drunkenness, carousing, and things like these. I am warning you, as I warned you before: those who do such things will not inherit the kingdom of God. (Gal 5:19–21)

> Do you not know that wrongdoers will not inherit the kingdom of God? Do not be deceived! Fornicators, idolaters, adulterers, male prostitutes, sodomites, thieves, the greedy, drunkards, revilers, robbers—none of these will inherit the kingdom of God. (1 Cor 6:9–10)

Remember that for Paul—and for Jesus—the "Kingdom of God" is an earthly reality, representing a radical religious and social shift in world order, and therefore is not Heaven, as some might assume.

Paul's theology is simple: The good will live and the evil will die. "For the wages of sin is death, but the free gift of God is eternal life in Christ Jesus our Lord" (Rom 6:23). In other words, for Paul, those who receive Christ are saved and will experience resurrection after death: "For since we believe that Jesus died and rose again, even so, through Jesus, God will bring with him those who have died" (1 Thess 4:14). Sinners (Gal 5:19–21; 1 Cor 6:9–10) and all those who reject Christ will simply cease to exist. Sending sinners to "hell" does not enter into Paul's theology.

The earliest reference we have to the *idea* of hell in the Bible is found in the Gospel of Mark:

> If your hand causes you to sin, cut it off. It is better for you to enter into life maimed than with two hands to go into Gehenna, into the unquenchable fire. And if your foot causes you to sin, cut it off. It is better for you to enter into life crippled than with two feet to be thrown into Gehenna. And if your eye causes you to sin, pluck it out. Better for you to enter into the kingdom of God with one eye than with two eyes to be thrown into Gehenna, where "their worm does not die, and the fire is not quenched." (Mark 9:43–48, NAB)

It is clear that at least by the time Mark writes his Gospel (70 CE) there is a literal place for the punishment of sinners. And Mark's description of this place includes some very specific details: The unrepentant soul is not only tortured by fire but also eaten by worms. Yikes!

Luke, who writes his version of the Jesus story in about 85 CE, does not mention Mark's chilling warning of eternal damnation, nor does Luke include Mark's description of the place of punishment (Mark 9:43–48). Luke does, however, confirm that this place—"Gehenna" in Mark and "Hades" in Luke—is a real place. In the Parable of the Rich Man and Lazarus, Luke condemns the actions of the rich man not because he lacks faith in Christ (lack of faith is also a central concern in both Paul and Mark) but because the rich man fails to help the poor man, Lazarus:

> There was a rich man who was dressed in purple and fine linen and who feasted sumptuously every day. And at his gate lay a poor man named Lazarus, covered with sores, who longed to satisfy his hunger with what fell from the rich man's table; even the dogs would come and lick his sores. The poor man died and was carried away by the angels to be with Abraham. The rich man also died and was buried. In Hades, where he was being tormented, he looked up and saw Abraham far away with Lazarus by his side. He called out, "Father Abraham, have mercy on me, and send Lazarus to dip the tip of his finger in water and cool my tongue; for I am in agony in these flames." But Abraham said, "Child, remember that during your lifetime you received your good things, and Lazarus in like manner evil things; but now he is comforted here, and you are in agony. Besides all this, between you and us a great chasm has been fixed, so that those who might want to pass from here to you cannot do so, and no one can cross from there to us." (Luke 16:19–26)

Luke's description of a postmortem torture chamber remains the most concrete portrayal of a dreaded after-death experience for the unrighteous in the New Testament. Curiously absent in Luke's description, however, is Satan. He makes no mention of the loathsome caretaker who will come to be associated with hell.

But, if Luke's vision of eternal punishment seems to be tempered in comparison to that in the Gospel of Mark, Matthew (who writes his Gospel in about 90 CE) turns up the flames under the pot. Matthew's Jesus makes a clear distinction between the righteous, who will be saved, and the evildoers, who will be punished. Not even so-called religious men can escape the coming wrath, as Jesus warns the Pharisees: "You serpents, you brood of vipers, how can you flee from the judgment of Gehenna?" (Matt 23:33, NAB).

Matthew depicts Gehenna as a place of annihilation and torture. The gnashing of teeth, weeping, and physical torment are persistent activities in Matthew's Gehenna. Matthew also makes it clear that it is the Son of Man who separates the righteous from the unrighteous before assigning the appropriate rewards (or punishments):

> And do not be afraid of those who kill the body but cannot kill the soul; rather be afraid of the one who can destroy both soul and body in Gehenna. (Matt 10:28, NAB)

> Just as the weeds are collected and burned up with fire, so will it be at the end of the age. The Son of Man will send his angels, and they will collect out of his kingdom all causes of sin and all evildoers, and they will throw them into the furnace of fire, where there will be weeping and gnashing of teeth. Then the righteous will shine like the sun in the kingdom of their Father. Let anyone with ears listen! (Matt 13:40–43)

> So it will be at the end of the age. The angels will come out and separate the evil from the righteous and throw them into the furnace of fire, where there will be weeping and gnashing of teeth. (Matt 13:49–50)

> As for this worthless slave, throw him into the outer darkness, where there will be weeping and gnashing of teeth. (Matt 25:30)

Aside from the fact that Matthew mentions this terrible place more times than the other Gospel writers, Matthew yields yet another important detail. In all of the previous references to after-death judgment, Satan (or the Devil) is never mentioned. But Matthew makes it clear that Satan and his evil comrades are permanent fixtures in this terrifying place:

> Then he will say to those at his left hand, "You that are accursed, depart from me into the eternal fire prepared for the devil and his angels." (Matt 25:41)

From these relatively few references in the Synoptic Gospels, it appears that "hell" as we understand it today is not the centerpiece of the earliest followers of the Jesus movement; in fact, in the Gospel of John, written around 95 CE, there is no mention of such a place. Of course, all of this presents us with a rather incomplete picture of hell. For a clearer picture, we need to adjust our viewfinder and turn to the book of Revelation.

And the devil who had deceived them was thrown into the lake of fire
and sulfur, where the beast and the false prophet were, and they will
be tormented day and night forever and ever. (Rev 20:10)

According to the author, John of Patmos, Christians must resist the
temptation to bow down to the strong-armed Roman authorities who
mandate veneration of the emperor. John's visions seem to imply that martyrdom is preferable to worshipping Rome, whom John usually calls "the
beast." Unfaithful Christians who *do* bow down to the Roman Emperor
are singled out for a special punishment, consisting of constant torture.
Moreover, reminiscent of the "watching eyes from Heaven" (cf. Luke
16:19–26), this posthumous torture-fest will be witnessed by none other
than Christ (often called "the Lamb" in Revelation) and the angels.

Then another angel, a third, followed them, crying with a loud voice,
"Those who worship the beast and its image, and receive a mark on
their foreheads or on their hands, they will also drink the wine of
God's wrath, poured unmixed into the cup of his anger, and they will
be tormented with fire and sulfur in the presence of the holy angels
and in the presence of the Lamb. And the smoke of their torment
goes up forever and ever. There is no rest day or night for those who
worship the beast and its image and for anyone who receives the
mark of its name." (Rev 14:9–11)

In Revelation, we see echoes of Paul's "categories of sinners" and Matthew's version of punishment, whereby a judgment takes place and each
individual is assigned to a particular postmortem fate (cf. Matt 13:40–43;
49–50; 25:41–46).

But as for the cowardly, the faithless, the polluted, the murderers,
the fornicators, the sorcerers, the idolaters, and all liars, their place
will be in the lake that burns with fire and sulfur, which is the second
death. (Rev 21:8)

And I saw the dead, great and small, standing before the throne, and
books were opened. Also another book was opened, the book of
life. And the dead were judged according to their works, as recorded
in the books. And the sea gave up the dead that were in it, Death
and Hades gave up the dead that were in them, and all were judged
according to what they had done. Then Death and Hades were
thrown into the lake of fire. This is the second death, the lake of fire;

and anyone whose name was not found written in the book of life
was thrown into the lake of fire. (Rev 20:12–15)

These terrifying, enduring images are the earliest road maps of what
will become the post-biblical hell. The fear of hell haunts God-fearing
Christians for centuries and becomes the inspiration behind countless
fire-and-brimstone sermons designed to keep the faithful in line. But Revelation is really just one of many sources that contributes to hell's final
form. During the first few centuries of the Common Era, a vast array of
other "apocalypses," including the Apocalypse of Peter, the Apocalypse
of Paul, and the Apocalypse of the Virgin, may have also influenced the
way we conceptualize hell. Some of these noncanonical works even feature
a guided tour of the underworld, a common motif found in other hellish tales. Finally, most scholars agree that the New Testament and post-
biblical versions of hell seem to have been influenced by other religions in
the Ancient Near East, most notably those of the Egyptians, Greeks, and
Persians. A brief exploration of each of these "hells" will help illuminate
this idea.

The Egyptian underworld is a place into which all mortals descend
after death to be judged. Because pharaohs are considered deities, they
alone are exempt from judgment. Anpu (or Anubis), the jackal-headed
god often featured in Egyptian funerary art, is in charge of weighing the
deceased's soul on a scale. If a person is judged to be good, he or she
continues to exist in this shadowy necropolis; but if the person is judged
to be evil, then he or she is tortured before being consumed by fire or by
hungry demons. The final place of this judgment is an underworld known
in Egyptian mythology as Tuat, the dark subterranean place of the dead.
In Egyptian religion, only the righteous, whose hearts balance against "the
feather of truth" on the scales of justice, enter this benign netherworld,
whereas in ancient Israelite religion, both the righteous and unrighteous
enter *Sheol*. The fate of the wicked in Egyptian eschatology includes annihilation by Amamet, a monster with the forelegs of a crocodile, the body
of a lion, and the hindquarters of a hippo. If a soul is deemed evil or bur-
dened by guilt, Amamet devours it. This idea may have influenced the later
Christian notion of hell whereby the wicked are often tortured by flames
and demons.

Like the Egyptians, the Greeks have a rather sophisticated vision of the
underworld that bears a striking resemblance to both the Jewish *Sheol* and
the Christian version of hell. The host of the Greek hell is Hades, a dark
and somber deity who can lurk about unseen with the help of a special
helmet that renders him invisible. Hades is not alone in his underworld

kingdom; in addition to the souls of the deceased, three terrifying god-desses called the Furies (sometimes referred to as the *Erinyes*, or the daugh-ters of Hades, in Greek poetry), and the goddess Hecate (usually associated with ghosts and black magic), round out his underworld posse. The Furies are particularly fearsome, depicted as being clad in blood-soaked garments with snakes instead of hair. As terrifying as these underworld figures are, however, it is perhaps the physical structure of the Greek underworld that is most frightening.

The underworld has a tripartite structure wherein the deceased spend eternity. The highest level, known as the Elysian Fields, is usually reserved for those who accomplish great things in life, such as war heroes, who enjoy a peaceful repose. This notion of a peaceful repose may have influ-enced one of the Christian notions of Heaven. The second level, called the Asphodel Fields, is a sort of Purgatory for those who are neither great nor evil. But the lowest level of the underworld, Tartarus, is a place of pure darkness, located in the deepest recesses of the Earth. This particu-lar level is the dwelling place for criminals and other evildoers, who are condemned to suffer eternal torture and punishment for their disreputable lives on Earth.

The Greek poet, Hesiod (eighth century BCE), writes that an anvil takes nine days and nights to fall from Heaven to Earth, and nine days and nights to fall from Earth to Tartarus. If we add some fire to Tartarus, it closely resembles the Christian concept of hell. In fact, Tartarus is said to have been the very inspiration behind Dante's *Inferno* and the prototype for the Christian hell.

If the Egyptian and Greek hells are not frightening enough, then take a look at the Persian version. The ancient Persian religion known as Zoroas-trianism, founded by Zoroaster probably in the sixth century BCE, depicts hell as an utterly horrifying place. A dramatic account of the Persian hell is described in gruesome detail in the *Vision of Arda Viraf*, written some-time between 226 and 641 CE. In this tale, the hero of the story, the pious Arda Viraf, is given a tour of Heaven, hell, and an in-between place similar to the Christian concept of Limbo, called *Hammistagan* ("place of the motionless ones"). Arda Viraf's description of hell is one of the more chill-ing accounts in literature:

> I saw the greedy jaws of hell: the most frightful pit, descending, in a very narrow, fearsome crevice and in darkness so murky that I was forced to feel my way, amid such stench that all who inhaled the air struggled, staggered, and fell, and in such confinement that existence seemed impossible. Each one thought: "I am alone."

The physical structure of the Persian hell greatly influences Dante Alighieri (1265–1321) and John Milton (1608–1674), whose geographical maps of hell in their respective masterpieces, *The Divine Comedy* and *Paradise Lost*, will become blueprints for our Western conception of the Devil's abode.

The Inferno, the first part of Dante's three-part *Divine Comedy*, recounts Dante's journey through a multilayered hell. "The Pilgrim" (Dante) is led by the ghost of the Roman poet Virgil, and together they navigate the nine circles of hell on a tour that reminds us of the hero's tour of the Persian hell as recounted in the *Vision of Arda Viraf*. As the two brave the Gates of Hell, it is the pitiable sounds of the accursed that first grip Dante:

> Here sighs, with lamentations and loud moans,
> Resounded through the air pierced by no star,
> That e'en I wept at entering. Various tongues,
> Horrible languages, outcries of woe,
> Accents of anger, voices deep and hoarse,
> With hands together smote that swell'd the sounds,
> Made up a tumult, that forever whirls
> Round through that air with solid darkness satin'd,
> Like to the sand that in whirlwind flies. (canto 3, 21–29)

In Dante's scheme, these nine circles narrow, like a funnel, into the Earth, and sinners are scattered among the rings, suffering punishments appropriate to their crimes. Once again, we see vestiges of Paul's "categories of sinners" and Matthew's concept of judgment. Dante paints a vivid picture of the different levels (or rings) of hell. The highest of the first four circles is Limbo, where Virgil himself lives and where no one is actually punished. This is a sort of no-man's-land—not quite Heaven and certainly not hell. Limbo and Purgatory (the latter of which is the focus of the second part of the *Divine Comedy*) become part of the Christian afterlife belief. Purgatory, in particular, and, to a lesser extent, Limbo are actually quite attractive to the masses, who for the most part do not view themselves as Heaven-ready, yet not so bad as to merit the flames of hell. Appealing as these afterlife nondestinations may seem, it is important to note that they have no basis in the Bible.

Returning to Dante's design of hell, the second ring is for the lustful, who must endure the infernal winds of desire for all eternity, while gluttons, who occupy the third circle, are condemned to live in a reeking garbage heap. Those dwelling in the fourth ring are the misers and spend-thrifts (many of whom, Dante notes, are priests), who must struggle with one another, while the angry and sullen occupants of the fifth ring are forced to languish in a loathsome swamp (choking on mud), part of the River Styx ("River of Hate"), which separates upper hell from lower hell.

Crossing the River Styx, Dante enters the City of Dis, the dwelling place of fallen angels and the housing project for the rest of hell. The sixth circle houses the heretics, who must spend eternity burning in their graves. Oddly, the fire we commonly associate with hell is present only within the walls of lower hell. But it is this image of hell as a fiery pit that captures the imagination of the masses and becomes the staple for most subsequent stories about hell.

The seventh ring is home to the most violent—murderers, thieves, and blasphemers—while the eighth ring houses those guilty of fraudulence and malice (fortunetellers, flatterers, hypocrites, and the like). Finally, at the center of hell, in a place reserved for traitors, is a frozen lake with Satan immobilized in the center.

> That Emperor, who sways
> The realm of sorrow, at mid breast from the ice
> Stood forth; and I in stature am more like
> A giant, than the giants are his arms.
> Mark now how great that whole must be, which suits
> With such a part. If he were beautiful
> As he is hideous now, and yet did dare
> To scowl upon his Maker, well from him
> May all our misery flow. Oh what a sight! (canto 34:27–35)

Though Dante's work is imaginative, it has a tremendous impact on popular Christian thought. In fact, Dante's work of fiction bleeds into popular Christian lore surrounding hell. What many Christians fail to realize, of course, is that this graphic description of hell does not come from the Bible, but from the brilliant mind of a poet.

John Milton's epic poem *Paradise Lost* offers an intriguing glimpse of another sort of hell that is a far cry from Dante's frozen lake. As mentioned briefly in chapter 1, Milton's work is hugely important in our investigation of hell. While most of *Paradise Lost* focuses on the Fall of humankind in the Garden of Eden, the first two books focus on hell. In the story, following a failed rebellion against God, Satan and his followers are banished from Heaven and cast into a fiery lake:

Hurled headlong flaming from the ethereal sky,
With hideous ruin and combustion, down
To bottomless perdition, there to dwell
In adamantine chains and penal fire,
Who durst defy the Omnipotent to arms.
Nine times the space that measures day and night
To mortal men, he, with his horrid crew,
Lay vanquished, rolling in the fiery gulf. (1:45–52; cf. Rev 20:12–15;
    21:8)

Milton's version of hell, in contrast to Heaven, is dim (even the fires of hell cannot make it more bright) and somewhat formless. Though it is not quite the loathsome place described by Dante, Milton's hell is a place of deep psychological and physical suffering:

Confounded, though immortal. But his doom
Reserved him to more wrath; for now the thought
Both of lost happiness and lasting pain
Torments him: round he throws his baleful eyes,
That witnessed huge affliction and dismay,
Mixed with obdurate pride and steadfast hate.
At once, as far as Angels ken, he views
The dismal situation waste and wild.
A dungeon horrible, on all sides round,
As one great furnace flamed; yet from those flames
No light; but rather darkness visible
Served only to discover sights of woe,
Regions of sorrow, doleful shades, where peace
And rest can never dwell, hope never comes
That comes to all, but torture without end
Still urges, and a fiery deluge, fed
With ever-burning sulphur unconsumed.
Such place Eternal Justice has prepared
For those rebellious; here their prison ordained
In utter darkness, and their portion set,
As far removed from God and light of Heaven
As from the centre thrice to th' utmost pole.
Oh how unlike the place from whence they fell!
There the companions of his fall, o'erwhelmed
With floods and whirlwinds of tempestuous fire. (1:53–77)

Not to be discouraged when they are banished from Heaven, Satan and his demonic companions crawl out of the fire, and as they plot revenge, they build a palace, aptly named Pandemonium ("all demons"), on the side of a volcano. The palace boasts a grand meeting hall where Satan and the other demons in hell gather to plot and scheme. Once again, such cosmic meetings remind us of the meetings of the Divine Council in the heavenly realm as detailed in the Hebrew Bible, particularly in the book of Job.

This is not the sort of hell we typically imagine when we think of Satan's underground dwelling, but the most important contributions of both *Paradise Lost* and *The Inferno*, in regard to hell, occur when the two are somehow merged in the reader's mind. The blending of these two poems (and the prevailing assumption that they are somehow biblically based) creates a particular version of hell that finds its way into the religious vernacular of the faithful. This, of course, points to the larger issue of biblical illiteracy, but it also serves as a warning: Sometimes stories, poems, and even movies can seep into biblical narratives, blurring the lines between what the Bible really says and imaginings from sources far removed from the Bible.

With this brief exploration of hell, let us return to our original assumptions, introduced at the beginning of this chapter:

1. The Bible describes Heaven and hell in great detail.
2. The Bible tells us that good people go to Heaven and bad people go to hell.
3. The Bible teaches us that Heaven is a place of repose, where the deceased reunite with dead relatives and enjoy the company of God for all eternity.
4. The Bible teaches us that hell is a place of unending torment, ruled by Satan.

We shall save assumption number three, which deals exclusively with Heaven, for later, but we can address assumptions one, two, and four. In general, we learned that there is no hell as we know it, and therefore no description of it in the Hebrew Bible (assumption number one). There is no concept of bad people (or *any* people, for that matter) going to hell after death (assumption number two) and certainly no fiery furnace and no Devil (assumption number four).

Influenced by other hells from other ancient peoples, the hell of the New Testament begins to take shape, but it is still indistinct (assumption number one). The categories of sinners who are destined to inhabit hell for eternity also begins to develop in the New Testament (assumption number two), as does the notion that hell has a terrifying overseer, Satan (assumption number four), but all of these concepts take many years to evolve into something approximating our modern notions of hell. In short, this "post-biblical hell" is really the result of an amalgamation of sources, including early Christian apocalypses and extra-biblical lore such as John Milton's *Paradise Lost* and Dante's *Inferno*. So, if we have a biblical hell, even in its rudimentary form, what about hell's polar opposite, Heaven? What does the Bible tell us about this place of peace and repose?

Going to Heaven

If hell is an evolving concept in the Bible—and beyond—Heaven, too, has its own complex history. Beginning with the Hebrew Bible, it is clear that there *is* a Heaven—but it is not what most people imagine. According to the Hebrew Bible, Heaven is God's special dwelling place; it is *not* for the repose of human souls whose good works on Earth merit eternal bliss in paradise. In fact, in the Hebrew Bible, there are no human souls in Heaven at all.

> The heavens are the LORD's
> heavens,
> but the earth he has given to
> human beings. (Ps 115:16)

Heaven is an exclusive club, and while humans may be dying to get in, the Hebrew Bible is clear: *God* lives in the heavenly realm and the Earth is the place God has graciously set aside for human habitation. We moderns often think of ourselves as dying, going to Heaven, and getting cozy with the King of the Universe, but in the Hebrew Bible, God draws a clear line of distinction between humans and the LORD:

> For my thoughts are not your
> thoughts,
> nor are your ways my ways,
> says the LORD.
> For as the heavens are higher than
> the earth,
> so are my ways higher than
> your ways
> and my thoughts than your
> thoughts. (Is 55:8–9)

There are, however, a few lucky mortals who manage to get a sneak peek into the Divine Abode, including Moses; his older brother, Aaron; and select members of the wilderness community who not only see Heaven and the LORD but apparently also have a little soirée:

> Then Moses and Aaron, Nadab, and Abihu, and seventy of the elders of Israel went up, and they saw the God of Israel. Under his feet there was something like a pavement of sapphire stone, like the very heaven for clearness. God did not lay his hand on the chief men of the people of Israel; also they beheld God, and they ate and drank. (Exod 24:9–11)

Moses and his colleagues see God's feet (in the ancient world, to see God's face would be such a powerful experience as to kill you) standing on a sidewalk of gems, but this brief passage, unfortunately, is lacking in detail.

Certain prophets also catch a glimpse of Heaven. The prophet Micaiah peers into Heaven and sees the LORD "sitting on his throne with all the host of Heaven standing beside him" (1 Kgs 22:19); Isaiah, too, sees the LORD sitting on his throne, attended by angelic figures (Is 6:1–8). Ezekiel offers a more detailed description of the LORD and his heavenly home (Ezekiel 1; 10), while Daniel sees "the Ancient One" in a terrifying apocalyptic vision (Dan 7:13–27). Though Micaiah, Isaiah, Ezekiel, and Daniel are all granted brief glimpses of the LORD in his heavenly home, none are invited houseguests, and none of these prophets are permitted to move in for good.

There, are, however, two individuals, Enoch (Gen 5:24) and Elijah (2 Kgs 2:1–12), who appear to become permanent residents of Heaven: "Enoch walked with God; then he was no more, because God took him" (Gen 5:24). But where did God take him? The text does not say, but later interpreters assert Enoch and God moseyed off together to Heaven. In a somewhat more dramatic departure, Elijah, who is preparing his protégé, Elisha, to succeed him, is suddenly whisked away on a chariot of fire: "As they continued walking and talking, a chariot of fire and horses of fire separated the two of them, and Elijah ascended in a whirlwind into Heaven" (2 Kgs 2:11). Though the Enoch passage is somewhat unclear regarding his final destination, Elijah's fate seems more explicit: He is taken into Heaven and can even correspond from there with humans on Earth (2 Chron 21:12–15).

Recall from chapter 4 that the physical environs of Heaven in the Hebrew Bible are similar to any royal residence and include a throne room and a throng of royal attendants known as the "sons of God" or *benay elohim*, whose chief function is to move between Heaven and Earth to carry out God's directives. Isaiah and Ezekiel describe them as angelic winged creatures who attend to the LORD (Is 6:1–8; Ezekiel 1; 10), and Micaiah speaks of "the host of Heaven" flanking the LORD as he sits on his throne (1 Kgs 22:19). Absent are the souls of faithfully departed humans in these heavenly scenarios. Hence, we have a Heaven in the Hebrew Bible that is the exclusive domain of the LORD. The idea of dying and then going to Heaven, as we understand it today, does not seem to be part of the plan.

While this is certainly the case, *in general*, there are two relatively late passages in the Hebrew Bible that indicate a shift in this perspective; that is, after death, perhaps human souls move beyond the confines of *Sheol* to a place of rest and repose. Although we still do not have a clear ascent into Heaven, these passages come close.

Mentioned in the introduction to this chapter, the book of Daniel seems to reference the concept of resurrection and eternal life. The text does not directly refer to Heaven, but many assert that mention of the stars is indicative of the Heavenly realm:

> Many of those who sleep in the dust of the earth shall awake, some to everlasting life, and some to shame and everlasting contempt. Those who are wise shall shine like the brightness of the sky, and those who lead many to righteousness, like the stars forever and ever. (Dan 12:2–3)

The Wisdom of Solomon, part of the Apocrypha in Protestant Bibles and an accepted part of the canon in Catholic Bibles, where it is known as the book of Wisdom, is probably written close to the end of the first century BCE. In this text, we find an even more explicit mention of the postmortem fate of humans:

> But the souls of the just are in the hand of
> God,
> and no torment shall touch them.
> They seemed, in the view of the foolish,
> to be dead,
> and their passing was thought an
> affliction,
> and their going forth from us, utter
> destruction.
> But they are in peace.

New International Version, the grounds for divorce are "marital unfaithfulness"; and in the King James Version, not only is the term used for divorce different (to "put away" one's wife), but so are the grounds for putting said wife away ("fornication"). All of this confusion stems from the way in which different translators render certain Greek words into English. As you can see, we are wading into murky waters here, where definitive answers to important questions may prove elusive.

When it comes to sex and gender in the Bible, many people, including most of my students, approach these topics with equal measures of interest and squeamishness. On the one hand, they are interested to know what the Bible teaches about these controversial topics, but on the other hand, they are reluctant, worried that they have failed to measure up to what must surely be a high moral standard that few, if any of us, can attain. Some harbor concerns about their own modern (or not-so-modern) views regarding gender roles and their own sexual histories or sexual orientations, while others simply dismiss what they view as the Bible's antiquated sexual ethics, embracing instead a more contemporary view that promotes equality of the sexes and acceptance of all forms of sexual expression. In our brief foray into this fascinating and complex topic, we begin, appropriately, with the first common assumption that deals with gender and gender roles.

Assumption One: The Bible Says That Men Are More Important Than Women

Today, in many parts of the world, especially in North America and Western Europe, the old rules that once governed gender roles have been rewritten, revised, and reevaluated. Dating, marriage, parenting, and who brings home the bacon are more or less determined by individuals on a case-by-case, family-by-family basis. It is no longer assumed, for instance, that mothers, by virtue of their gender, should act as the primary caregivers of children or that men will supply the bulk of the family income. Economics, politics, religion, culture, and personal preferences all come into play these days as families decide what is right for them.

While some families embrace and retain what they feel are "traditional" gender roles within families—which usually includes women at home with children and men in the workplace—many other families reject these traditional roles in favor of more creative responses to the demands of modern life. Those who assume the more traditional model often cite the Bible as a definitive source for their choices. Others may argue that such attitudes are based on an outdated form of patriarchy that really has no place in contemporary society. Of course, we must remember that today, in many parts of the world (including the West), things like patriarchy, virginity, chastity, and modesty are still very much a part of daily life, culturally, and in some places, such attitudes are religiously mandated.

This chapter has no interest in promoting one lifestyle choice over another, for such choices are always extremely personal. I mention the notion of traditional gender roles versus modern ideas about the roles of women and men only because many people assume that traditional notions of gender come to us from the pages of the Bible. While this is true to some extent, a fuller reading of the biblical text, particularly those passages that feature stories about women, reveals the fact that during biblical times, women assume many roles, in the home and outside it. In order for us to better understand gender roles in the Bible, we must look at several important aspects of life for both men and women. These key aspects include marriage, family, work, leadership roles, land ownership, and other legal matters, including divorce.

As we explore these crucial areas of life, we must first concede that the Bible is undeniably written with a patriarchic bias. Many of my students find this reality off-putting at first, but I remind them that the biblical authors did not *invent* patriarchy, for patriarchy is well entrenched in the ANE before a single word of the Bible is ever written. Still, patriarchy is the norm, and few people in biblical antiquity, including most of the biblical writers, ever give it much thought; it is simply the way the world operates.

In patriarchal societies, the overwhelming majority of men and women marry and have children because it is expected of them. In biblical times, families are the bedrock of the community, and it is a strong communal identity that allows Judaism and eventually Christianity to flourish. Once wed, in the largely agrarian culture that dominates ancient Israel, most men work long days in the field, tending their crops and livestock, while women remain in the home to care for the house and children. Women are expected to have many children, and each child is viewed as a cherished gift from God. It is considered unnatural not to want children, and despite the high infant mortality rate (scholars speculate that as many as half of all children born never reach adulthood) and great personal risk (complications during childbirth and postpartum infections are the leading causes of death for women), it is clear that most women very much want to become mothers.

While children are considered great blessings from God, what can be said of those who are not so blessed? Infertility or "barrenness" is seen as a terrible curse and always the "fault" of the woman. In the ancient world, the medical causes of infertility are unknown, and male sterility is rarely considered to be the cause of the problem. Hence, the barren woman not only feels incomplete in her expected roles as wife and mother but she is also socially ostracized and the likely victim of sidelong glances, gossip, and ridicule among the townspeople, most of whom view her situation as a punishment from God. Barrenness is a common theme in the Bible; for example, all of the matriarchs (Sarah, Rebekah, and Rachel) are barren at some point—that is, until God miraculously removes their barrenness. Such stories offer hope to childless couples, but probably do little to mitigate the day-to-day longing, guilt, and sorrow that surely accompanies infertility in ancient Israel.

Though patriarchy is the norm, there are many exceptions—instances in the Bible where women assume leadership roles in the military, within the monarchy, and even in business. Some notable examples include the great judge Deborah (Judges 4–5), who acts as a strong military leader and prophetess; Bathsheba, a powerful queen who manipulates events in order to promote her son Solomon to succeed his father, King David—ahead of Adonijah, the son who is next in line to the throne (1 Kings 1–2); and Lydia, who, in Acts of the Apostles, is described as a wealthy, influential merchant involved in the production of costly purple fabric and a leader in one of the many house churches founded by Paul (Acts 16:11–15, 40). There are, in fact, scores of biblical stories that feature women outwitting, outsmarting, and outmaneuvering their male counterparts. In many such stories, it is the woman who assumes the central role and who is entrusted to carry out God's plan. Many readers are surprised to learn that despite the fact that the Bible is steeped in patriarchy, women often occupy a central role in many pivotal stories. Though scholars have differing opinions as to why this is so, most agree that the stories about women often feature women as trickster characters who manage to beat the odds and prevail. The tales about women are really metaphorical, and they reflect the reality of ancient Israel, a nation that is often the underdog among Ancient Near Eastern empires, yet somehow manages to survive.

Recall that in a patriarchal system, men own most of the land, which is passed on from father to son, unless he has no sons. Though this is the norm, there *are* cases of female inheritance in the Bible. For example, in chapter 6, I mentioned the five daughters of Zelophehad (Num 27:1–7), whose father dies without a son to inherit his property. The daughters feel that it is their right to inherit their father's possessions, and they approach Moses to see if he will permit it. Moses consults the LORD, and the LORD sides with the daughters: "If a man dies, and has no son, then you shall pass his inheritance on to his daughter. If he has no daughter, then you shall give his inheritance to his brothers" (Num 27:8–9). Here, the daughters are regarded as more important than their uncles, a very unpatriarchal concept.

Evidence from outside the pages of the Bible also supports the notion that women could inherit property. Documents uncovered from a Jewish military outpost in Elephantine, Egypt (sixth to fourth centuries BCE), clearly show that women are allowed to buy and sell property. In some cases, women even inherit land over and above their male siblings. Archaeologists found similar documents dating from 93 to 132 CE. Often referred to as the Babata Archive, these documents, thirty-five in all, were discovered in 1960–1961 in the "Cave of Letters" in Nahal Hever in southern Israel. Forced to flee the Romans, seventeen people hid in the cave and perished there. Along with their skeletons archaeologists found various artifacts, including what is essentially the purse of a woman named Babata. Inside the purse, wrapped into neat bundles, were Babata's (mostly) legal documents, including marriage certificates (Babata was married twice), various lawsuits, and property transactions that indicate that Babata had inherited land from her mother as well as from her second husband.

Though most might assume that in a patriarchal system the legal tribunals are exclusively male, this does not seem to have been the case. For example, the judge, Deborah, appears to have been part of the legal assembly at "the gate" (Judg 5:11–12). What is the meaning of "the gate"? In biblical times, the elders of the town or city convene at the city gate to hear grievances and render judgments regarding criminal activity (Ps 69:12; Amos 5:10, 12; Is 29:21). So "the gate" is essentially an ancient court. Though most of those presiding at the gate are male, Deborah seems to have been at least one exception. While women, on rare occasions, may have been involved in rendering judgments, they are nonetheless generally considered to be unreliable *witnesses* in court proceedings. But again, there are some notable exceptions, as in the case of a rebellious son:

> If someone has a stubborn and rebellious son who will not obey his father and mother, who does not heed them when they discipline him, then his father and his mother shall take hold of him and bring him out to the elders of his town at the gate of that place. They shall say to the elders of his town, "This son of ours is stubborn and rebellious. He will not obey us. He is a glutton and a drunkard." Then all the men of the town shall stone him to death. So you shall purge the evil from your midst; and all Israel will hear, and be afraid. (Deut 21:18–21)

Ouch! Is it any wonder that most children during biblical times are obedient to their parents?

Overall, in both the Hebrew Bible and New Testament, women have less legal rights than men. For instance, a father may sell his daughter into slavery (Exod 21:7), and though there is a rule that requires male slaves to be freed after six years (Lev 25:40), there is no such rule for female slaves. When it comes to divorce, it is generally assumed that, once again, men hold all the cards. But not so fast. While it is true that passages in the Hebrew Bible seem to indicate that only men could initiate divorce (Deut 24:1–4; Jer 3:8), the Elephantine documents indicate that women not only could initiate divorce but after the divorce they could also retain the possessions they brought to the marriage. There are even special provisions in cases involving abuse.

The New Testament has very little to say about divorce and offers conflicting views that today often pit the miserably married against the staunch custodians of the faith. In the Gospel of Mark, Jesus seems to part ways with the Mosaic provision for divorce (Deut 24:1–4) and forbids it for any reason (Mark 10:2–12).

> Some Pharisees came, and to test him they asked, "Is it lawful for a man to divorce his wife?" He answered them, "What did Moses command you?" They said, "Moses allowed a man to write a certificate of dismissal and to divorce her." But Jesus said to them, "Because of your hardness of heart he wrote this commandment for you. But from the beginning of creation, 'God made them male and female.' 'For this reason a man shall leave his father and mother and be joined to his wife, and the two shall become one flesh.' So they are no longer two, but one flesh. Therefore what God has joined together, let no one separate." (Mark 10:2–9)

In Mark 10:2–9, as is so often the case in the Gospels, the Pharisees question Jesus, most likely for entrapment purposes. A brief historical note brings this passage into clearer focus. During this time, a debate of sorts is raging between two schools of thought concerning Jewish divorce. One position, based on the teachings of the great Rabbi Hillel, allows a man to divorce his wife for any reason, including ineptitude in the kitchen! The other, more conservative position, espoused by another prominent rabbi, Shammai, reserves this right only in cases of "unchasity." Jesus at first sidesteps the apparent snare and instead links marriage to the Creation account in Gen 2:24. He appears to be saying that what God has joined, humans cannot dissolve.

But in both Mark (70 CE) and Luke (85 CE), Jesus goes a step further, stating that remarriage after divorce is adultery: "Whoever divorces his wife and marries another commits adultery against her; and if she divorces her husband and marries another, she commits adultery" (Mark 10:12; Luke 16:18). In Matthew's version (90 CE), discussed briefly at the opening of this chapter, Jesus seems to mellow and comes closer to the Shammai school of thought, which allows for divorce in cases of adultery (Matt 5:31–32; 19:3–9), sometimes interpreted as "unchastity." The Greek word translated as "adultery" is *porneia*, the meaning of which has been hotly debated. I will say more about *porneia* when I discuss the third commonly held assumption ("The Bible says that women must remain virgins until they are married"). But the general consensus is that *porneia* here refers to marital infidelity. It is noteworthy that many scholars feel that Matthew's version reflects more the emerging Church's position rather than Jesus' views, while others reject this idea.

To add to the confusion, Paul seems to permit divorce in favor of the faith; that is, if a non-Christian no longer wishes to be married to a Christian, then they may divorce (1 Cor 7:10–17). Curiously, Paul states that if a woman separates from her husband, she should not remarry (1 Cor 7:11), and although he says that a husband should not divorce his wife, he says nothing about a husband remarrying if he does divorce her (1 Cor 7:11). All of this confusion has resulted in a cavalcade of theological interpretations that will make your head spin. Trying to reach a definitive conclusion, given the conflicting reports of what Jesus says about this topic, is nearly impossible. But what can be said of divorce insofar as gender is concerned? It would seem that divorce is undesirable, but, in certain cases, it is something that both men and, to a lesser degree, women are able to initiate.

Though gender roles are clearly defined, there are many cases of women and men stepping out of those roles. In the Hebrew Bible, for example, the great patriarch Jacob is fond of cooking (Gen 25:29), a chore in the Bible usually associated with women. Though most soldiers are male, the judge Deborah assumes a military role and helps to engineer the defeat Jabin of Hazor and his general, Sisera (Judges 4–5). In the New Testament, Jesus ignores the strict rules that govern male-female interaction (which is usually limited to family members) and includes women in his healing ministry (Matt 9:18–26; Mark 5:21–43; Luke 8:40–56; 13:10–17) and inner circle (Luke 8:1–3).

While men dominate most aspects of religious life in both the Hebrew Bible and New Testament, in the Hebrew Bible, women do perform certain religious duties and are even permitted to take religious vows (Numbers 6; 30:3–5, 9). In the New Testament, women not only help to finance Jesus' ministry (Luke 8:1–3) but also work to spread the Gospel message alongside Paul and others (Romans 16; Phil 4:2), and apparently preside over house churches (1 Cor 1:11; Acts 12:12; 16:14–15, 40). Some of these early church leaders include Mary, the mother of John Mark, who leads services in her home in Jerusalem (Acts 12:12–17); Nympha in Laodicea (Col 4:15); Apphia in Colossae (Philemon 2); and Phoebe in a place called Cenchreae, in Greece (Rom 16:1). House churches would later grow into a more institutionalized structure, and the era of relative equality between the sexes in the early years of the Jesus movement (during his lifetime and immediately after his death) is soon replaced with a form of patriarchic sexism that relegates women to an inferior status (Eph 5:22–24; 1 Tim 2:11–15).

What are we to make, then, of this rather complex history regarding gender in the Bible? In returning to our first assumption ("The Bible says that men are more important than women"), we find passages in the Hebrew Bible and New Testament that both confirm and deny this assertion. Archaeological evidence and texts outside the pages of the Bible are often at odds with certain biblical texts, too, indicating a more egalitarian society than the Bible would have us believe, but such evidence is by no means conclusive. What we *can* say for certain is that the biblical authors are products of their particular time and space in history, and their writings reflect the social norms, including gender roles, of their particular carbon footprints. Perhaps the simplest statement about gender in the Bible is that, in general, it appears that men are more highly regarded than women, with some notable exceptions. This provisional and tentative statement precludes a definitive response to our first assumption, a quiet reminder that we must be cautious in making generalizations about such complex material.

Speaking of general statements, the next commonly held assumption is the one I hear most when I question students about what they think that Bible says about sex.

Assumption Two: The Bible Says That Sex Is Bad/Evil/Dirty/ Wrong and Should Be Done for Procreation Purposes Only

Sex in the Bible begins with the story of the first woman and man in the Garden of Eden (Genesis 2–3). This foundational tale teaches us many things, including the importance of obedience in following God's commands; the challenges involved in resisting temptation, and the desire to have something that is forbidden. But the story of Adam and Eve is also a story of sexual attraction and marriage (Gen 2:24–25). Because of this, I must introduce the topic of sex in the Bible fairly early in the semester. I often begin my introduction with a simple question: "What do you think the Bible says about sex?" I ask students not to think much about this question, but instead to blurt out their first thoughts on the matter. More often than not, they respond with statements such as the following: The Bible says that sex is "bad" or "dirty" or "evil" and should be done only "to make babies."

Sex in the Bible is a vast topic with many references in both the Hebrew Bible and New Testament. In response to our second commonly held assumption, we begin with an exploration of sex in marriage, including procreation, followed by a brief discussion of the laws in the Bible designed to help regulate sexual behavior. Contrary to popular belief, during biblical times, sex is not viewed as something bad, dirty, or evil. It is a healthy, normal, and important part of marriage. Which points us to our first reality: Sex is something reserved strictly for marriage. Both men and women are expected to marry and have children; the idea of remaining single or not wanting children is unheard of. One of the chief functions of marriage is "to be fruitful and multiply" (Gen 1:28), and there are many stories that center on the Children of Israel making more Children of Israel. The Patriarchal History that spans the bulk of the book of Genesis (Genesis 12–50) details the joys and frustrations of this enterprise.

God promises Abraham (whose name means "the father of a multitude") that his descendants will be as numerous as the dust of the Earth (Gen 13:16) and the stars in the heavens (Gen 15:5). Despite the fact that Abraham and his wife, Sarah, are elderly and childless, this unlikely promise comes to fruition (Gen 21:2). In fact, the people of Israel grow at such an astonishing rate that in the second book of the Bible, Exodus, the Egyptian Pharaoh attempts to reduce their census by issuing a death decree for all Hebrew male newborns (Exod 1:15–16, 22). This desire to heed God's command to procreate in order to populate may also help to explain the practice of polygamy and the common practice of married men taking on "secondary" wives as concubines.

In any case, women are expected to remain virgins until they marry (I will speak more about virginity when I address assumption three) and married couples view sex as an important aspect of marriage. In fact, a newly married man could be granted a leave of absence for up to a year from military service or business to concentrate on his lovemaking skills (Deut 24:5)! Indeed, sex is more than just "to have babies"—it must also function as an expression of love (Gen 24:67; 29:18) and respect (Heb 13:4) and must be fulfilling for both partners (Deut 24:5). But, if this is the case, where do we get the idea that the Bible condemns sex as something bad or dirty or unwholesome?

While the Bible affirms sex as an integral part of marriage, there are certain sexual acts that are considered perverse, a laundry list of which can be found in the so-called "Holiness Code" section in the book of Leviticus in chapters 17–26. Regulations that specifically address sex are found mainly in Leviticus 18 and 20. In exploring the sexual regulations in Leviticus, we must be aware from the get-go that the string of forbidden sexual behaviors mentioned in Leviticus 18 and 20 are associated with foreign cults in Egypt and Canaan.

> You shall not do as they do in the land of Egypt, where you lived, and you shall not do as they do in the land of Canaan, to which I am bringing you. You shall not follow their statutes. (Lev 18:3)

This association is important for two reasons: First, it clearly implies that the sexual practices mentioned are commonplace among the Canaanites and, to a lesser extent, the Egyptians. This is significant because the author wishes to demonize both nations, for they are considered enemies of the Israelites. I have mentioned this convention in previous chapters—that is, the tendency of some of the biblical writers to exaggerate certain behaviors related to their foes. But in this case, there is little evidence (either in texts outside the Bible or in the archaeological record) that the Egyptians and Canaanites are as perverse as the author of this material would have us believe. And second, the sexual regulations are closely tied with purity laws and profoundly connected to the acquisition of the land. The previous inhabitants—the Canaanites—are driven from the land because they defile it; the people of Israel are admonished to discontinue the practices of their neighbors, lest they defile the land and suffer the same fate (Lev 18:24–30). With these two facts in mind, many scholars assert that the regulations set forth regarding sexual conduct are more about the condemnation of Israel's enemies and less about the acts themselves. In fact, a careful reading of the litany of no-no behaviors may be understood more as a warning against idolatry, given that most of the behaviors on the naughty list are connected to the worship of foreign gods. The mention of the fiery Canaanite deity, Molech, to whom little Canaanite children are purportedly sometimes sacrificed, helps to bolster this claim (Lev 18:21; 20:3).

In any case, the index of sexually forbidden behaviors includes a prohibition of nearly every degree of incest (Lev 18:6–12; 20:11–12, 14, 17–21), sex with a menstruating woman (Lev 18:19), bestiality (Lev 18:23; 20:15–16), adultery (Lev 20:10), and male homosexual sex (Lev 18:22; 20:13), which I will discuss in more detail in the final common assumption. In addition to the list in Leviticus, there are many other stories that demonstrate the negative consequences of what the author(s) view as deviant sexual behaviors. For example, the incestuous union between Lot and his daughters (Gen 19:30–38) results in the birth of sons who become the progenitors of the Moabite and Ammonite peoples, sworn enemies of the Israelites. This is another "demonizing" story, but it also carries the lesson that fathers and daughters must not have sex with one another. In another incestuous tale, Amnon, a son of King David and next in line to the throne, rapes his sister, Tamar (2 Samuel 13). His actions unleash subsequent acts of revenge and murder as the house of David collapses.

The crime of rape in the Bible is varied and complex. In the world of biblical antiquity, rape is largely viewed as a crime of disordered lust. Today, we know that it is about much more, but in the Bible, if an unengaged virgin is raped, she may actually be required to marry her rapist, and the rapist must pay the girl's father a fee for defiling his daughter (Deut 22:28–29)! Though Deuteronomy stipulates the death penalty for the rape of an engaged female (Deut 22:25–27), there are numerous cases of vigilante justice for victims of rape (Gen 34:25–29; Judges 19–20; 2 Sam 13:22–29), which leads us to conclude that perhaps in ancient Israel, the long arm of the law often falls short when it comes to rape.

The following is a case in point. In Genesis 34, a petty young prince named Shechem rapes Jacob's daughter, Dinah (Gen 34:2). In keeping with the custom of his day, he then asks for her hand in marriage (Gen 34:4). But since the rapist is an outsider, the laws of Israel do not apply. Jacob's sons are outraged that their sister has been defiled and decide to seek revenge. They lie and tell the rapist that he can marry their sister only if he and all the men in his town submit to the Israelite covenantal practice of circumcision (Gen 34:13–17). I can imagine that no one would have been thrilled with this proviso, but in the end, all the men in the town are circumcised (Gen 34:24). As they are weak and recovering from their circumcisions, Dinah's brothers attack, slaughter the lot of them, and loot their village (Gen 34:25–30).

Returning to the Levitical list of sexual taboos, curiously missing from the list is any mention of masturbation. Many people assume that this, too, is forbidden, but the truth is, the word *masturbation* is never specifically mentioned in the Bible, though some argue that it is implied (and also condemned) in several places. The story cited most often is found in Genesis 38 and involves a twice-widowed and very resourceful widow named Tamar (not the same Tamar just mentioned in 2 Samuel 13). The story begins with Judah, one of Jacob's twelve sons, leaving his family and settling just outside Bethlehem. He marries a local Canaanite woman, and they are blessed with three sons, Er, Onan, and Shelah (Gen 38:2–5). When the eldest, Er, is ready for a wife, Judah arranges for him to marry Tamar. Unfortunately, Er does something—the Bible does not tell us what—that greatly offends God and God kills him (Gen 38:7). There is a specific law in such instances, the law of levirate (Deut 25:5–10), which decrees that a surviving brother must marry his dead brother's widow. In compliance with this law, Judah gives Tamar to Er's younger brother, Onan. If Tamar has a son with Onan, according to the levirate law, her firstborn son is recognized as *Er's* and assumes Er's inheritance. Obviously, it is not in Onan's best financial interest to have a child with Tamar, so he practices *coitus interruptus*, an action that prompts the LORD to kill him too: "But since Onan knew that the offspring would not be his, he spilled his semen on the ground whenever he went in to his brother's wife, so that he would not give offspring to his brother" (Gen 38:9).

For centuries, this obscure passage has been used as an indictment against masturbation, though it is not masturbation at all. Moreover, it is not Onan's sexual behavior that provokes God; rather, it is his refusal to honor the law of levirate. This is an important distinction because, over time, the myths of blindness, hair growing on the palms, and impotency, just to name a few, become linked to masturbation and have connections to the story of Onan. The term *onanism*, taken from Onan's name, is an eponymous term for masturbation. As recent as the nineteenth century, onanism is considered both a sin and a medical condition that affects the brain and nervous system. Elaborate medical devices are prescribed for particularly stubborn cases to aid the afflicted in keeping his hands off of himself. While all of this may seem preposterous to contemporary readers, it is no joke, for it points to the very real problem that this book seeks to address: biblical illiteracy. Onan's story illustrates how such faulty understandings of Scripture distort its true meaning.

But if Onan's story is not about masturbation, then where in the Bible is the practice forbidden? Some commentators conclude that the word *porneia*—a word already discussed in the first two assumptions—is a catchall term to include all forms of unchastity, including masturbation, but others vehemently disagree. In the book of Leviticus, there is explicit mention of purity regulations regarding semen that seem to emanate from either masturbation or possibly nocturnal emission:

> If a man has an emission of semen, he shall bathe his whole body in water, and be unclean until the evening. Everything made of cloth or of skin on which the semen falls shall be washed with water, and be unclean until the evening. (Lev 15:16–17)

None of this, however, represents a clear condemnation of masturbation.

As we move toward definitive conclusions regarding our second common assumption, we turn to the Song of Solomon. Sometimes referred to as the Song of Songs, this particular text is the most explicit example in the Bible that affirms human sexuality as something wholesome, normal, and, I daresay, desirable. Authorship is often ascribed to King Solomon, a legendary lover who had seven hundred wives and three hundred concubines (1 Kgs 11:3; cf. Song 1:5; 8:11–12), but with all those women to please, it seems unlikely that Solomon had time to write much of anything! Indeed, most scholars agree that the text is composed sometime during the postexilic period, which of course precludes Solomonic authorship.

The Song of Solomon is basically a series of erotic love poems that celebrates romantic and physical love between a man and a woman. We might even describe it as "pillow talk" between two lovers. A more provincial interpretation of Songs is that it is a collection of poetry (or songs) that expresses the love between Yhwh and his people. Most scholars have largely abandoned this somewhat chaste and conservative interpretation, however, and you need only to read a few verses to see why. In Song of Solomon 7, for example, a man blinded by love praises his lover's beautiful, naked body in highly suggestive terms:

Your rounded thighs are like
jewels,
the work of a master hand. Your navel is a rounded bowl
that never lacks mixed wine. Your belly is a heap of wheat,
encircled with lilies. Your two breasts are like two
fawns,
twins of a gazelle. . . .
How fair and pleasant you are,
O loved one, delectable
maiden! (Song 7:1–3, 6)

Barely able to contain his passion, he poetically expresses his unbridled sexual desires in metaphorical language.

You are stately as a palm tree,
and your breasts are like its
clusters.
I say I will climb the palm tree
and lay hold of its branches.
Oh, may your breasts be like
clusters of the vine,

and the scent of your breath like
apples,
and your kisses like the best wine
that goes down smoothly,
gliding over lips and teeth. (Song 7:7–9)

The woman apparently likes what she hears and responds with a series of
sexually laden metaphors of her own, including vines with buds, blossoms
that open, pomegranates in bloom, and mandrakes, considered an aphrodi-
siac in the ancient world. Her seductive words are just as erotic as the man's,
which implies a certain level of sexual mutuality, rather than the female
sexual subordination we might expect in the patriarchic culture of the Bible.

I am my beloved's,
and his desire is for me.
Come, my beloved,
let us go forth into the fields,
and lodge in the villages;
let us go out early to the vineyards,
and see whether the vines
have budded,
whether the grape blossoms have
opened
and the pomegranates are
in bloom.
There I will give you my love.
The mandrakes give forth
fragrance,
and over our doors are all choice fruits,
new as well as old,
which I have laid up for you,
O my beloved. (Song 7:10–13)

Aside from the steamy imagery and erotic nature of the Song of Solomon,
it is, at its essence, a moving commemoration of human sexuality and love.

In returning to our second common assumption ("The Bible says that
sex is bad/evil/dirty/wrong and should be done for procreation purposes
only"), we can say with reasonable certainty that this assumption is false.
There are certain sexual behaviors that are regarded as perverse, but, as
the Song of Solomon and other texts demonstrate, sex for pleasure as
well as sex for procreative purposes, within the confines of marriage, is

considered to be the norm. Our next common assumption addresses sex before marriage, and that is a totally different story.

Assumption Three: The Bible Says That Women Must Remain Virgins Until They Are Married

Female virginity is highly prized in ancient Israel, not only because of its religious implications, but also because virginity indicates a certain measure of self-control and obedience, qualities desirable in a wife and predicative of marital fidelity. Since girls marry quite young, usually around age thirteen or fourteen, and live at home under the strict guardianship of their parents until they are married, their chastity is protected. But notice here that we are talking about *female* virginity. For, while the Bible's stipulation for female virginity is clear, interestingly, it has no specific stipulations for male virginity. Some scholars, however, point to the Commandment, "You shall not commit adultery" (Exod 20:14), which forbids sexual relations outside marriage, as a general injunction against premarital sex aimed at both men and women.

In the Hebrew Bible and New Testament, marriage is considered the natural state for men and women, and although there are certainly instances where Jewish men (and, rarely, Jewish women) are not married, this is the exception rather than the norm. Most women marry quite young, usually soon after the onset of menstruation, which, of course, heralds fertility. Marriages are usually brokered between families and most women have little or no say in the matter.

Men typically marry later (in their twenties, or even thirties) and thus most men are older than their wives. Since the life expectancy for women is shorter than for men (women generally live to about age thirty and men to age forty), this arrangement makes sense. As I mentioned earlier in this chapter, pregnancy and childbirth complications, especially infections, are the leading causes of death for women. For this reason, many women die young, and men often remarry more than once and have more children with their new wives, creating what we call today "blended families." Women are expected to be virgins when they marry, but it is likely that some are not. If a husband suspects that his wife is not a virgin on their wedding night, he can reject her, which would be a great humiliation for both the new bride and her family. The girl's family, however, is not without recourse. If her parents can offer evidence that their daughter is indeed a virgin, in the form of a bloody marital sheet (Deut 22:13–21), then her husband will not be allowed to divorce her. Setting aside the way in which the parents might obtain this sheet, if the elders of the town examine the sheet and find evidence of the woman's virginity, then the husband is fined and his request for divorce denied. If, however, the town elders find in favor of the aggrieved husband, then the woman is brought to her father's house and stoned to death by the townsmen (Deut 22:20–21).

Although the New Testament is not as specific as the Hebrew Bible—for example, Jesus does not explicitly address virginity—it is nonetheless clear that women are expected to remain virgins until they marry. The most obvious example of this is found in the story of Mary, Jesus' mother. According to Matthew, Mary, who is a virgin, and Joseph are engaged when she conceives by the power of the Holy Spirit. Apparently, Joseph and Mary have a signed marital contract (or *ketubah*), but the marital ceremony has not yet taken place. Jewish marriages are a two-step process. In the first step, the *ketubah*, which is a legal document that spells out the bride and groom's obligations to one another, is signed in the presence of two witnesses. The *ketubah*, among other things, protects women financially in the case of the husband's death or divorce. Once this contract is signed, then a wedding ceremony takes place. Mary and Joseph are in the in-between stage when she informs him that she is pregnant (Matt 1:18). Joseph decides to dismiss or "divorce" Mary rather than subject her to public disgrace, but an angel appears to him in a dream and convinces him that Mary is telling the truth: She really *did* conceive by the power of the Holy Spirit (Matt 1:19–20). Much more can be said of this story, but I mention it here only as an example of the importance of virginity during the first century.

Let us now briefly return to the word *porneia*, discussed earlier. Recall that in Matthew's version of the Jesus story, when Jesus addresses divorce, he seems to permit it in cases of adultery (Matt 5:31–32; 19:3–9), or *porneia* in Greek. Although the general consensus regarding the meaning of the word *porneia* in the context of Matt 5:31–32; 19:3–9 seems to be "adultery" or "marital infidelity," this opinion is by no means unanimous. Several translators feel that a better reading of the word *porneia* is "unchastity"—which opens the door for a whole variety of meanings. Thus, *porneia* could point to a number of sexual sins, including incest, adultery, and even premarital intercourse. If this indeed is the case, and there are some who unequivocally assert that it is, then Jesus does address the issue of virginity as a prerequisite for marriage.

Regardless of the debate surrounding the correct translation of *porneia*, it seems clear that female virginity in both the Hebrew Bible and New Testament is something that is encouraged and, indeed, expected, thus confirming our third commonly held assumption. Let us now explore our final commonly held assumption to see what the Bible has to say about homosexuality.

Assumption Four: The Bible Says That It Is a Sin to Be Gay

This last assumption is by far the most controversial and is often at the center of emotionally charged discussions between the religious right and those with less conservative beliefs. Those on the far right often cite the Bible as their definitive source for the condemnation and even hatred of homosexuals, while those on the left and the moderates in between contend either that religious conservatives misunderstand the Bible's teachings on homosexuality or that the Bible, because of its antiquity, cannot be a definitive resource when it comes to homosexuality. It is thus clear that there are few issues that elicit such strong feelings as the topic of homosexuality in the Bible.

Before I discuss the relatively few biblical passages that address homosexuality, it is important to first say a few words about sexual orientation. Sexual orientation refers to the range of physical, emotional, and romantic feelings an individual has toward another. One may have a heterosexual orientation (attraction to the opposite sex), a homosexual orientation (attraction to the same sex), an orientation to both sexes (bisexuality), or neither (asexuality). Though there is certainly some disagreement regarding sexual orientation, most scientists agree that one's sexual orientation is influenced by a combination of environmental, emotional, biological, and genetic factors and that it is in place at a very young age, perhaps even before birth. The general consensus among experts is that one's sexual orientation is not a choice and cannot be changed.

Sexual orientation is different from sexual activity, which refers to specific behaviors of a sexual nature with a partner of the opposite or of the same sex. In the world of biblical antiquity, the concept of sexual orientation is unknown. What this means is that all homosexual activity is thought to take place within a heterosexual orientation. Moreover, in the patriarchal world of the Bible, men are men and women are women. Although there are a few exceptions, some of which have already been noted in this chapter, gender roles are fairly rigid. Both of these factors may account for some of the Bible's statements regarding homosexuality. While many on the religious right are wont to cite dozens of passages that purportedly address homosexuality, including, for example, the Creation account in Genesis that speaks of a man (Adam) and his partner (Eve) in heterosexual terms, there are actually only a few that specifically address homosexuality. Accordingly, I will confine my remarks to passages in which homosexuality is clearly addressed or undeniably implied.

The first and perhaps most popular story in which homosexuality is mentioned is found in Genesis 19, the story of Sodom and Gomorrah. In order to better understand this story, you must first read Genesis 18—specifically, Gen 18:16–33. In Genesis 18, the LORD and two of his attendants (variously called "men" or "angels") are on a fact-finding mission to see if Sodom and Gomorrah are as disreputable as has been reported (Gen 18:20–21). The patriarch Abraham intercedes on Sodom's behalf in a somewhat comical conversation with the LORD (Gen 18:23–33), asking the King of the Universe if he will destroy the city if ten good men can be found within its walls. Abraham's nephew, Lot, and his family live in Sodom; hence Abraham has a personal interest in preserving the doomed city. In any case, God promises not to destroy the city if ten good men are among the townspeople. But, apparently, good men are hard to find in Sodom. The LORD drops out of the picture and instead sends his "angels" to Sodom to scope out the situation. Though Lot, like his Uncle Abe, displays typical Middle Eastern hospitality (Gen 18:1–8; 19:1–3), the rest of the town could use a crash course in manners. Lot graciously offers the angels—who appear as mere men—a meal and a place to sleep for the evening. This sort of hospitality is common and very much expected during this time period, when few are able to afford travel and those who could afford it often have trouble finding a safe place to bed down for the night.

But the travelers never have the chance to tuck in, because, shortly after dinner, all the men of Sodom surround the house, intent on gang-raping Lot's visitors:

> But before they lay down, the men of the city, the men of Sodom, both young and old, all the people to the last man, surrounded the house; and they called to Lot, "Where are the men who came to you tonight? Bring them out to us, so that we may know them." (Gen 19:4–5)

As I have mentioned before, in the Bible, the verb "to know" is often a euphemism for sexual intercourse. This violence—and rape then and now is considered an act of extreme violence—is intended to humiliate the visitors. What happens next, however, is equally disturbing. Because Lot takes seriously the hospitality law (an obligation so sacred, I often call it the eleventh commandment), he offers his virgin daughters to the rabble in lieu of his houseguests (Gen 19:8)! At this point we must step back and look at this situation from the perspective of the storyteller. What exactly is the ancient author trying to say?

First, Lot's actions make it clear that this is a story about hospitality, or, in this case, the lack of it. Indeed, the overwhelming scholarly opinion regarding the crime of Sodom that warrants its destruction has to do with the violation of hospitality, not homosexuality. For centuries, due to a lack of knowledge about Ancient Near Eastern customs, individuals have misinterpreted this story and used it as fodder for discrimination and hatred of homosexuals. That Lot is obliged to protect his visitors at all costs—even to the point of offering his own daughters to the crowd of men—drives home the extreme importance of the law of hospitality, and the ancient reader would have sympathized with Lot's quandary. That the would-be rapists and their intended victims are male is really secondary, for all rapes, whether heterosexual or homosexual, are intended to assert power and control. The townsmen's behavior demonstrates the opposite of what is expected of them under the law of hospitality, and this is precisely the author's point. Remember that the Bible often teaches us by showing us what not to do. In this case, the author first highlights proper hospitality in Gen 18:1–8: Abraham greets his guests, feeds them, and offers them rest. In Genesis 19, the guests are not so lucky.

The importance of the law of hospitality is even more apparent in Judges 19, a story that is very similar to the tale of Sodom. This time, it is a Levite and his concubine who enter the town of Gibeah in search of a place to stay for the night. An old man—an outsider, just like Lot (who migrates to Canaan with Abraham but then parts ways with him to make his home in the ill-fated Sodom)—is the only person who offers them a place to stay (Judg 19:15–21). While the couple and the old man are enjoying a meal, the townsmen surround the home and demand that the Levite be turned over to them so that they can "have intercourse with him" (Judg 19:21–22). As in Genesis 19, the old man takes very seriously his duty to protect the man to whom he is offering hospitality and, like Lot, offers the licentious crowd his virgin daughter and the Levite's concubine instead (Judg 19:23–24). Apparently annoyed at the interruption of his evening, the Levite takes matters into his own hands and tosses out his concubine to the crowd. They rape and abuse her all night while her husband slumbers peacefully in the home of the old man (Judg 19:25–26). The Levite gets up the next morning to continue his journey and finds his concubine lying outside the door, either dead or unconscious. The text is unclear which, but let us hope it is the former, because upon their arrival home, the Levite hacks her body into twelve pieces and sends a body part to each of the twelve tribes, a symbolic gesture designed to highlight the lack of hospitality in Gibeah (Judg 19:27–30). This utter disregard for the law of hospitality actually triggers a civil war.

Much more can be said of these terrifying tales, not the least of which is the heinous way in which the women in both Sodom and Gibeah are treated, but the central issue has to do with the violation of the code of hospitality. And although homosexual gang rape is an element in each story, it is peripheral and not the point of either story.

The next text that specifically refers to homosexuality is, however, more explicit. Found in the Holiness Code section of Leviticus, this verse is often touted as the Bible's definitive statement regarding the sinfulness of homosexuality. I discussed Leviticus 18 in the second common assumption, and I encourage you to stop for a moment and re-read Leviticus 18 and to review my commentary there.

I remember driving past a hate rally many years ago and seeing "Leviticus 18:22" printed on a sign carried by one of the participants. If you look at Lev 18:22, which reads, "You shall not lie with a male as with a woman; it is an abomination," it may seem pretty clear. But reading this verse in isolation reminds us that we must be wary of reading any biblical passage out of its given context. So what is the context of this statement? Recall that Leviticus 18 and 20 contain lists of forbidden sexual behaviors associated with foreign cults in Egypt and Canaan and that the author's intent is to demonize both nations. As you reread Leviticus 18, try to put on your scholar's hat, for the moment setting aside your personal feelings about homosexuality, and simply read the words in front of you. If you do, it should be clear that the author is referring to certain behaviors associated with pagan cult worship. In fact, the word rendered in English as "abomination" in Lev 18:22 comes from the Hebrew word *to'ebah*, a word that means something like "ritually impure" and is usually associated with foreign religious cults. For an Israelite to participate in such a cult would be a form of *idolatry*. We must also remember that in the ancient mind, all homosexual acts are committed by those with heterosexual orientations and therefore are considered, at the very least, unnatural.

Notice, too, that although Leviticus 18 has a long list of taboo sexual practices, curiously absent from the list is the prohibition of father-daughter incest and lesbian sex. If we are to take this list seriously, then what do these two glaring omissions mean? The point I am trying to make is that Leviticus 18 is a tirade against foreign cults and a strict warning to the followers of Yhwh to abstain from any participation in such cults. Incidentally, the word *to'ebah* (usually translated as "abomination" or "detestable" in English Bibles) is used in many other places. Those who take this word literally must necessarily abstain from eating shellfish (Lev 11:9-11), from wearing slacks (if you are female) (Deut 22:5), reading your horoscope (Deut 18:10–12), and a whole a host of other "abominations" that modern folks do not seem to find so abominable.

So far, we have covered the passages in the Hebrew Bible that explicitly mention male homosexuality (there are no passages that expressly address lesbian sexual behavior in the Hebrew Bible). But what does the New Testament have to say about this topic? Since today much of the outcry against homosexuals comes from within the ranks of the Christian right, surely there must be scores of passages in which Jesus condemns such behavior. The truth is, Jesus never once discusses homosexual behavior, much less condemns it. But Paul mentions it in two of his seven authentic letters: 1 Corinthians and Romans. We will examine the reference in 1 Corinthians first.

Why Paul decides to start a church in Corinth has confounded me for years. Corinth, in the world of antiquity, is a busy port city located in southern Greece. With so many people coming in and out of the city, it proves to be fertile ground for prostitutes, both male and female. Moreover, pagan worship of nearly every type can be found in Corinth. Paul must have seen promise in Corinth, however, and his hunch that he could net converts to the Jesus movement proves to be a good one. History and the archaeological record indicate that there is a thriving, albeit confused, fledgling church in Corinth. But for some of these new converts, parting ways with their old pagan practices is a challenge. The so-called Corinthian correspondence (1–2 Corinthians) reveals these challenges in vivid detail.

The purpose of 1 Corinthians is to deal with a number of specific problems. Paul takes up several topics raised by the Corinthians themselves in a letter he receives from them (1 Cor 7:1) and although we do not have that original letter, we can piece it together based on Paul's response. Apparently, "Chloe's people" (Chloe is a church leader) inform Paul that various factions have developed, threatening the church's unity (1 Cor 1:11–12), and that a man who is having an incestuous relationship with his stepmother has gone undisciplined by the congregation (1 Corinthians 5). These matters are addressed in 1 Corinthians 1–6. Paul also addresses concerns about sexual relationships, marriage, and divorce (1 Corinthians 7), Christians eating food sacrificed to idols (1 Corinthians 8–10), and various matters pertaining to Christian worship, including speaking in tongues (1 Corinthians 11–14). He goes on to answer questions concerning the resurrection of the dead (1 Corinthians 15), and questions regarding the collection for the Jerusalem church, which Paul solicits from them earlier (1 Corinthians 16). But, for our purposes, we will focus on 1 Cor 6:9–10, a section of the letter that contains a list of behaviors that might prevent one from inheriting the Kingdom of God (a similar list appears in 1 Tim 1:9–11).

> Do you not know that wrongdoers will not inherit the kingdom of
> God? Do not be deceived! Fornicators, idolaters, adulterers, male

prostitutes, sodomites, thieves, the greedy, drunkards, revilers, robbers—none of these will inherit the kingdom of God.

This passage has been translated in various English Bibles to read quite differently. Of course the key words in which we are interested have to do with whether or not Paul is referring to homosexuals. In the New Revised Standard Version (NRSV) just quoted, those key words are translated as "male prostitutes" and "sodomites." This translation is by no means universal, however; the King James Version (KJV), for example, translates 1 Cor 6:9–10 this way:

> Know ye not that the unrighteous shall not inherit the kingdom of God? Be not deceived: neither fornicators, nor idolaters, nor adulterers, nor effeminate, nor abusers of themselves with mankind, nor thieves, nor covetous, nor drunkards, nor revilers, nor extortioners, shall inherit the kingdom of God.

And the New International Version (NIV) chooses the word "homosexual" in its translation:

> Do you not know that the wicked will not inherit the kingdom of God? Do not be deceived: Neither the sexually immoral nor idolaters nor adulterers nor male prostitutes nor homosexual offenders nor thieves nor the greedy nor drunkards nor slanderers nor swindlers will inherit the kingdom of God.

Again, these are all English translations of the same Greek passage. So how can one translation use the words "male prostitutes" and "sodomites," and another "effeminate" and "abusers of mankind," and still another "male prostitutes" and "homosexuals"? We are running into the same problem mentioned at the outset of this chapter—that is, the difficulty of translating ancient Greek into English. Anyone who speaks a foreign language will tell you that sometimes there simply is not an equivalent word in another language that means the same thing. So what are Paul's original words?

The Greek word *malakoi* translated variously as "male prostitutes" (NRSV, NIV) or "effeminate" (KJV) can mean several things, including "soft" or "delicate," but can also be used to indicate an effeminate male. The Greek word *arsenokoitai*, translated as "sodomites" in the NRSV, as "abusers of themselves with mankind" in the KJV, and "homosexual offenders" in the NIV, means something approximating "male going to bed." It is difficult to find this word in other ancient Greek texts, and its meaning is confusing. Translating *arsenokoitai* to "sodomite" is a particularly poor translation, since "sodomite" is not actually a biblical word at all. As already noted, the sin of Sodom is gross neglect of hospitality, and later biblical references to the doomed cities (including a reference by Jesus) indicate this widespread belief (cf. Ezek 16:46–58; Matt 10:15). Hence, "sodomite" simply refers to someone from Sodom. It is only later, when the story in Genesis 19 is misinterpreted as an indictment against homosexuality, that this word comes to be associated with homosexual intercourse.

If Paul wants to indicate homosexuals in his list, why does he not simply use the Greek word for homosexual (*paiderasste*)? This is exactly the question scholars have asked for ages! As a result, great theories and not a few tedious tomes have been produced, all claiming to accurately capture Paul's "true meaning" in 1 Cor 6:9–10. One of the leading theories is that Paul is referring to the ancient Greek practice of pederasty, whereby an adult male takes to his bed (*arsenokoitai*) a young boy. Considering the context of the overall letter and the place and people to whom it is addressed, this theory makes a great deal of sense. Remember that the port city of Corinth is a bustling center of trade in the Roman Empire. Thousands of people flock in and out of the city each day from all parts of the empire and beyond. Bars, brothels, and pagan cults dot the landscape. All of this is part of life in most port cities in antiquity, including Corinth. But so is pederasty. In fact, it is a fairly widespread practice among educated Greeks. Paul is a Roman citizen and well traveled. Since he is what we might call "worldly," he is surely aware of a practice so common in the Roman Empire. But Paul is also a Jew, and for Jews, pederasty is considered sinful, so he might be condemning the practice.

Another theory is that Paul, an educated Pharisee, may have been alluding to the passages we have already discussed in Leviticus (18:22 and 20:13), in which men are forbidden to lie down with other men in the context of pagan cult worship. Paul would have been aware of these and other references to cult prostitutes—some of whom are male, often called "dogs"—in the Hebrew Bible (Deut 23:17–18; 1 Kgs 14:23–24; 15:12; 22:46; 2 Kgs 23:7). If this is the case, perhaps Paul is trying to condemn male prostitution, an apparently thriving trade in Corinth.

While all of these theories, and I am sure there are dozens more, are interesting, the ambiguity remains, and we simply cannot know for certain what Paul means by the Greek terms *arsenokoitai* and *malakoi* in 1 Cor 6:9–10. But what about Paul's other reference to homosexuality, found in his letter to the Romans?

Paul's letter to the Romans is the longest of his seven authentic epistles, and it contains the fullest expression of Paul's gospel. The primary intention of Romans is to promote unity among the followers of Christ—specifically, between Jewish and Gentile Christians. In Rom 1:18–3:31, Paul indicts Jews and Gentiles for their failure to live in accordance with God's demands. This failure incurs God's wrath, and the sole remedy for the situation is faith in Christ. In Rom 1:18–25, Paul points out the failure of humans to worship God and the deleterious effects of paganism. This willful rejection of God results in a perversion of natural law:

> For this reason God gave them up to degrading passions. Their women exchanged natural intercourse for unnatural, and in the same way also the men, giving up natural intercourse with women, were consumed with passion for one another. Men committed shameless acts with men and received in their own persons the due penalty for their error. (Rom 1:26–27)

Here, there are no tricky, indecipherable Greek words; Paul is clearly talking about homosexual activity involving both men and, for the first and only time in the Bible, women. This sort of behavior is common among Roman and Greek cults, but Paul views such behavior as unnatural. In this passage, Paul understands such behavior as a rebellion against God by essentially rejecting one's natural state. But, once again, we must remember that he is talking about homosexual acts that are performed between what he perceives as heterosexual persons. And this leads us back to our central point: In the world of biblical antiquity, homosexual orientation is unknown, and all homosexual acts are therefore thought to occur within the context of a heterosexual orientation.

If there are passages that are either correctly or incorrectly interpreted as a condemnation of homosexuality, are there instances in the Bible where homosexuals are affirmed? Some scholars insist that there are at least two places in the Hebrew Bible in which homosexual relationships may be approved. The first is found in the book of Ruth. The character of Ruth is the model of filial devotion, loyalty, and friendship. Such a characterization may seem surprising given the fact that Ruth is a Moabite, a suspicious foreigner from across the Jordan River. Descendants from the incestuous union between Lot and his eldest daughter (Gen 19:37), the Moabites are the enemies of the Israelites and known for their apostasy and sexual immorality.

As the book opens (Ruth 1:1–5), it reveals a desperate situation. Naomi, along with her husband, Elimelech, and their two sons, Mahlon and Chilion, leave their home in the famine-stricken Bethlehem and settle in Moab, where they live peacefully for ten years. At some point, Elimelech dies and eventually both boys marry local Moabite girls. Mahlon marries Ruth and Chilion marries Orpah, and sometime after this, Naomi's sons also die, leaving their widows childless.

Learning that the famine in Bethlehem is now over, Naomi makes the decision to return to her homeland and her people. Ruth and Orpah set out with her, but Orpah turns back to her family in Moab (Ruth 1:14–15). Ruth, however, remains with Naomi; in fact, she "clings" to her (Ruth 1:14). Some scholars assert that the use of this verb (*dabaq* in Hebrew) is evocative of Adam and Eve, who "cling" to each other in a sexual embrace (Gen 2:24). As the parting scene continues, despite Naomi's persistent urgings for Ruth to stay in Moab with her family, Ruth refuses to abandon her mother-in-law. Ruth's declaration of love and loyalty represents one of the most moving passages in the entire Bible:

> Where you go, I will go;
> where you lodge, I will lodge;
> your people shall be my people;
> and your God, my God.
> Where you die, I will die—
> there I will be buried.
> May the LORD do thus and so
> to me,
> and more as well,
> if even death parts me from you. (Ruth 1:16–17)

It is Ruth's passionate confession of love and devotion—both to her mother-in-law and to Naomi's God—that has raised a few eyebrows. Moreover, any woman who has ever had a mother-in-law must marvel at Ruth's close relationship with Naomi. But does Ruth's desire to "cling" to Naomi and her heartfelt speech indicate a more intimate relationship with her mother-in-law? Though some scholars (and others) insist that it does, the rest of the story does not seem to support this notion. Women during biblical times often form close attachments to one another, not unlike today's modern females. They are also more overtly expressive of their feelings, and Ruth is no exception. But beyond these obvious gender traits is the fact that the prime objective of both women is to secure a man to redeem them from their poverty.

Boaz, a distant relative of Naomi's deceased husband, is the object of Ruth's affection, and it is Naomi who recognizes Boaz as a possible redeemer (*go'el*). In the Bible, the term *go'el* usually refers to either a blood avenger for a relative who has been murdered (Num 35:31–34; Deut 19:6–12) or a male relation who acts as a protector to vulnerable relatives in danger of losing ancestral property (Lev 25: 25–55). It is likely that Naomi views Boaz in terms of the latter. Later in the Bible, *go-el* is a term used for the LORD and is associated with God's saving actions (Is 41:14; 43:1).

Naomi scripts a seduction that helps Ruth to get her man (Ruth 3:1–18). The scene is filled with sexual innuendos, including the euphemistic word "feet," which may refer to the genitals (Ruth 3:4, 7, 8, 14), and the repeated use of the verbs "to lie down" (Ruth 3:4, 7, 8, 13, 14) and "to know" (Ruth 3:3, 14), both of which connote sexual intercourse. Still, the text does not explicitly state that Ruth and Boaz have sexual relations. But Ruth 3 does depict a steamy love scene between Boaz and Ruth, which all but negates the notion that Ruth and Naomi are lesbians.

There is another story in the Hebrew Bible that is a bit more ambiguous. The tale of David and Jonathan (1 Samuel 13–2 Samuel 1) is often used as the singular model of a loving male homosexual relationship in the Bible, but is this an accurate characterization of the relationship between these two men? David is one of the most highly developed characters in the Bible. David's relationship with Jonathan, Saul's son, precedes David's ascension to the throne. Recall in my previous discussions of Saul (in chapters 1 and 5) that he is the antithesis of David. The young Saul is described as a rather shy and a reluctant monarch, while David, on the other hand, is a politically savvy operator who manipulates people and events in his favor.

King Saul eventually falls from grace, and the story of his personal and political demise is one of the most tragic stories in the Bible. Saul's undoing begins in 1 Samuel 13, when he takes credit for a military victory won by his son, Jonathan. Then, growing impatient before a battle with the Philistines, Saul fails to wait for Samuel, the priest and prophet, to arrive to offer the prebattle sacrifice; instead, he offers the sacrifice himself, a cultic no-no. Samuel, who arrives just after Saul has performed a religious function normally reserved for Israel's priests, makes it clear that Saul's actions will not go unpunished: "Samuel said to Saul, 'You have done foolishly; you have not kept the commandment of the LORD your God. . . . Your kingdom will not continue'" (1 Sam 13:13–14).

The prophet's words come to sad fruition, as Saul slowly loses control—of his kingdom, his family, and ultimately his very senses. He swears rash oaths (which, in the ancient world, are seen as binding) and begins to fight battles not so much for the glory of *God* as for his own glory (something that always yields disastrous consequences in the Bible). For these and other sins, God sends a "tormenting spirit" that renders Saul mentally incapacitated (1 Sam 16:14). David (a "man after the LORD's heart," 1 Sam 13:14) capitalizes on this and he grows in popularity. In fact, even Saul's own son, Jonathan, aligns himself with David and appears to be quite smitten with him: "The soul of Jonathan was bound to the soul of David, and Jonathan loved him as his own soul" (1 Sam 18:1).

The two men make a covenant with each other (1 Sam 18:3), and Jonathan gives David his most prized possessions (1 Sam 18:4). Saul views David as a threat and seeks to kill him (1 Samuel 19–20), but Jonathan protects David and sends David into hiding. One evening, Saul confronts Jonathan at the dinner table—"Do I not know that you have chosen the son of Jesse to your own shame?" (1 Sam 20:30)—and makes it clear that Jonathan's relationship with David will prevent Jonathan from inheriting the throne (1 Sam 20:31). Saul demands to know David's whereabouts, but Jonathan refuses to tell Saul where David is hiding. The argument escalates to the point where Saul throws a spear at his son (1 Sam 20:31–34).

Jonathan leaves his father's house and goes to the place where David is hiding. The two have a prearranged, "all clear" signal, and David emerges from his hiding place (1 Sam 20:35–40):

> David rose from beside the stone heap and prostrated himself with his face to the ground. He bowed three times, and they [David and Jonathan] kissed each other, and wept with each other. David wept the more. (1 Sam 20:41)

When later, Jonathan, along with brothers and his father, Saul, die in battle, David, who will rise to the throne, is deeply distressed. He recites or sings an elegy that includes the following:

> Jonathan lies slain upon your high
> places.
> I am distressed for you, my
> brother, Jonathan;
> greatly beloved were you to me;
> your love to me was wonderful,
> passing the love of women. (2 Sam 1:25–26)

The question at hand seems to be this: Do these passages, and others like them, indicate a close male friendship or something more? While this sort of relationship between two men is virtually unheard of in the rest of the Bible, we cannot say for certain that the relationship between David and Jonathan is of a sexual nature. If it is sexual, the authors offer no negative critique of it. Of course, it is also possible that David is using

Jonathan to further his own ambitions, something totally in keeping with David's character.

Still, both men assume what is then the traditional role for adult males—they each marry and have children—but this alone does not preclude the possibility that there is something more to their relationship beyond the bonds of friendship. The point here is that we cannot know for certain what is on the mind of the ancient author who writes this material.

Which brings us to our less than conclusive conclusion to the fourth and final commonly held assumption ("The Bible says that being gay is a sin"). We can definitively state that this assumption is, in fact, erroneous because in the world of biblical antiquity the concept of a sexual orientation other than heterosexual is unknown. The term *gay* is also a relatively new designation for someone with a homosexual orientation, and this alone makes the assumption false. Furthermore, if a gay or lesbian orientation is a natural condition, as most people understand it today, then how can it be sinful? The Hebrew Bible and New Testament consistently affirm the goodness of human beings as reflections of the Creator. But we also know that the question is far more nuanced and beyond merely one's sexual orientation. Indeed, some accuse scholars of dancing around the heart of the issue with fancy footwork that focuses on such things as word origins and the difficulties involved in deciphering ancient texts. This is not simply a matter of choreography, however, because words and what they mean matter and are central to gaining a fuller understanding of the Bible.

The average person just wants to know if the Bible says that it is sinful to engage in sexual relations with a person of the same sex. This is a simple, honest question, but the answer is not so simple. The Bible makes it clear that sex within the confines of a loving marriage is not only healthy but also expected. It remains silent, however, when it comes to loving, committed, sexual relationships between persons of the same gender. And, in many ways, it is unfair to expect a collection of ancient texts, written centuries before the advent of modern medicine and psychology, to provide definitive answers to such contemporary concerns. This leaves readers with the responsibility to learn more about what it is they are reading, but also to read the Bible with a discerning heart, following the quiet voice of God in their acceptance or judgment of others.

Fair Is Fair

THE ESSENTIAL ASPECTS OF
BIBLICAL LAW AND JUSTICE

At his best, man is the noblest of all animals;
separated from law and justice he is the worst.

—ARISTOTLE

The topics of biblical law and justice are among the most discussed, debated, and written about subjects in theological circles. Great libraries of books, articles, and manifestoes attest to the variety of interpretations of various biblical texts that deal specifically with the Law (or Torah) and justice. New theologies and social movements have emerged as interpreters of every spiritual, political, and social stripe expound upon the *real* meaning of select passages. The purpose of this chapter, however, is not to offer a definitive interpretation of any particular text, but to explore certain assumptions many people hold about the topics of law and justice in the Bible. As always, the challenge for you, the faithful reader, is to probe the text for meaning by reading it alongside your Bible commentary, both in its context and in light of what you have already learned about the Bible from previous chapters.

In my college Bible courses, the topics of the Law and fairness (justice) come up early in the semester, largely because the foundation for Israel's laws can be found in Torah. When I ask my socially minded students what they think the Bible has to say about things like law, social justice, and basically the manner in which we should treat one another, I get a variety of answers. What follows are the top four responses.

1. The Bible has the Ten Commandments, which are laws that must be followed.
2. The Bible teaches that when you break a law, you will be punished ("an eye for an eye").
3. The Bible says we should treat others the way we want to be treated (the so-called Golden Rule).
4. The Bible says we should take care of those less fortunate.

Before we plunge into the four commonly held assumptions about what the Bible says about the Law and justice, we must first define what it means when we speak of *biblical law* and *biblical justice*. The Bible is filled with all sorts of laws, prohibitions, and injunctions that regulate how humans ought to behave in the world created by God. Most of these laws are familiar to us because they have laid the foundation for our own legal system. Law, in so-called civilized societies, forbids certain behaviors and actions because they impinge upon the welfare and safety of others in the community. For example, we are not allowed to kill, steal, rape, abuse, coerce, slander, or otherwise cause harm to another person (or animal), lest we suffer consequences ranging from fines to incarceration and in some cases, even capital punishment. Our laws create societal order, and in a sense, they are designed to regulate and control our behavior and to protect the innocent. While the same can be said of the Law in ancient Israel, there are some major differences.

Israel's legal system is grounded in its unique connection to God. In the Bible, God creates the Earth and forms a people (Israel) he calls his own. He gives his people an ethic by which to live, and the people accept this ethic. This is usually referred to as a covenant. Thus, in the Bible, when the people of Israel "follow the Law," they are demonstrating their love of God and their adherence to the covenant. Remember that obedience to God is highly prized in ancient Israel, and so it seems logical that strict observance of the Law (or Torah) is viewed favorably. The religious and moral overtones found in much of ancient Israel's laws illustrate the fact that we are talking about a *relationship* between God and his people, as implied in the covenant.

Today, when most preachers and teachers speak of biblical justice, they often discuss it as something different from Israel's laws. But, in truth, justice is really at the center of Israel's legal system because God is at the heart of both the Law and justice. Israel's notion of justice is not to simply be fair or equitable, but is profoundly connected to one's relationship to God who is the embodiment of justice. When God's people treat others fairly; when they are mindful of the weak, downtrodden, poor, and oppressed; and when they demonstrate compassion and mercy, they exemplify the intimate nature of the covenant and act in the same manner as God acts in the world.

Similar notions of law and justice resonate throughout both the Hebrew Bible and New Testament and help to the shape the consciousness of believers. With this very basic understanding of biblical law and justice in mind, let us now move forward and explore the four commonly held assumptions many people have about what the Bible says about rules and fairness.

Assumption One: The Bible Has the Ten Commandments, Which Are Laws That Must Be Followed

The logical starting place in trying to discern what the Bible teaches us about law and justice seems to be with our first assumption. Most of us are familiar with the Ten Commandments—even if we fall short of actually recalling all ten (in my college classroom, until I teach the Exodus story, most students can name fewer than six). In any case, the first assumption is indeed correct, insofar as it assumes that the Ten Commandments are laws given to the people by God and that people are expected to follow his rules. Scholars often refer to the laws contained in the Ten Commandments as *apodictic*, or formulaic prohibitions ("You must not . . .") that do not contain penalties for infractions. The first few Commandments deal with Israel's relationship to God, and the others mandate how members of the community must treat one another. But the Ten Commandments are not the only laws given to the people. There are, in fact, 613 laws in the Torah alone, ranging from the prohibitions against getting a tattoo (Lev 19:28) and consulting sorcerers (Deut 18:10) to the commands to love one's neighbor (Lev 19:18) and to uphold justice in court proceedings (Deut 16:18–20). But since our first common assumption expressly cites the Ten Commandments, and in the interest of keeping this chapter under a thousand pages, we will explore the ten laws given to Moses by God. Before we do that, however, let us briefly discuss the events leading up to that moment on Mount Sinai.

The Exodus story is the most important event in the Torah and provides the answer to the question: Who is your God? The story solidifies God's relationship with his Chosen People as he fights on the side of the Israelites and frees them from the despotic Egyptian Pharaoh (Exodus 3–15). Themes from the Exodus tale eventually become favored themes in the prophetic literature, which we will consider later. We briefly discussed Moses in chapter 1, identifying him as the unlikely liberator of the Hebrews enslaved in Egypt.

As the Israelites joyfully leave their captors, they march toward the sea. But Pharaoh suddenly changes his mind and sends his army after the former slaves, catching up with them and trapping them at the edge of the Red Sea. Moses appeals to the LORD for help, and the sea parts, allowing the Israelites to safely cross to the other side. Pharaoh's army, however, is not so lucky. As they pursue the Children of Israel, the sea closes in upon them and they all perish (Exod 14:5–29).

In gratitude for God's rescue, Moses leads the people in song (Exod 15:1–19), but this spate of merriment is short-lived. As they follow Moses around the wilderness for some forty years—Bible-speak for "a long time"—the people begin to whine and "murmur" against him (Exod 15:24; 16:2–3; 17:2–4; Num 11:1–6). They complain of thirst and hunger, and they grow impatient with Moses. Despite the people's moaning and groaning, the LORD provides for them (Exod 15:25; 16:13–15). The central concern in the story now focuses on the formation of a covenant community. In a terrifying encounter with God, the people learn that as God's Chosen Ones, they must behave accordingly (Exodus 19–20).

The giving of the Ten Commandments is really at the heart of the Torah. Through our brief examination of the Ten Commandments, you will not only understand what they mean but also glimpse the basic spirit of all God's laws. This event can be broken down into four stages, and I encourage you to stop and read the pertinent chapters and verses for each stage. In the first stage, Israel prepares to meet the LORD (Exodus 19). In stage two (Exod 20:1–17), the LORD gives general laws, or the Ten Commandments. We will return to stage two and discuss each Commandment in a moment. More specific laws and punishments for breaking these laws are given in Exod 20:22–23:33. This section is often referred to as the "Covenant Code." And, finally, in Exod 24:3–8, Israel accepts the LORD's laws in a covenant ceremony.

This is the short version of a very complex narrative, but it serves as a framework for understanding the context of the Decalogue (Ten Commandments). Let us now return to Exodus 20 and discuss the meaning of each of the Ten Commandments (a similar list of the Commandments can be found in Deuteronomy 5). The first thing you might notice when reading Exod 20:1–17 is that it is a little confusing. For one thing, there seem to be more than just ten Commandments—some scholars note fourteen or fifteen; for another, in some sections, it is unclear where one Commandment ends and another begins. This has led to different interpretations and even different lists of the Ten Commandments among Jews and Christians; there is even debate among different denominations of Christians concerning the official list. For instance, Jews feel that the First Commandment is "I am the LORD your God" (Exod 20:2), whereas Christians, for the most part, view this statement as just part of the First Commandment, which continues, "you shall have no other gods before me" (Exod 20:3).

Minor differences in the way various Christian groups order the Ten Commandments do not detract from the fact that these foundational laws have always been an important aspect of Christian faith. Jesus himself affirms this truth:

> Do not think that I have come to abolish the law or the prophets; I have come not to abolish but to fulfill. . . . Therefore, whoever breaks one of these least commandments, and teaches others to do the same, will be called least in the kingdom of heaven. (Matt 5:17, 19)

Paul also insists that followers of Jesus fulfill God's laws (Rom 13:8–10).

As we take a brief look at each Commandment, I will follow the general format for the Ten Commandments held by the majority of Protestant churches, but noting differences between Jews and Catholics and Lutherans (the latter two generally follow the same list of the Big Ten). I will also parenthetically note certain (not all) New Testament passages that reference or expound upon the Commandment under consideration. Those readers who are interested in such a connection are urged to pause for a moment and review those New Testament verses before moving on to the next Commandment.

The First Commandment, "You shall have no other gods before me" (Exod 20:3), forbids the worship of other gods. Notice that it does not say that no other gods exist, but declares that for the Israelites, Yhwh, and Yhwh alone, is the only god worthy of Israel's devotion. We have already discussed the evolution of monotheism in Israel, and this Commandment seems to support the notion that provisionally, at least, the Israelites are henotheists—that is, people who worship one god but at the same time acknowledge the existence of other gods for other peoples. As already mentioned, for Jews "I am the LORD your God" (Exod 20:2) is the First Commandment and "You shall have no other gods before me" constitutes part of the Second Commandment (cf. Matt 4:10; Luke 4:8).

The Second Commandment, "You shall not make for yourself an idol" (Exod 20:4), is understood as a prohibition of idolatry, which is common in the ANE. The worshipping of idols, such as a bull statue, is strictly forbidden. The belief in a transcendent deity that cannot be contained in wood or stone is somewhat unique to ancient Israel. Further, God warns his people that he is "a jealous God" (Exod 20:5) and will severely punish the religiously fickle. For Jews, "You shall not make for yourself an idol" is considered part of the Second Commandment, while for Catholic and Lutheran Christians, it is part of the First Commandment (cf. Acts 15:20; 17:29; 1 Cor 5:10–11; 10:7, 14, 19; 12:2; 2 Cor 6:16; Gal 5:20).

The Third Commandment, "You shall not make wrongful use of the name of the LORD your God" (Exod 20:7), forbids the use of God's name in an irreverent way. When I discuss this Commandment in my university classroom, students typically think this means that believers should refrain from certain swear words ("goddamnit" is the swear word cited most often). While this is not totally correct, there is a great deal of truth in their assumption. Most scholars note that misuse of God's name springs from the ancient belief that if you use a god's name in prayer or in swearing an oath, that god is somehow magically forced to do your will. This may seem a little odd to us today, but remember that in ancient Israel, curses, oaths, and blessings are viewed as irrevocable and binding. For Catholics and Lutherans, "You shall not make wrongful use of the name of the LORD your God" is the Second Commandment (cf. Matt 5:33–34).

The Fourth Commandment enjoins God's people to "Remember the sabbath day and keep it holy" (Exod 20:8). This Commandment is based on the Creation account (Gen 2:2–3) that designates the Sabbath as a day set aside for the worship of God, relaxation, and the promotion of family life. The followers of Jesus shift the Sabbath from Saturday (technically, in Judaism, it is from Friday evening to Saturday evening) to Sunday, in honor of Jesus' resurrection. "Remember the sabbath day and keep it holy" is the Third Commandment for Catholic and Lutheran Christians (cf. Matt 12:8; Mark 1:21; 2:27–28; Luke 4:16, 31; 6:5; Acts 17:1–2).

The injunction to "Honor your father and your mother" (Exod 20:12) is the Fifth Commandment for most Protestants and Jews and the Fourth Commandment for Catholics and Lutherans. Though we typically associate this Commandment with young children's obedience to their parents, the spirit of the Commandment is really intended more for adult children to care for their aging parents (cf. Matt 15:4; 19:19; Mark 7:10; 10:19; Luke 18:20).

"You shall not murder" (Exod 20:13) is the Sixth Commandment and refers to actions such as premeditated murder or manslaughter. Execution of convicted criminals or the killing that takes place during wars is considered "legal killing." Moreover, during biblical times, blood feuds often wipe out whole tribes, and this Commandment prohibits such violence. In the New Testament, Jesus forbids the actions that can often lead to murder, such as anger, vicious gossip, and hatred (Matt 5:21–23). For Catholics and Lutherans, this is the Fifth Commandment, but the wording is slightly different. Catholic and Lutherans accept "You shall not kill" as the correct wording, and while some argue that it is the same thing, others feel that "murder" and "kill" have two very different connotations. For example, a farmer "kills" a chicken and cooks it for dinner; few people would use the word "murder" to describe the farmer's actions regarding the chicken (cf. Matt 19:18; Mark 7:21; 10:19; Luke 18:20–21; Rom 1:29; 13:9).

The Seventh Commandment, "You shall not commit adultery" (Exod 20:14), forbids sexual relations outside marriage. This means that married people can have sex with their spouses only and that unmarried persons must remain celibate until marriage. The penalty in Israelite society for those convicted of committing adultery is death. The primary intention of this Commandment is to protect the family, because the survival of the community depends on the strength of individual families. Adultery also leads to blood feuds, which disrupts the *shalom* (peace) and tears families apart. The prohibition of adultery indirectly addresses the persistent lure of Israel's more promiscuous neighbors, whose exotic women seem irresistible for many Israelite men. "You shall not commit adultery" is the Sixth Commandment for Catholics and Lutherans (cf. Matt 5:27–28; 19:18; Mark 7:22; 10:19; Luke 16:18; 18:20; Rom 2:22; 13:9; 1 Cor 5:11; 6:9, 18).

"You shall not steal" (Exod 20:15) is the Eighth Commandment for Jews and most Protestants, and the Seventh Commandment for Catholics and Lutherans. Stealing, of course, is viewed today as a sin against one's neighbor. In ancient times, stealing is connected more with God, implying that the thief feels that God is not properly caring for him or her. According to the Talmud (an encyclopedic collection of ancient rabbinic writings on laws and Jewish traditions), this Commandment is really an injunction against kidnapping, which, unlike stealing, is considered to be a capital offense (cf. Matt 19:18; Mark 7:22; 10:19; Luke 18:20; Rom 2:22; 13:9; 1 Cor 5:10–11; 6:9–10, 18; Gal 5:19).

The Ninth Commandment, "You shall not bear false witness against your neighbor" (Exod 20:16), prohibits giving false testimony, especially during court proceedings, and the penalty for perjury is death. "You shall not bear false witness against your neighbor" is the Eighth Commandment for Catholics and Lutherans (cf. Matt 15:19; 19:18; Mark 10:19; Luke 18:20).

And finally, the Tenth Commandment, "You shall not covet your neighbor's house; you shall not covet your neighbor's wife, or male or female slave, or ox, or donkey, or anything that belongs to your neighbor" (Exod 20:17), has to do with covetousness or greediness. It speaks to the human inclination to want something that belongs to someone else and the desire to have more of what we already have. Craving and greed can lead to greater sins and be psychologically destructive. For example, coveting a neighbor's wife is the first step toward committing adultery. Catholics and Lutherans break this final Commandment into two. For most Lutherans, the Ninth Commandment is "You shall not covet your neighbor's house," and the Tenth Commandment is "You shall not covet your neighbor's wife," while Catholics, following the order of the Commandments in Deut 5:21, list "You shall not covet your neighbor's wife" as the Ninth Commandment and "You shall not covet your neighbor's house" as the final Commandment (cf. Luke 12:15; Acts 20:33; Rom 1:29; 7:7; 1 Cor 5:10–11; 6:10).

Contained in the larger epic of Israel's liberation from Egyptian bondage, the Ten Commandments are at the core of Israel's laws. It is important to note that these laws come from God rather than from an earthly monarch, religious leader, or government official, making Israel's laws unique in the world of the ANE. The people's acceptance of God's Commandments in a covenant ceremony (Exod 24:3–8) exemplifies the intimate connection between God, God's Law, and God's Chosen People. Thus, in reference to the first commonly held assumption ("The Bible has the Ten Commandments, which are laws that must be followed"), we must conclude that this assumption is indeed correct. So, the Ten Commandments prohibit or demand certain behaviors, but what happens when you break one of God's laws? This question leads us to examine the second commonly held assumption.

Assumption Two: The Bible Teaches That When You Break a Law, You Will Be Punished ("An eye for an eye")

The idea that God will punish the transgressor and reward the faithful is a concept that reverberates throughout the Bible and captures the spirit of our second assumption. But is the sort of retributive justice implied in our second assumption ("an eye for an eye") normative in the Bible? If so, where does this idea of justice originate? Must the punishment fit the crime? These are important questions that can help us to better understand the biblical notions of crime and punishment.

Generally speaking, there are two basic types of laws found in the Bible. We have already explored examples of what scholars call *apodictic* laws in our discussion of the Ten Commandments in assumption one. These types of laws are more like statements prohibiting certain behaviors, and they do not contain punishments for lawbreakers. The second type of law found in the Bible is *casuistic* or case law, which addresses a particular case. Most of these types of laws are found in Exodus and Deuteronomy, and they typically follow a pattern of "when or if . . . then they must or shall." For example:

> When someone borrows an animal from another and it is injured or dies, the owner not being present, full restitution shall be made. If the owner was present, there shall be no restitution; if it was hired, only the hiring fee is due. (Exod 22:14–15)

Casuistic law is common in the ANE and is based on previous judgments in various court cases. In a sense, it is based on tradition. For example, the Babylonian King Hammurabi (1700 BCE) fashions a specific legal system based largely on case law. Hammurabi's Code and other Ancient Near Eastern laws greatly influence the form and function of Israel's laws, but with one important exception: Israel's laws are from God to his people. Other Ancient Near Eastern cultures receive laws from their rulers.

The *lex talionis* (usually casuistic) is alluded to in our second commonly held assumption. This particular reference, "an eye for an eye," is well known and constitutes most people's belief that biblical law is retributive in nature. A quick glance at the passage seems to demand that a perpetrator *literally* receive a punishment equal to his or her crime: "You shall give life for life, eye for eye, tooth for tooth, hand for hand, foot for foot, burn for burn, wound for wound, stripe for stripe" (Exod 21:23–25; cf. Lev 24:19–20 and Deut 19:21). But a fuller examination of the verses that precede the often-quoted abbreviated version helps to clarify its meaning:

> When people who are fighting injure a pregnant woman so that there is a miscarriage, and yet no further harm follows, the one responsible shall be fined what the woman's husband demands, paying as much as the judges determine. If any harm follows, you shall give life for life, eye for eye, tooth for tooth, hand for hand, foot for foot, burn for burn, wound for wound, stripe for stripe. (Exod 21:22–25)

What we see here is a case in which brawling persons harm a pregnant woman, causing either miscarriage or maternal demise. For the former, monetary restitution is required, but if the woman dies from her injuries, the penalty for the perpetrators is death. Scholars have debated whether or not this type of biblical law is meant to be taken literally or if it is a way of figuratively asserting that the "punishment must fit the crime." Given the propensity of these types of laws in the Torah, it seems likely that their primary function is to deter revenge killing by clearly delineating appropriate punishments for nearly every imaginable crime.

In the New Testament, Jesus and Paul offer us a mixed testimony concerning crime and punishment. In some cases, they seem to support the Mosaic Law, but in other instances, seem to diverge from it. Their support or rejection of the Law, of course, is key, for it is the Law that determines crime and punishment. Once again, scholars often disagree when it comes to this issue, and there is ample evidence in the New Testament to support a variety of scholarly opinions regarding Jesus and Paul and the Law.

As far as Jesus' position is concerned, there are passages in which he aligns himself with the Mosaic Law: "Do not think that I have come to abolish the law or the prophets; I have come not to abolish but to fulfill" (Matt 5:17); "But it is easier for heaven and earth to pass away, than for one stroke of a letter in the law to be dropped" (Luke 16:17). There are also instances in which he seems to amplify the Law—"You have heard that it was said, 'You shall not commit adultery.' But I say to you that everyone who looks at a woman with lust has already committed adultery with her in his heart" (Matt 5:27–28)—and passages in which he seems to place himself above the Law—"For the Son of Man is lord of the Sabbath" (Matt 12:8). So, how are we to view Jesus in terms of the Law? The general consensus is that Jesus views the Law as an authoritative source, but that he denounces the hypocrisy of certain religious leaders who pervert the Law and use it for their own personal gain (Matthew 23).

If Jesus affirms the validity of the Law, then it follows that he also accepts the punishments therein. However, some scholars point to several texts in the Gospels as evidence that Jesus rejects some of the strict punishments demanded by the Law. The first refers directly to our second common assumption and the *lex talionis* discussed earlier: "You have heard that it was said, 'An eye for an eye and a tooth for a tooth.' But I say to you, Do not resist an evildoer. But if anyone strikes you on the right cheek, turn the other also" (Matt 5:38–39). To be sure, this passage does not condone violence between individual persons, but it is unclear whether or not Jesus also seeks to address the prevailing legality of retributive justice.

The second often-cited passage takes place during Jesus' arrest in the Garden of Gethsemane, when a member of his entourage draws his sword and attacks a slave of the high priest, cutting off the slave's ear (Matt 26:51). In Luke's version of this event, Jesus reaches out and heals the servant's severed ear (Luke 22:50–51), but in Matthew's version, he does not. In both versions, however, Jesus condemns such violence: "Put your sword back into its place; for all who take the sword will perish by the sword" (Matt 26:52); "No more of this!" (Luke 22:51). Jesus' condemnation seems to indicate a belief that violence begets violence, but his admonitions do not seem to be aimed at redressing all of Israel's laws of retribution.

In the story of a woman caught in adultery (John 8:3–11), Jesus challenges the woman's accusers, saying whoever is without sin should "be the first to throw a stone at her" (John 8:7) (the penalty for adultery is death by stoning), and one by one, they all drift away. Jesus warns the woman to reform her life, and she goes on her way. This very powerful story is added to the Gospel of John sometime around the fifth century and is not part of the original Gospel. John 8:3–11 is closely associated with the Jesus tradition and may have been passed down orally before being appended to John's Gospel. For our purposes, the story does not question the Law, but only the motives of the woman's accusers.

We can tentatively conclude that the Gospels present Jesus as someone who generally upholds the Mosaic Law but also, in some cases, questions it and offers his own unique interpretation. He clearly distains distortions in the Law and gratuitous violence, but all in all, it is difficult to know his views regarding particular case laws from the Hebrew Bible. If Jesus' position regarding crime and punishment seems unclear, Paul, the man responsible for the propagation of the Jesus movement, is even more puzzling.

Paul's missionary activities throughout much of the Roman Empire bring about many changes in the strictly Jewish sect that remains in Jerusalem after Jesus' death. The most pivotal change occurs when he begins bringing Gentiles into the fold. In order to give Gentiles card-carrying membership in the new Christian faith, Paul has to dispense with certain aspects of the Mosaic Law, including circumcision and Jewish dietary regulations. Paul faces a great deal of opposition from those who insist that converts must observe Jewish customs, such as circumcision (Galatians 2; Acts 15). His opponents cause him a great deal of consternation throughout much of his missionary career (Gal 6:12–13; Phil 3:2–21; Rom 3:8, 31; 1 Thess 2:2–6; 2 Cor 10–12); in the end, however, he carries the day, and Gentiles become the lifeblood of the Jesus movement.

Paul's letters present a complex struggle with the Law, but perhaps the best way to describe Paul's position is that faith in Christ takes precedence over everything, including the Law (Romans 1–4; Gal 2:16; Philippians 3). Paul is often accused of preaching a "Law-free" Gospel (Gal 5:13; 1 Cor 6:12), and while he may have some strong opinions regarding the Law, many of the behaviors he strictly prohibits are rooted in the Law.

Now the works of the flesh are obvious: fornication, impurity, licentiousness, idolatry, sorcery, enmities, strife, jealousy, anger, quarrels, dissensions, factions, envy, drunkenness, carousing, and things like these. I am warning you, as I warned you before: those who do such things will not inherit the kingdom of God. (Gal 5:19–21; cf. 1 Cor 6:9–10)

In another case, Paul upholds the Mosaic Law by forbidding a man to live with his stepmother (1 Cor 5:1–5; Deut 22:30; 27:20; Lev 18:7–8) and demands that he be cut off from the community. So it appears that perhaps Paul supports the morality of the Mosaic Law while demurring much of the proscribed rituals under the Law.

In returning to the second commonly held assumption ("The Bible teaches that when you break a law, you will be punished—'an eye for an eye'"), we can, with some degree of certainty, affirm this assumption in both the Hebrew Bible and New Testament. We can further affirm that Israel's Law (Torah), unlike the laws of its neighbors, are grounded in devotion to God. This love of God governs the way in which they worship and in the way they behave toward others. Which brings us to our third commonly held assumption.

Assumption Three: The Bible Says to Treat Others the Way We Want to Be Treated (the So-Called Golden Rule)

Our third commonly held assumption speaks to the idea of justice; we should strive to treat others equitably and expect the same in return. This sort of ethic of reciprocity is implied in the so-called Golden Rule. Most people attribute the Golden Rule to Jesus, but the truth is there is some version of it in nearly every religious system all over the world. In the Hebrew Bible, we find echoes of it in Leviticus: "You shall not take vengeance or bear a grudge against any of your people, but you shall love your neighbor as yourself" (Lev 19:18, 34). Sometimes called the Great Commandment or the Silver Rule, this ethic is meant to govern relationships, to make them reciprocal and fair. Simply put, Lev 19:18 asserts that God's people should treat their neighbors not with disrespect, but with love.

Jesus would definitely concur with the Hebrew Bible's ethic of reciprocity and proclaims as much in the Gospels of Matthew and Luke: "In everything do to others as you would have them do to you" (Matt 7:12); "Do to others as you would have them do to you" (Luke 6:31). Notice, however, that the wording is slightly different from Lev 19:18. Scholars often note that Jesus' use of the Golden Rule captures the spirit of Lev 19:18, but that it espouses more proactive measures. In other words, simply avoiding harming our neighbor is taken a step further, as Jesus enjoins us to actively work toward the good. In my college classroom, I typically turn to the Parable of the Good Samaritan (Luke 10:25–37) to further clarify Jesus' meaning. Unique to the Gospel of Luke, the Parable of the Good Samaritan is one of the best known of Jesus' parables, and you are probably already familiar with it. But consider taking a few moments to read it again, as I will simply summarize it here.

The parable is designed to answer a question posed by a lawyer in a crowd of people gathered around Jesus. The question is this: Who is my neighbor? (Luke 10:29). In order to better understand the parable, it is important to mention that during Jesus' day, Jews and Samaritans despise one another. That Jesus makes the kind-hearted Samaritan the hero in the story is what contributes to its surprising twist.

The tale begins when a man, presumably a Jew, is robbed, beaten, and left for dead on the side of the road (Luke 10:30). Two temple officials, a priest and then a Levite, pass by the injured man and do nothing (Luke 10:31–32). But when a Samaritan traveler notices the man on the side of the road, he tends to his wounds, takes him to an inn, and pays the innkeeper to care for the wounded man until he (the Samaritan) returns for him (Luke 10:33–35). When Jesus finishes telling the story, he turns to the lawyer, and presumably the crowd, and asks, "Which of these three, do you think, was a neighbor to the man who fell into the hands of the robbers?" (Luke 10: 36), to which the lawyer responds, "The one who showed him mercy" (Luke 10:37). Jesus instructs the lawyer to "Go and do likewise" (Luke 10:37), thus providing a response to the lawyer's question: "Who is my neighbor?" If you missed the point, the answer to this question is *everyone*. In the divisive world of ancient Israel—where Jews and Samaritans are sworn enemies—this is a radical message. We can almost hear the gasps of shock as Jesus tells the story. Of course, the parable is one of Jesus' primary methods of teaching, precisely because of the shock value parables often provide. What better way to educate his listeners than to include life lessons within the context of a great story!

Paul, despite having a few issues with the Mosaic Law, says that the ethic of reciprocity captures the spirit of the Law and all of God's Commandments: "For the whole law is summed up in a single commandment, 'You shall love your neighbor as yourself'" (Gal 5:14; Rom 13:9). In this, Paul asserts the primacy of the so-called Silver Rule (Lev 19:18). He also echoes Jesus' proactive stance when it comes to the Golden Rule. For example, Paul encourages husbands and wives to treat one another similarly as they work toward a reciprocal sexual relationship:

> The husband should give to his wife her conjugal rights, and likewise the wife to her husband. For the wife does not have authority over

her own body, but the husband does; likewise the husband does not have authority over his own body, but the wife does. (1 Cor 7:3–4)

In reference to our third common assumption ("The Bible says we should treat others the way we want to be treated—the so-called Golden Rule"), we must conclude that this assumption finds support in both the Hebrew Bible and New Testament. The ethic of reciprocity speaks to a basic notion of fairness, something that is likewise implied in Israel's legal codes. In a sense, much of what we have covered thus far seems quite simple: Treat others justly. But how does the Bible understand justice? Since this question is better answered in the context of fair treatment of those less fortunate, let us move on to our final common assumption.

Assumption Four: The Bible Says We Should Take Care of Those Less Fortunate

In chapter 6, we briefly explored the Bible's position regarding wealth and riches and determined that the Bible clearly delineates the obligations the rich have toward the economically poor. We will not revisit the areas covered in chapter 6 here; instead, we will focus on the manner in which the Bible identifies "those less fortunate" and God's imperative to render them assistance.

We begin by first reviewing the biblical concept of justice. Justice, as noted earlier, means treating others with fairness. The Law in Israel is constructed around this concept, and practicing justice not only is demanded by God but also reflects God's own nature. Just actions are expected in all areas of life—between persons, within governments, and within religious institutions. Sometimes the term "righteousness" is used in the Bible to indicate justice, and though some scholars argue that justice and righteousness are different, most agree that they are basically the same thing. In this brief discussion, we will assume that they are rooted in the same idea.

The fourth common assumption implies that an aspect of justice means taking care of those less fortunate, but who exactly are we talking about when we discuss the "less fortunate"? Generally speaking, in the Bible, this means anyone who has been oppressed or deprived of basic human rights. This class of people is referred to by several names, but the most common is the *anawim*, from the Hebrew meaning "bent down" or "being low." Widows and orphans are most often cited. Without the protection of a male figure, widows and fatherless children are vulnerable and often exploited. God admonishes his people to care for them (Exod 22:22–24; Deut 14:28–29; 24:17–22; Ps 82:3–4; Prov 23:10; Is 1:17, 23;

10:1–2; Job 29:12–13; 31:16–23; Zech 7:10; Jer 7:6–7; Mal 3:5), but the prophets indicate that widespread neglect, and even abuse, is common.

The needy also include the poor and the sick, the disenfranchised and the swindled, the enslaved and sojourners, and many more wretched folk who somehow feel the pain of life's unfairness (Job 29:12–17; Ps 146:7–9; Matt 9:35–38). As already noted in the previous commonly held assumptions, Israel's laws stipulate fair and equitable treatment for all of God's people. And the Law and the prophets make it clear that God is on the side of those less fortunate. When things go awry, God dispenses special envoys—the prophets—to speak on his behalf.

The classical prophetic tradition is usually dated from 750 to 400 BCE and is uniquely tied to the institution of the monarchy. It is no coincidence that the prophetic movement parallels a period of great social, economic, and religious change in Israel. The nation—which is by this time divided, with Israel to the north and Judah to the south—is riddled with injustice.

The rich, ruling class forsakes the Law (Amos 8:4–6; Is 10:1–2), neglects the poor (Amos 2:6–8; Is 3:13–15; Mic 2:8–9), and rejects the LORD in favor of the Canaanite fertility cults (Hos 1:2–9; 2:5–7; Jer 32:31–35). Those entrusted to care for the people and those with the power and the means to do so are instead the instigators of social injustice. Israel's kings are notoriously guilty (Jer 23:1–3; Ezek 22:6–22). God makes his expectations clear, however; kings are to treat their subjects fairly and to be mindful of the less fortunate:

> Act with justice and righteousness, and deliver from the hand of the oppressor anyone who has been robbed. And do no wrong or violence to the alien, the orphan, and the widow, or shed innocent blood. (Jer 22:3)

But, in speaking to the corrupt King Jehoiakim, the prophet Jeremiah asserts that the opposite is the case:

> But your eyes and heart are only on your dishonest gain,
> for shedding innocent blood,
> and for practicing oppression
> and violence. (Jer 22:17)

This sort of despotic behavior is characteristic of many of Israel's kings and, according to the prophets, contributes to the Exile (Jeremiah 21; 22:11–12). The prophets hone the idea that foreign powers are summoned by the LORD to be used as his rod in the punishment of guilty nations (Amos 3:6; 5:1–3; Is 10:5–6).

Even the court officials, who are called to render just and fair decisions, abrogate their duties by abusing the needy and accepting bribes:

> For I know how many are your transgressions,
> and how great are your sins—
> you who afflict the righteous, who
> take a bribe,
> and push aside the needy in
> the gate. (Amos 5:12; cf. Jer 5:28)

The wealthy elite, as a class, are likewise condemned (Ezek 22:1–16), including the spoiled and pampered wives of rich men (Is 3:16–17; Amos 4:1).

> The LORD enters into judgment
> with the elders and princes of
> his people: It is you who have devoured the
> vineyard;
> the spoil of the poor is in your
> houses. What do you mean by crushing
> my people,
> by grinding the face of the
> poor? says the LORD God
> of hosts. (Is 3:14–15)

The rich reduce others to poverty by illegally seizing their property (Is 3:13–15; Mic 2:1–2, 8–9), cheating them in business transactions (Amos 8:4–5; Hos 12:7; Mic 6:10–11), and calling in debts that the poor cannot repay, reducing some to slavery (Amos 2:4–6).

The situation painted by the prophets is a bleak one. The rampant social injustice and mistreatment of the *anawim* continue into the first century, when Jesus confronts it head on. In the Gospels, Jesus demonstrates that he is on the side of the needy and publicly proclaims himself as the fulfillment of Isaiah's messianic vision (Is 61:1–2):

> "The Spirit of the Lord is upon
> me,
> because he has anointed me
> to bring good news to the

Making the God Connection
COMMUNICATING WITH GOD THROUGH PRAYER AND WORSHIP

I have lived to thank God that not all my prayers have been answered.

—JEAN INGELOW

T he way in which humans pray and worship the Divine is as old as religion itself. From the earliest human records, primitive people have turned to God or the gods for help—for success in the hunt, rains to nourish the fields, and protection against enemies. Big questions— such as what happens to us after we die—are on the minds of even the earliest humans. For example, the belief in some sort of afterlife can be dated to about 125,000–30,000 BCE with the Neanderthals, who are the first to ritually bury their dead. Tools, food, and offerings to the gods have been found in many prehistoric and ancient gravesites, perhaps viewed as necessary accoutrements for the deceased in the next world.

Simply defined, prayer is the way in which humans communicate with God or the gods. This communication can be between the Divine and an individual, or it can be communal in nature. Worship can and usually does incorporate prayer and refers to the way in which an individual or group expresses their religious devotion to God or the gods. Every religion has its own unique set of prayers, rituals, and modes of worship, and exploring these is one of the most fascinating aspects of religious studies. From the quiet contemplation of a Buddhist monk to the prostrating Muslim who prays facing Mecca five times each day to the enthusiastic Southern Baptist who sways in ecstatic praise of Jesus, prayers are as diverse as the many faces of religious faith. In this, our final chapter, we will explore what the Bible has to say about prayer and worship in the Judeo-Christian tradition in light of common assumptions held by the majority of my students and others.

As I prepared to write this chapter, I thought about many things, including my own prayer life. I recalled the many times I cried out to God during times of grief, when I was experiencing physical or emotional pain, or when I felt afraid. I thought about my prayers of gratitude for God's many blessings and felt a rush of shame when I realized that I am less likely to praise God when things are going well and much more likely to complain to God when they are not. I remembered teaching my children how to pray when they were just toddlers and snuggling close to them just before they were tucked into bed for the night, listening to their sweet words to God before they drifted off to sleep. I often told them that God pays special attention to the prayers of children, and I like to think this is so.

I also reflected upon the many different types of worship services I have attended over the years. As a religious studies professor, I have been privileged to attend all sorts of religious services beyond those of my own tribe. I have gained much insight and have a greater understanding and respect for other religious traditions as a result. Now, I ask you to take a moment and review your own prayer and worship histories and the meaning they hold for you (or do not hold for you) in your life today. Having some sense of your own personal views on these topics may help you to better appreciate the variety of religious expression the Bible offers us.

Of course, the topics of prayer and worship fall into the realm of spirituality, a sensitive area for most people, as there are many cherished beliefs individuals and groups hold dear. Some of these cherished expressions of faith are grounded in the Bible, and some are from traditions that developed beyond the pages of the Bible. Articulating your own beliefs, either in writing or through reflection, is beneficial and important, but we must be careful about bringing our own modern attitudes and beliefs about prayer and worship—either positive or negative—to our present investigation, thus reading the Bible in a biased or unilateral way. Prayer and worship in the Bible are as rich and diverse as the people of biblical antiquity. The ancient followers of Yhwh, for example, feel comfortable crying out to God in prayer for rescue while at the same time wondering why it is taking him so long to act.

> But you, O LORD, do not be far
> away!
> O my help, come quickly to
> my aid!
> Deliver my soul from the sword,
> my life from the power of the
> dog!
> Save me from the mouth of the
> lion!
> From the horns of the wild oxen
> you have rescued me. (Ps 22:19–21)

> My God, my God, why have you
> forsaken me? Why are you so far from
> helping me, from the
> words of my groaning?
> O my God, I cry by day, but you
> do not answer;
> and by night, but find no rest. (Ps 22:1–2)

They also see nothing wrong with cursing their enemies in prayer, even to the point of praying that their enemies' children will be smashed against rocks (Ps 137:8–9). As with the other topics considered in this book, we must allow the ancient writers to speak to us and approach the Bible's prayer and worship practices with both intellectual curiosity and reverence for the spiritual aspects of this type of literature.

Today, when I bring up the subjects of prayer and worship in my university classroom, most of my students look a little worried. Some have flashbacks to unfulfilling and even painful Sunday school experiences, while others view prayer, religious rituals, and worship as practices that have little or no value in their lives. For such students, a lecture or discussion about such topics makes them uneasy, mostly because they fear a sermon, and there is nothing students dislike more than a preachy professor. Other students confess that they really do not know how to pray. Few have any sort of prayer life at all. And so the topics of prayer and worship must be approached with great sensitivity, allowing for a wide variety of opinions and attitudes.

When I ask my students to focus not on their personal opinions regarding prayer and worship, but instead on what they think the Bible might have to say about these topics, they usually offer the following assumptions:

1. The Bible contains many important prayers and people are supposed to pray often.
2. The Bible says that we should pray to God to help us and that God will answer our prayers.
3. The Bible says people should regularly go to temple/church to worship God.

In past chapters, with the exception of chapter 4, I have listed four common assumptions. Usually, there are many more, but I selected only the most popular. In this chapter, I list only three; this is because students have less to say about the topics of prayer and worship, and what they do offer is often very similar in content. For example, students often state a common assumption such as "The Bible contains many prayers," or they cite a particular prayer, such as Psalm 23 ("The LORD is my shepherd") or the "Lord's Prayer." When I ask them follow-up questions such as "Why do you think there are so many prayers in the Bible?" they usually respond, "Because people are expected to pray a lot." These two concepts are so closely connected, I decided to list them as single assumption. With this brief clarification in mind, let us move forward to explore our first common assumption.

Assumption One: The Bible Contains Many Important Prayers and People Are Supposed to Pray Often

Even a novice student of the Scriptures cannot help but notice that there seems to be a lot of praying going on in the Bible. And I am referring not only to the 150 psalms in the Psalter but also to the hundreds of prayers that are scattered throughout the Hebrew Bible and New Testament. The preponderance of prayers in the Bible indicates the importance of praying in the lives of the faithful and provides a living, breathing legacy for people of faith today. Since the second half of our first common assumption, which presumes that the faithful must pray frequently, is easier to answer than the first part, which requires a more detailed exploration of the various types of prayers found in the Bible, we will begin with an examination of what the Bible says about how often the faithful should pray.

In the Hebrew Bible, most scholars cite Dan 6:6–10 as evidence that faithful are expected to pray three times each day. In this story, the prophet Daniel is cast into a pit of lions but miraculously survives. Just prior to his internment in the lion's den, Daniel prays, which apparently violates his enemies' month-long edict banning prayer directed to anyone other than the king (Dan 6:12). Daniel's opponents report his prayer activity to the king:

> Then they responded to the king, "Daniel, one of the exiles from Judah, pays no attention to you, O king, or to the interdict you have signed, but he is saying his prayers three times a day." (Dan 6:13)

The king, obliged to enforce his decree, tosses Daniel to the lions (Dan 6:16). The obligation to pray three times per day—morning, noon, and evening—is supported by Ps 55:17:

> Evening and morning and at noon
> I utter my complaint and moan,
> and he will hear my voice.

Additional prayers are recited on the Sabbath (Psalm 92) and on special feast days, but many of these come from later traditions outside the pages of the Hebrew Bible.

While praying three times each day is generally accepted as the norm, there is some evidence in the Psalms, which we will consider in a moment, that the faithful are called to incessantly praise God:

> I will bless the LORD at all times;
> his praise shall continually be in
> my mouth. (Ps 34:1)

> Upon you I have leaned from my
> birth;
> it was you who took me from
> my mother's womb.
> My praise is continually of you. (Ps 71:6)

In the New Testament, Paul echoes the psalmist's sentiments as he urges the faithful to "pray without ceasing" (1 Thess 5:17). And if you thumb through the Gospels, you will note that Jesus not only prays often (Matt 6:9–13; 14:23; Mark 1:35; Luke 10:21–24; John 17) but also urges his followers to do likewise: "Then Jesus told them a parable about their need to pray always and not to lose heart" (Luke 18:1). Indeed, there are dozens of verses in which Jesus prays, and we will explore some of them when we discuss the various types of prayers. Several other New Testament figures also "pray without ceasing," including the prophetess Anna, who prays and fasts night and day (Luke 2:37), the followers of John the Baptist, and the Pharisees (Luke 5:33).

We can conclude that the second part of our first common assumption is indeed correct; it does appear that God's people are supposed to pray often. But how do they pray? This, as I have already mentioned, is a far more complicated question, and my commentary regarding the types of prayer will be somewhat lengthy. Though hardly exhaustive, I will provide a framework here, in our first assumption, which will help guide us through the other two assumptions, which will be much briefer.

There are basically four different types of prayers found in the Bible. The first type is the prayer of praise, designed to glorify God for simply being God. Second are the prayers of thanksgiving; closely related to the prayer of praise, prayers of thanksgiving express gratitude for something that God has done. The third type is the penitential prayer, offered by an individual or community seeking God's forgiveness for some sort of transgression. The final type of prayer is the prayer of petition or supplication; these are prayers that ask for something, such as God's protection in the face of harm. What follows is an explanation of each type of prayer with examples. As always, I encourage you to read all of the cited passages, as well as the surrounding material in the Bible. Remember to pay close attention to the footnotes in your study Bible and consult your commentary as needed.

We will use the book of Psalms as our primary anchor in our discussion of prayer in this chapter. For this reason, a more detailed discussion of the Psalter seems warranted. The book of Psalms is actually a collection of different kinds of poetry spanning many centuries of history. Most biblical scholars date this book to the period of the Babylonian Exile and beyond (Psalm 137, for example, is clearly from the period of the Exile). As far as who wrote them, many psalms contain ascriptions to David, a great but flawed king who plays the harp, but the scholarly consensus and current dating of the Psalms preclude Davidic authorship. And, like many other books in the Bible, we cannot know for certain who wrote them.

The Psalter is usually divided into five books. These divisions or books are as follows: Book One: Psalms 1–41; Book Two: Psalms 42–72; Book Three: Psalms 73–89; Book Four: Psalms 90–106; and Book Five: Psalms 107–150. The notion that there are five distinct books comes from the use of the word "amen," which seems to conclude one book and begin another. Psalm 150 concludes the Psalter as a whole.

Poetic prayers set to music and meant to be sung, the Psalms are both used in communal worship and recited by individuals. The language is metaphorical and symbolic. A sharp eye will note vestiges of musical instruction to ancient choirmasters. For example, many psalms call for musical accompaniment, such as "stringed instruments" (cf. Psalms 4, 6, 54, 55, 61, and 67) or "flutes" (Psalm 5). Some psalms are to be sung to a familiar tune known to the ancient congregation, but for the most part, the music remains a mystery to us today. Such tunes include "The Deer of the Dawn" (Psalm 22), "Lilies" (cf. Psalms 45 and 69), and "The Dove on Far-off Terebinths" (Psalm 56). Other "instructions" include the word *selah* in the margins to the right of the verse, which probably means "pause," perhaps for silent prayer or for a musical interlude (cf. Ps 3:2, 4, 8).

In chapter 9, I mentioned briefly the various categories or forms of the Psalms. Scholars recognize that the Psalms have certain patterns, themes, and structures that tend to recur, which points to their liturgical use. Most communal prayers—in religious traditions all over the world—have set patterns that are familiar to worshippers, and this encourages participation and aids in memory. Scholars have noted several common structural elements in the Psalms, the most common of which is parallelism, the arrangement of two or more lines in sequential order to complete a thought. Once you understand the types of parallelism, you will begin to notice its prevalence throughout the Psalter.

One type of parallelism is *synonymous parallelism*. This is when the second line repeats the first in words or ideas:

> The earth is the LORD's and all that is in it,
> the world, and those who live in it. (Ps 24:1)

In psalms that employ the use of *antithetical parallelism*, the second line reverses the first line in words or ideas:

> For the LORD watches over the way of the righteous,
> but the way of the wicked will perish. (Ps 1:6)

Synthetic parallelism is when the second line develops or supplements the first line:

> O sing to the LORD a new song, for he has done marvelous things,
> His right hand and his holy arm have gotten him victory. (Ps 98:1)

Psalm 93 is an example of what scholars often call *staircase parallelism*. Here, you will notice that certain words—"the floods have lifted"—are repeated from the first line to amplify its meaning:

> The floods have lifted up, O LORD,
> the floods have lifted up their voice;
> the floods lift up their roaring. (Ps 93:3)

Finally, some psalms use a form of *chiastic parallelism*. The word "chiastic" is derived from the Greek letter *chi*, which is written like an X. In this type of parallelism, you can literally draw an X to create a pattern, as in the following example from Psalm 91, which describes how God will protect the psalmist. Notice the X parallel, between "He will cover you" and "you will find refuge" and "with pinions" and "under his wings" (*pinions* is just another name for wings).

> He will cover you with his pinions,
> and under his wings you will find refuge. (Ps 91:4)

In addition to these nifty structural elements, scholars also note certain forms. The various forms of the Psalms include psalms of praise (hymns), psalms of lament (the majority of psalms fall into this category), psalms of trust, royal psalms, and wisdom psalms. With this brief excursus into the structure and form of the Psalms, we now return to the various types of prayers found in the Bible.

Prayers of Praise

Sometimes referred to as a hymn, the prayer of praise expresses devotion to God. Devotion, of course, can be demonstrated in a variety of ways, such as through music, poetry, or caring for others, but our focus here is on prayer. It is common for God's people to offer him praise because they understand that all blessings come from God. For example, Hannah, the mother of the great prophet Samuel, praises God in a moving song that has deep connections to Mary's Magnificat in the Gospel of Luke (Luke 1:46–55):

> My heart exults in the LORD;
> my strength is exulted in my
> God. . . .
> There is no Holy One like the
> LORD,
> no one besides you. (1 Sam 2:1–2)

Hannah is a pious figure who, like the matriarchs Sarah, Rebekah, and Rachel, is barren. She prays for a son, and God answers her prayers; in return, she gives up her son so that he may serve the LORD at the temple in Shiloh (1 Sam 1:24). The temple at Shiloh precedes the building of the great Temple in Jerusalem under King Solomon. If you read your footnote in your study Bible, you will notice that Hannah's prayer is probably written at a later date and inserted into 1 Samuel 2 by an ancient editor and reflects later concerns associated with the monarchy. In any case, her prayer, among other things, praises God and extols his many virtues.

The prophet known as First Isaiah also celebrates God's majesty:

O LORD, you are my God;
I will exalt you, I will praise
your name;
for you have done wonderful
things. (Is 25:1)

Third Isaiah asserts that humans are, in a sense, created to praise the LORD:

[T]he people whom I formed
for myself
so that they might declare
my praise. (Is 43:21)

There are many prayers of praise in the New Testament that reflect Third Isaiah's conviction, such as Mary's Magnificat (Luke 1:46–55), just mentioned, and the hymn of praise intoned by the heavenly host in the night sky above the shepherds' field on Christmas Eve, known as the *Gloria in excelsis* (Luke 2:14). But the most concentrated prayers of all five types, including the prayers of praise, are found in the Psalter. Most of the Psalms, regardless of form, contain elements of praise, but it is the hymns that are designed specifically to glorify God's goodness, justice, love, and faithfulness.

Praise the LORD, all you nations!
Extol him, all you peoples!
For great is his steadfast love
toward us,
and the faithfulness of the LORD
endures forever.
Praise the LORD! (Psalm 117)

Many hymns assert the notions that God is deserving of praise and that all of creation should join in extolling the LORD's glory.

> Praise the LORD from the earth,
> you sea monsters and all deeps,
> fire and hail, snow and frost,
> stormy wind fulfilling his
> command!
> Mountains and all hills,
> fruit trees and all cedars!
> Wild animals and all cattle,
> creeping things and flying birds! (Ps 148:7–10)

Other psalms of praise include Psalms 8, 19, 29, 33, 100, 103, 104, 111, 113, 114, 117, 135, 136, and 145–150. One final comment about the hymns of praise: Psalm 136 contains an *antiphonal response*, indicative of the liturgical use of this psalm. Such psalms contain what scholars presume to be a congregational response that follows each proclamation—in this case, the congregation responds with "for his steadfast love endures forever."

> O gives thanks to the LORD, for he
> is good,
> for his steadfast love endures
> forever.
> O give thanks to the God of gods,
> for his steadfast love endures
> forever.
> O give thanks to the Lord of
> lords,
> for his steadfast love endures
> forever. (Ps 136:1–3)

Prayers of Thanksgiving

The second type of prayer found in the Bible is one of thanksgiving. These prayers have a joyous element associated with them and are close cousins to the hymns or prayers of praise. There are prayers of thanksgiving throughout the Hebrew Bible and New Testament. For example, Moses and Miriam lead the people in a song of thanksgiving after they cross the sea and escape Pharaoh's army (Exod 15:1–21), and the prophet Jonah thanks God for delivering him from the belly of the great fish (Jon 2:1–9).

King David formalizes the prayer of thanksgiving among the people with a moving psalm (1 Chron 16:8–36) as the Ark of the Convent is brought back to Jerusalem.

In the New Testament, Paul offers thanksgiving to God for the members of his congregations (Phil 1:3) even as he thanks them for their prayers (2 Cor 1:11). In fact, most of Paul's letters begin with thanksgiving. Certain actions, in Paul's opinion, are also intended as thanksgiving, including observing the LORD's Day, grace before meals, and fasting (Romans 14).

In the Gospels, Jesus also offers many prayers of thanksgiving. For example, he thanks God that the pure of heart (here called "infants") have received his message, for it is intended for them. The arrogant Temple hierarchy (in the Gospels, usually the Pharisees and Scribes), who by virtue of their education should recognize the Messiah, do not.

> I thank you, Father, Lord of heaven and earth, because you have hidden these things from the wise and the intelligent and have revealed them to infants; yes, Father, for such was your gracious will. (Matt 11:25–26; cf. Luke 10:21)

In the "feeding stories" Jesus also gives thanks before nourishing the multitudes that have come to hear him preach:

> Taking the five loaves and the two fish, he looked up to heaven, and blessed and broke the loaves, and gave them to his disciples to set before the people; and he divided the two fish among them all. (Mark 6:41)

And, in what is perhaps his most moving miracle, Jesus prays before raising his friend Lazarus from the dead. His prayer, in front of the crowd of mourners who witness this miracle, inspires the faithful to believe that God is always attentive to their prayers:

> So they took away the stone. And Jesus looked upward and said, "Father, I thank you for having heard me. I knew that you always hear me, but I have said this for the sake of the crowd standing here, so that they may believe that you sent me." (John 11:41–42)

Though there are thanksgiving prayers scattered throughout the Bible, the Psalter contains more thanksgiving prayers than any other book in the Bible. As with all prayers of thanksgiving, the thanksgiving psalms express gratitude for God's many gifts or saving actions and can either be individual or communal in nature. Some thanksgiving psalms offer appreciation to God for his steadfast love and faithfulness and for creating the world (Ps 118:1; 138:2). Others offer thanks to God for rescuing the psalmist from his or her enemies:

> I will give thanks to the LORD
> with my whole heart;
> I will tell of all your wonderful
> deeds.
> I will be glad and exult in you;
> I will sing praise to your name,
> O Most High.
> When my enemies turned back,
> they stumbled and perished
> before you. (Ps 9:1–3)

Psalm 9 is an excellent example of an individual thanksgiving psalm (cf. Psalms 32, 34, 41, 92, 116, and 138), but it is also an *acrostic* psalm. Depending on which study Bible you are using, you will likely see mention of this in the footnote associated with Psalm 9. Acrostic psalms are those in which sequential letters of the Hebrew alphabet begin every verse, line, or (in this case) every second verse. Other acrostic psalms include Psalms 10, 25, 34, 37, 111, 112, 119, and 145.

Psalm 67 is a good example of a communal thanksgiving prayer. In this particular psalm, the community offers gratitude to God for a good harvest:

> The earth has yielded its increase;
> God, our God, has blessed us.
> May God continue to bless us;
> let all the ends of the earth
> revere him. (Ps 67:6–7)

Other communal thanksgiving psalms include Psalms 68, 75, 118, and 124. As you read some of these psalms, you will undoubtedly notice an outpouring of gratitude as the psalmist celebrates God's generosity.

Penitential Prayers

The third type of prayer is a prayer of contrition and one in which the individual or group confesses his/her/their sins and asks for God's forgiveness.

This type of prayer is relatively rare in the Bible, despite the fact that God's Chosen Ones often fall woefully short of keeping up their end of the covenant. There are a few instances when the transgressor admits his or her wrongdoing, such as when David concedes that maybe it was not such a good idea for him to take the wife of Uriah, impregnate her, and then arrange to have her husband conveniently murdered (2 Samuel 11–12). But while David admits that he "sinned against the LORD" (2 Sam 12:13), his admission is not really a prayer.

Aside from the Psalter, we will look at three often-cited penitential prayers in the Hebrew Bible. There are others, of course, but we will concentrate on the three most popular. All of these prayers are postexilic and all are in prose form, as opposed to the poetic form found in the Psalms. The first comes to us from the books of Ezra and Nehemiah, a set of complex texts that help us to understand the period of Jewish return after the Exile. There is much debate surrounding Ezra and Nehemiah in scholarly circles, including questions about whether we are really dealing with two texts or just one and concerns that relate to the final editing and arrangement of material in both books. The composition of the books of Ezra and Nehemiah, named after the starring characters in each text, is uncertain. Authorship is equally uncertain, but the general consensus is that the same hand responsible for 1–2 Chronicles writes much of the material found in Ezra-Nehemiah and that Ezra and Nehemiah are written around the beginning of the fourth century BCE. Scholars by and large agree that despite the arrangement of these two books in the canon (Ezra precedes Nehemiah), historically, Nehemiah should come first. The individual known only as Nehemiah serves as a sort of puppet governor in Judah under the watchful eye of the Persian Empire and is instrumental in the rebuilding of the wall surrounding Jerusalem. Ezra is a priest and a scribe who seeks purification of the Jewish people through adherence to the Mosaic Covenant.

Both Ezra and Nehemiah are active in the restoration of Israel after the Exile. The books that bear their names reflect an interest in rebuilding the Temple and the repatriation of the community of believers. In order for things to go smoothly, the people must adhere to the covenant. When Ezra hears that this is not the case and that some men have married foreign wives, a practice clearly forbidden in the Torah (Deut 7:3–4), he falls to his knees and offers a rather lengthy penitential prayer on behalf of his impious community (Ezra 9:6–15):

O my God, I am too ashamed and embarrassed to lift my face to you, my God, for our iniquities have risen higher than our heads, and our guilt has mounted up to the heavens. (Ezra 9:6)

After expressing his humiliation, Ezra recounts God's saving grace in delivering the people from the Exile, despite the fact that the people continually fail to live up to their covenantal responsibilities. Such a failure in the past led to the Exile, but God in his mercy eventually liberates them. Is this is how they demonstrate their gratitude—by marrying foreign brides? Ezra is clearly distressed with the pollution of the cult with non-Jewish wives and the possible reprisals that may be coming (Ezra 9:8–15).

Another prayer attributed to Ezra is found in Neh 9:6–37. This prayer is also one of contrition and recounts Israel's crimes with a rap sheet that includes idolatry (Neh 9:18), murder, and blasphemy (Neh 9:26). Despite the people's iniquitous history and failure to honor the covenant, however, God once again demonstrates mercy (Neh 9:31). Nehemiah also offers a penitential prayer on behalf of his sinful people: "I now pray before you day and night for your servants, the people of Israel, confessing the sins of the people of Israel, which we have sinned against you" (Neh 1:6). Nehemiah includes his own family—along with the family of Israel—as transgressors who fail to keep the LORD's Commandments (Neh 1:6–8).

The postexilic prophet Daniel offers a similar prayer of contrition and, like Ezra, indicts all the people as guilty, including the kings, officials, priests, and ancestors:

> Open shame, O LORD, falls on us, our kings, our officials, and our ancestors, because we have sinned against you. To the LORD our God belong mercy and forgiveness, for we have rebelled against him, and have not obeyed the voice of the LORD our God by following his laws, which he set before us by his servants the prophets. (Dan 9:8–10; cf. Neh 9:33–34)

Daniel fasts and prays for his people as he reflects upon passages from Jeremiah (Jer 25:11–12; 29:10), which indicate a seventy-year exile from the land (Dan 9:2). It is clear to Daniel that the crimes of the people warrant punishment from God (Dan 9:4–6), but he nonetheless concludes his prayer with a plea for forgiveness and mercy, elements common to most penitential prayers: "O Lord, hear; O Lord, forgive; O Lord, listen and act and do not delay!" (Dan 9:19).

Before we examine the penitential prayers in the Psalter, let us briefly explore the New Testament's version of prayers of contrition. Interestingly, the New Testament has very few structured prayers—certainly nothing even approximating the Psalms—and so there are few penitential prayers for us to consider. Paul's letters sometimes speak of the need for repentance (Rom 2:4), but he does not provide us with any formal penitential prayers as such. The accent on prayer in the Gospels seems more concerned with teaching people how to pray (Matt 6:5–13; Luke 11:2–4). For instance, when Jesus recites the Lord's Prayer (or the Our Father), he demonstrates the way in which his followers should pray (Matt 6:9–13; cf. Luke 11:2–4). The Lord's Prayer, considered by Christians to be foundational to their faith, is really a mixed prayer of praise, petition, and penitence. Forgiveness, of course, is an important aspect of the prayer of penitence (Matt 6:14–15), and in the Lord's Prayer believers are to both ask for and offer forgiveness:

> And forgive us our debts,
> as we also have forgiven
> our debtors. (Matt 6:12)

One of the most heartfelt prayers of contrition in the New Testament is that of the tax collector featured in one of Jesus' parables in the Gospel of Luke. Continuing a common motif from the Hebrew Bible, Jesus contrasts one who does the right thing versus one who does the wrong thing. In this case, the phony piety of the Pharisee versus the contrite heart of the tax collector—the latter of whom is reviled by ancient Jews, who view tax collectors as nothing short of collaborators with Rome. In the parable, the Pharisee offers this prayer:

> God, I thank you that I am not like other people: thieves, rogues, adulterers, or even like this tax collector. I fast twice a week; I give a tenth of all my income. (Luke 18:11–12)

His prayer is full of arrogance and self-congratulatory praise for observing the letter of the Law. Jesus then describes the prayer of the despised tax collector: "But the tax collector, standing far off, would not even look up to heaven, but was beating his breast and saying, 'God, be merciful to me, a sinner!'" (Luke 18:13). The tax collector echoes Daniel and Ezra in his humble and contrite manner before God (Dan 9:8; Ezra 9:6). Jesus uses the tax collector's penitential prayer as an occasion to further instruct his followers how to pray—with a sincere heart rather than for show (Luke 18:14).

This attitude of contriteness has roots in the seven penitential psalms in the Psalter. Psalms 6, 32, 38, 51, 102, 130, and 143 are often called psalms of confession or penitence; however, except for Psalm 32, an individual prayer of thanksgiving, they are structurally and thematically individual lament psalms. Because of the tenor of repentance in these psalms, however, they have been grouped together since about the seventh century. I encourage you to take a moment and read each of the seven penitential psalms; I personally find them among the most moving prayers in the Psalter.

There are both individual and communal laments in the Psalter and, as I mentioned earlier, the lament represents the most common genre in the book of Psalms. Laments function as an expression of fear, pain, bewilderment, and terror in the face of physical or emotional illness or under threat from one's adversaries. A forward motion can be detected—indeed, felt—in the lament. This motion brings the psalmist from despair to joy as he or she envisions God's rescue. As with most psalms, there is a sequential structure. In laments, this includes an address to God and description of the crisis or complaint, an expression of trust in God's ability to save, deliverance or assurance of future help, and praise of God's actions, either in the present moment or at some future date.

The penitential psalms all have elements typically associated with penitential prayers such as confession (Pss 32:5; 38:18), supplication (Pss 6:9; 143:1), forgiveness (Pss 32:1; 51:1–4, 9; 130:4), and sorrow or contriteness for one's deeds (Ps 51:17). While space does not afford us a close reading of all seven penitential psalms, two deserve special mention: Psalm 51 and Psalm 130.

Psalm 51 is perhaps one of the most well-known psalms in the Psalter. Often referred to as the *Miserere* (from the Latin translation of the first verse *Miserere mei, Deus*—Have mercy on me, O God), most scholars feel the psalmist is sick and in need of healing. It is unclear whether this condition is physical or emotional, but in the Hebrew Bible illness of any type is directly linked to sin. The psalmist is painfully aware that past actions have occasioned the present crisis and does not attempt to whitewash the past, but instead pleads for God's mercy:

> Have mercy on me,
> O God, according to your steadfast love;
> according to your abundant mercy
> blot out my transgressions.
> Wash me thoroughly from my
> iniquity,
> and cleanse me from my sin.
> For I know my transgressions,
> and my sin is ever before me.
> Against you, you alone, have I
> sinned,

and done what is evil in your
sight,
so that you are justified in your
sentence
and blameless when you pass
judgment. (Ps 51:1–4)

The plea for forgiveness resonates throughout Psalm 51 with phrases such as "blot out," "wash me," "cleanse me," and "purge me" (Ps 51:1–2, 7, 9–10). The contrition is real, palpable, and sincere (Ps 51:17).

Psalm 130, often referred to as *De profundis* (from the Latin translation of part of the first verse, "Out of the depths"), reflects a similar sense of deep distress. Scholars typically assume "the depths" to mean the creepy, dark underworld of *Sheol*, a place from which rescue seems impossible. Yet the psalmist expresses hope that God, in his mercy and love, will deliver him or her:

I wait for the LORD, my soul
waits,
and in his word I hope. (Ps 130:5)

The crisis that occasions the psalmist's plea is unknown, but even from the pit of despair, there is an abiding trust that God will come to the rescue (Ps 130:6–7). Perhaps this is why Psalm 130 has such deep meaning for Jews and Christians today.

In our exploration of three of the four types of prayers found in the Bible—the prayers of praise, thanksgiving, and penitence—we can deduce that our first common assumption is indeed on the mark: In the Bible, there *are* many different types of prayer, and there seems to be an expectation that God and his people should maintain a fairly constant dialogue. As we consider the final type of prayer found in the Bible, the prayer of petition, we must move on to our second common assumption, which directly addresses this type of prayer.

Assumption Two: The Bible Says That We Should Pray to God to Help Us and That God Will Answer Our Prayers

At the heart of our second common assumption is our fourth and final type of prayer: the prayer of petition. This particular type of prayer is probably most familiar to us today—in fact, when I discuss prayer with my students, some of them define prayer as simply "asking God for something."

As we have already seen, there are many other types of prayer—prayers that praise or thank God and prayers of contrition—but most of the time, prayer in the Bible involves bringing to God certain needs and asking for God's help—and this is a prayer of petition. These needs include such things as healing from a physical illness (2 Kgs 20:3; Ps 22:14–15), the alleviation of emotional duress (Pss 6:2–3; 34:18; Jer 17:14), or deliverance from one's foes (Gen 32:11; Ps 59:1). We have already noted many such needs in our discussion of the first assumption. Some petitions, however, are for more ineffable needs, such as King Solomon's prayer for wisdom (1 Kgs 3:5–9) or Jesus' prayer for strength on the eve of his crucifixion (Matt 26:36–44; Mark 14:32–42; Luke 22:40–46). Often, petitions are made on behalf of another and are called intercessory prayers (Gen 18:22–32; Exod 5:22–23; 2 Sam 12:16; 1 Kgs 17:20–21; 2 Kgs 4:32–33; Amos 7:1–6; Rom 15:13; Phil 1:9–11). There are dozens of psalms of petition, usually classified as laments, a form that is undoubtedly familiar to you by now.

The most well-known prayer of petition in the New Testament is the Lord's Prayer (Matt 6:9–13; Luke 11:2–4). I mentioned the Lord's Prayer earlier in our first assumption and classified it as a "mixed" prayer, for it contains elements of praise (Matt 6:9), penitence (Matt 6:12), and petition (Matt 6:10–13).

Central to the second common assumption is a two-pronged notion that God both hears the prayers of his people and that human prayers invite a response from God. The ancient supplicant certainly feels this is the case, as we have already observed (Pss 34:15; 65:1–2; Matt 7:11). In fact, there is an *expectation* that when the faithful "cry out" to God for help, God listens and is moved to respond (Psalm 18). This expectation is based on Israel's salvation history; that is, God always saves his people when they are in peril. This idea is most clearly reflected in the Psalms, particularly in the psalms of lament. When the psalmist cries out for help, the complaint is followed by an expression of trust that God will come to the rescue. This usually includes a reminder of God's majesty and sovereignty, indicative of God's *ability* to render assistance, but also a *recollection* of God's saving actions in the past. In Psalm 22, for example, we note a shift from the distressed psalmist's complaint in verses 1–2 to a sort of self-consoling reminder of who God is as well as God's historical record of preservation in verses 3–5:

> My God, my God, why have you
> forsaken me?
> Why are you so far from
> helping me, from the

words of my groaning?
O my God, I cry by day, but you
do not answer;
and by night, but find no rest.
Yet you are holy,
enthroned on the praises of
Israel.
In you our ancestors trusted;
they trusted, and you delivered them.
To you they cried, and were
saved;
in you they trusted, and were
not put to shame. (Ps 22:1–5)

By looking to the past, the psalmist finds hope in the midst of despair. If God rescued one's ancestors, perhaps God can rescue the psalmist too.

Sometimes in the Bible, an individual or community cries out to God because of a difficult situation. For example, the Hebrews enslaved under the cruel and nameless Egyptian Pharaoh in the Exodus story "cry out" to God for liberation (Exod 2:23), thus reminding God of the covenant with his people (Exod 2:24–25). There is no mention, of course, of how God would have forgotten that his people are languishing in the mud pits of Egypt, but for the author, the very act of crying out is sufficient to jog God's memory. Crying out to God for physical or emotional healing is also common, particularly in the lament psalms (Pss 22; 51; 107:17–20). Jesus seems to reflect this practice, reciting Psalm 22 as he suffers the pain of crucifixion (Matt 27:46).

While petition prayers are offered with the hope or expectation of rescue, there are a few conditions. As simple as it may seem, the faithful must first ask for help. In other words, the petitioner must initiate the conversation between himself or herself and God: "Ask, and it will be given to you; search, and you will find; knock, and the door will be opened for you" (Matt 7:7); "So I tell you, whatever you ask for in prayer, believe that you have received it, and it will be yours" (Mark 11:24). Second, the petitioner must trust in God: "[F]or they cried to God in the battle, and he granted their entreaty because they trusted in him" (1 Chron 5:20). And finally, the supplicant must humble himself or herself and turn away from sin, a condition that separates humans from God:

If my people who are called by my name humble themselves, pray, seek my face, and turn from their wicked ways, then I will hear from heaven, and will forgive their sin and heal their land. Now my eyes will be open and my ears attentive to the prayer that is made in this place. (2 Chron 7:14–15; cf. Is 59:12)

Our second common assumption ("The Bible says that we should pray to God to help us and that God will answer our prayers") seems to accurately capture the biblical understanding of the prayer of petition. Contemporary thinkers, and ancient ones, too, do not have to look very far, however, to find many instances when the opposite seems to be the case—when God seems to neither hear nor save. The highway of human history is littered with innumerable atrocities, punctuated by the haunting pleas of innocent victims who cry out to an unmovable God for rescue. So how can we reconcile both the biblical teaching that imagines God as the One who pays attention to our petitions and acts versus the silent and unforthcoming Deity who stands in the midst of tragedy and appears to be looking the other way? The faithful usually posit several theories regarding unanswered prayers, the most common of which interprets God's perceived silence as really an answer—and that answer is "no" (or "not yet"). Petitioners must therefore accept the fact that certain requests will not be granted—for whatever reason—or they must wait for God to render assistance at a time God deems appropriate.

Others assert that God always answers our prayers, but often the answer is not what we desire or expect. If we wait long enough, however, we will someday understand the wisdom of God's response. This position gains credence when, in hindsight, we might view some of our prayers as ill conceived. For example, a friend recently confided that she often prayed for strength and healing in her marriage; it was only after the marriage ended that she found both. In any case, prayers of petition—and all forms of prayer in the Bible—provide a "God connection" that sustains and comforts the faithful and is a central component of both Jewish and Christian worship.

Assumption Three: The Bible Says People Should Regularly Go to Temple/Church to Worship God

According to the Bible the earliest forms of worship are not in temples or churches, but in the open air. Genesis 4 is a very important chapter for many reasons, but for our purposes, it provides for us the first act of worship in the Bible. In the story, the brothers Cain and Abel each offer the LORD a sacrifice from their respective professions. The farmer, Cain, offers a sacrifice from the fruits of his fields (Gen 4:3), while the shepherd,

Abel, offers an animal sacrifice (Gen 4:4). We do not know for certain why God looks with favor on Abel's offering while rejecting Cain's, but most scholars assume that this reflects conflicts between the nomadic shepherds and farmers so common during the author's lifetime. This is a complicated conflict that goes beyond mere lifestyle choices. For instance, sheep are the most common livestock for shepherds; but when sheep graze, they graze down to the roots, effectively ruining the land. This, of course, does not endear shepherds to the farmers who wish to cultivate the land.

Equally uncertain in Genesis 4 is the reason why the brothers offer sacrifices in the first place, as there are not as yet any stipulations in the Bible that require such offerings to God. We can conjecture that perhaps the act of sacrifice is a way of thanking God or that the intention is to demonstrate faithfulness in the hopes of continued abundance, or both.

These early sacrifices seem to be spontaneous and informal, as when Noah makes his offering to the LORD after the flood (Gen 8:20) or when Jacob pours oil on a stone (Gen 28:18–22). Before the institution of the monarchy in Israel, worship is conducted outside, using earthen or stone altars (Exod 20:24–26). In Exodus, Moses receives instructions for the construction of a tabernacle—an enclosed tent structure that is to house an altar and specific instruments to be used for ritual sacrifices (Exodus 27). Eventually, the Ark of the Covenant, the box used to hold the tablets inscribed with the Ten Commandments, is also housed in the tent in a special place called the Holy of Holies. Ordained priests emerge from the tribe of Levi to oversee cultic sacrifices; the first of these priests are Moses' brother Aaron—designated as the high priest—and Aaron's four sons.

Leviticus 1–7 describes the various types of sacrifices and the regulations that must be observed when offering either an animal or cereal sacrifice. Sacrificial animals range from birds to lambs to bulls, but they all must be unblemished male animals. Grain offerings must also include a splash of oil and frankincense, the latter seeming to support the notion that the sacrifice must have a pleasing smell for the LORD (Lev 2:1–2).

There are four basic methods of sacrifice: the burnt offering, the cereal offering, the sin or trespass offering, and the peace offering. The burnt offering is an animal sacrifice used to atone for sin. This type of sacrifice demands that the entire animal be burned and none of it is set aside for human consumption. The cereal offering, also a sacrifice of atonement, stipulates that the priest may consume part of the sacrifice (Lev 2:3). The sin or trespass offering is for unintentional infractions, such as ritual impurity after childbirth (Leviticus 12; Luke 2:24). This type of sacrifice can be used to expiate the sins of an individual, community, or even the clergy. Depending upon the circumstances and economic status of those offering the sacrifice, an animal, cereal, or monetary offering may be made. The final type of sacrifice is the peace offering, used as a means to praise God. This type of sacrifice includes both animal and cereal offerings and allows a portion of each to be consumed by the priests and the others in attendance.

Israelite worship becomes more regulated—and more corrupt—under Israel's kings. King Solomon builds the great Temple in Jerusalem (the details of which can be found in 1 Kings 6–7 and 2 Chronicles 3–4) and the Temple becomes the central place of worship. Consequently, the clergy grows, both in number and in power. Priestly duties expand beyond performing sacrifices to include such things as purification rites for the ritually unclean, temple maintenance and repair, and the diagnosis and treatment of diseases. At various times, the Temple is defiled and subjected to the idolatrous and greedy whims of various kings (2 Kings 21). But, for the most part, it remains a place of pilgrimage, prayer, and, most important, the sacred place where Yhwh lives.

Our final common assumption presumes that the Bible legislates how often the faithful must congregate, and to some extent, we can note a movement from a rather loose mode of worship to a more structured one in both Judaism and Christianity. During the period of the monarchy, from about 1000 BCE to 587 BCE, the Israelites are expected to honor the Sabbath and to attend services on certain Jewish holidays, including Passover (which celebrates the liberation of the Hebrew slaves from Egyptian bondage), Shavuot (commemorating the giving of the Torah), and Sukkoth (a harvest festival). While they are expected to observe these feast days, there does not seem to have been a rigid system of penalties for those who do not participate.

The Temple is destroyed in 587 BCE when the Babylonians lay siege to Jerusalem and much of the populace is exiled to Babylonia. During the Exile, with no Temple, the practice of animal sacrifice is abandoned and many Jews adopt the religious customs of their captors. Others simply become more orthodox and cling to the old ways. During this time period, the faithful gather together to read the Torah and pray. This tradition constitutes the beginning of the synagogue—a Greek word meaning "a gathering together." Led by a special teacher (*rabbi*), the practice of gathering together continues after the Exile (Nehemiah 8) when the Jews return to rebuild and refurbish their house of worship (Ezra 1:2; 5:13). The priesthood expands to include non-Levites (Ezra 1:5) and many of the priests, especially the high priest, begin to wield considerable power.

During the time of Jesus, three dominant Jewish factions develop: the Sadducees, the Essenes, and the Pharisees. Often from aristocratic families, the Sadducees, members of the priestly class, are intellectuals who adhere to a strict observance of the Mosaic Law. They are often part of the ruling assembly (the Sanhedrin) and many collaborate with Rome. Interpreters of the Law, the Pharisees are men who come largely from the middle class. Unlike the Sadducees, the Pharisees believe in the resurrection of the dead and the coming of the Messiah (Acts 23:1–8). Paul describes himself as a Pharisee (Phil 3:5; Acts 23:6), and many scholars, including this one, believe that Jesus is also a Pharisee. The Essenes, the first-century inhabitants of the desert community of Qumran, are an austere, ultra-orthodox, secretive group who withdraw from society to form their own monastic community. The purported authors of the Dead Sea Scrolls, the Essenes are exclusively male, dress only in white garments, and practice celibacy. There are considerable conflicts—both religious and political—between these three factions, attesting to the diverse nature of Judaism during the first century.

The Temple remains the center of worship for Jesus and for the first generation of post-resurrection Christians, who are considered to be just another Jewish sect (Acts 2:46; 3:1). The Gospels record that Jesus attends Sabbath services and even teaches in the synagogue (Mark 6:2; cf. Matt 13:54; Luke 4:16–22). As a faithful Jew, he is incensed by the corruption of the Temple hierarchy, whose nitpicky reading of the Law unnecessarily burdens the faithful (Matthew 23). The Gospels tell of Jesus chasing from the Temple the money changers and sellers of animals for ritual sacrifice, who, for Jesus, are symbolic of this corruption.

> Then Jesus entered the temple and drove out all who were selling and buying in the temple, and he overturned the tables of the money changers and the seats of those who sold doves. He said to them,
>
> > "It is written,
> > 'My house shall be called a house
> > of prayer'; but you are making it a den of robbers." (Matt 21:12–13; cf. Mark 11:11, 15–19; Luke 19:45–48; John 2:13–17)

Like Jesus, Paul respects the synagogue and preaches there (Acts 17:2). As the early Christian movement expands, however, and becomes a distinct religion and not just another Jewish faction, changes in worship are inevitable. The most obvious change is in the observation of the Sabbath, which Christians move to Sunday in honor of Jesus' resurrection. There is also a change in venue, from synagogues to "house churches" (Rom 16:5).

Sacrifice moves from animal offerings to the sacrifice of the Lord's Supper (1 Cor 11:17–26) and the way in which the assembly of believers view themselves also changes. Paul asserts that Christians are "the body of Christ" (Rom 12:5; 1 Cor 12:12), an idea that promotes Christian unity, fosters solidarity, and creates a whole new identity for the ever-expanding Christian Church. There are some indications that Christians gather on the first day of the week to celebrate the Lord's Supper (Acts 20:7; 1 Cor 16:2), but this seems to be something that early Christians simply want to do rather than a requirement. If they do see themselves as Paul describes— as members of the Body of Christ—then coming together to worship seems to follow.

Returning to our third assumption ("The Bible says people should regularly go to temple/church to worship God"), we note an implication that there are certain requirements found in the Bible regarding temple/ church attendance. While there appear to be some regulations for Jews, these are largely based on the sacrificial system, which is eventually abandoned and replaced by the sacrifice of prayer. There is, however, no legislation requiring that the Christian faithful "go to church." We can therefore conclude that although the *spirit* of our third assumption is indeed correct, the Bible remains somewhat vague when it comes to specifics. We must remember that the cultic rituals, place of worship, and leadership roles within the temple/synagogue/church are evolving entities over the course of many years and that they continue to grow and change even today. Indeed, many of today's worship rituals and practices have little or no connection to the Bible, but find deep roots in cherished traditions woven into the fabric of both Judaism and Christianity.

Concluding Notes

MOVING FORWARD

From the end spring new beginnings.

—PLINY THE ELDER

In the introduction, I stated that this book is intended for a mixed audience of Christians and Jews, and those of other or no religious affiliation who are simply curious about the Bible. It is my hope that the curiosity that led you to read this book in the first place will continue to guide you and inspire you to learn more about the Bible and the fascinating world of biblical antiquity. Indeed, my primary intention in writing this book is not to provide all the answers, but to simply stimulate further interest, in hopes that you will continue to read and find meaning in the collection of ancient texts that has captured the hearts and minds of millions.

In chapter 1, the Sixty-Second Super-Easy Bible Quiz served to launch us headlong into the problem of biblical illiteracy while chapter 2 explored the historical the roots of the Problem. All subsequent chapters focused on the Solution. Chapter 3, a reference chapter, covered the Bible basics, including such things as the history and geography of the Ancient Near East as well as authorship and arrangement of the various biblical texts.

Chapters 4–10 were designed to cultivate and improve your exegetical skills through the exploration of seven important biblical themes: suffering; Heaven and hell; wealth and riches; sexuality and gender; law and justice; the environment; and, finally, prayer and worship. Regardless of the theme or passage under consideration, I asked you to pause and ask yourself three fundamental questions:

1. What does this passage have to say about God?
2. What does this passage have to say about me?
3. What does this passage have to say about others (community)?

I am hoping that you will make it your practice to ask these fundamental questions as you continue to study the Bible.

To that end, I hope that I have provided you with some valuable tools that have enabled you to feel confident in reading and interpreting the Bible. And I also hope you will continue to consider the enormous collection of books, articles, and commentaries produced by biblical scholars as means to continue your education. I have included a sizable list of resources that aided me in writing this book, and I encourage you to take a few moments to peruse the resources section to see which texts might be of interest to you.

In addition to further reading and study, you might also consider teaching something of what you have learned to others. It has been one of my greatest joys in this life to share my passion for the Bible with my students and to take them to lands associated with the Bible through student travel programs. Whether you share your newfound skills with youngsters through a religious education program, by leading a Bible study group for adults, or in simply sharing some of the Bible's rich and enduring lessons with those dear to you, I hope you will continue to do your part to help facilitate biblical literacy.

Resources

Achtemeier, Paul J. *HarperCollins Bible Dictionary*. San Francisco: Harper San Francisco, 1996.

Akenson, Donald Harmon. *Surpassing Wonder: The Invention of the Bible and the Talmuds*. Chicago: University of Chicago Press, 1998.

Albright, William Foxwell. *Archaeology and the Religion of Israel*. 5th ed. Garden City, N.Y.: Doubleday, 1968.

———. *Yahweh and the Gods of Canaan: An Historical Analysis of Two Contrasting Faiths*. Winona Lake, Ind.: Eisenbrauns, 1990.

Alighieri, Dante. *The Divine Comedy: Inferno*. Translated by Mark Musa. New York: Penguin Books, 2002.

Alter, Robert. *The Art of Biblical Narrative*. New York: Basic Books, 1981.

Anderson, Berhard W., and Katheryn Pfisterer Darr. *Understanding the Old Testament*. 4th ed. Englewood Cliffs, N.J.: Prentice Hall, 1998.

Armstrong, Karen. *A History of God*. New York: Knopf, 1993.

———. *The Bible: Books That Changed the World*. New York: Grove Press, 2007.

Bamberger, Bernard J. *Fallen Angels*. Philadelphia: Jewish Publication Society of America, 1952.

Barclay, William. *The Revelation of John*. Vol. 1. Philadelphia: Westminster, 1976.

Barrera, Julio Trebolle. *The Jewish and the Christian Bible: An Introduction to the History of the Bible*. Translated by Wilfred G. E. Watson. Grand Rapids, Mich.: Eerdmans, 1998.

Bauckham, Richard. *The Bible and Ecology: Rediscovering the Community of Creation*. Waco, Tex.: Baylor University Press, 2010.

Beasley-Murray, G. R. "The Interpretation of Daniel 7." *Catholic Bible Quarterly* 45 (1983): 44–58.

Belis, Alice Ogden. *Helpmates, Harlots, and Heroes: Women's Stories in the Hebrew Bible*. Louisville, Ky.: Westminster/John Knox Press, 1994.

Bergant, Dianne. *Job, Ecclesiastes*. Old Testament Message 18. Wilmington, Del.: Michael Glazier, 1982.

———. *Song of Songs: The Love Poetry of Scripture*. Hyde Park, N.Y.: New City Press, 1998.

Berlin, Adele, and Marc Zvi Brettler. *The Jewish Study Bible*. New York: Oxford University Press, 2004.

Berry, R. J., ed. *Environmental Stewardship: Critical Perspectives—Past and Present*. London: T & T Clark International, 2006.

Blenkinsopp, Joseph. *The Pentateuch: An Introduction to the First Five Books of the Bible*. New York: Doubleday, 1992.

Blomberg, Craig L. "Neither Poverty nor Riches: A Biblical Theology of Possessions." Vol. 7 of *New Studies in Biblical Theology*, series editor, D. A. Carson. Leicester, U.K.: Apollos, 1999.

Bos, Johanna. "Out of the Shadows: Genesis 38; Judges 4:17–22; Ruth 3." *Semeia* 42 (1988): 37–67.

Breytenbach, C., and P. L. Day. "Satan." In van der Toorn et al., *Dictionary of Deities and Demons in the Bible*, 726–32.

Brown, Raymond E., Joseph Fitzmyer, and Roland E. Murphy, eds. *The Jerome Biblical Commentary*. Englewood Cliffs, N.J.: Prentice-Hall, 1968.

———. *The New Jerome Biblical Commentary*. Englewood Cliffs, N.J.: Prentice-Hall, 1990.

Brueggemann, Walter. *Theology of the Old Testament: Testimony, Dispute, Advocacy*. Minneapolis, Minn.: Fortress Press, 1997.

Burns, Rita. *Old Testament Message 3: Exodus, Leviticus, Numbers*. Wilmington, Del.: Michael Glazier, Inc., 1983.

Carus, Paul. *The History of the Devil and the Idea of Evil*. New York: Gramercy Books, 1996.

Charlesworth, James H., ed. *The Old Testament Pseudepigrapha*. 2 vols. New York: Doubleday, 1983.

Collins, Raymond F. "Divorce in the New Testament." Vol. 38 of *Good News Studies*, consulting editor, Robert J. Karris, O.F.M. Collegeville, Minn.: The Liturgical Press, 1992.

———. "Sexual Ethics and the New Testament: Behavior and Belief." *Companions to the New Testament*. New York: Crossroad, 2000.

Clifford, Richard, S.J. *Old Testament Message 4: Deuteronomy*. Wilmington, Del.: Michael Glazier, Inc., 1989.

Coogan, Michael David, ed. *The New Oxford Annotated Bible with the Apocryphal/Deuterocanonical Books*. 3rd ed. New York: Oxford University Press, 2001.

Cook, Stephen L. *Prophecy and Apocalypticism: The Postexilic Social Setting*. Minneapolis, Minn.: Fortress Press, 1995.

Crim, Keith. *The Perennial Dictionary of World Religions*. San Francisco: Harper San Francisco, 1989.

Cross, Frank Moore. *Canaanite Myth and Hebrew Epic: Essays in the History of the Religion of Israel*. Cambridge, Mass.: Harvard University Press, 1973.

Dahood, Mitchell. "Three Parallel Pairs in Ecclesiastes 10:18." *Jewish Quarterly Review* 62 (1971): 84–85.

Dalley, Stephanie. *Myths from Mesopotamia*: Oxford World's Classics. Oxford: Oxford University Press, 2000.

D'Aragon, Jean-Louis. "The Apocalypse." In Brown et al., *The Jerome Biblical Commentary*, 482 (NT).

Davies, Philip. *Scribes and Schools: The Canonization of the Hebrew Scriptures*. Louisville, Ky.: Westminster John Knox, 1998.

Day, Peggy L. *An Adversary in Heaven: "Satan" in the Hebrew Bible*. Atlanta, Ga.: Scholars Press, 1988.

Deen, Edith. *All the Women of the Bible*. New York: Harper Collins, 1988.

De Hamel, Christopher. *The Book: A History of the Bible*. London: Phaidon, 2001.

Demers, Patricia. *Women as Interpreters of the Bible*. New York: Paulist Press, 1992.

Dempsey, Carol J. *Justice: A Biblical Perspective*. St. Louis, Mo.: Chalice Press, 2008.

Ehrman, Bart D. *A Brief Introduction to the New Testament*. New York: Oxford University Press, 2008.

Eisenman, R., and M. Wise. *The Dead Sea Scrolls Uncovered*. New York: Barnes & Noble, 1992.

Fee, Gordon D., and Douglas Stuart. *How to Read the Bible for All Its Worth*. Grand Rapids, Mich.: Zondervan, 2003.

Finkelstein, Israel, and Neil Asher Silberman. *The Bible Unearthed: Archaeology's New Vision of Ancient Israel and the Origin of Its Sacred Texts*. New York: Simon & Schuster, 2002.

Fitzmeyer, Joseph A. "The Letter to the Romans." In Brown et al., *The Jerome Biblical Commentary*, 330 (NT).

Forsyth, Neil. *The Old Enemy: Satan and the Combat Myth*. Princeton, N.J.: Princeton University Press, 1987.

Foster, Charles. *The Selfless Gene: Living with God and Darwin*. London: Hodder & Stoughton, 2009.

Freedman, David Noel, ed. *Anchor Bible Dictionary*. 6 vols. New York: Doubleday, 1992.

Friedman, Richard Elliot. *Commentary on the Torah: With a New English Translation*. New York: Harper San Francisco, 2001.

Futato, Mark D. "Interpreting the Psalms: An Exegetical Handbook." In *Handbooks for Old Testament Exegesis*, series editor, David M. Howard Jr. Grand Rapids, Mich.: Kregel, 2007.

Garbini, Giovanni. *History and Ideology in Ancient Israel*. Translated by John Bowden. New York: Crossroad, 1988.

George, Andrew. *The Epic of Gilgamesh: A New Translation*. New York: Barnes & Noble, 1999.

Getty, Mary Ann. "1 Corinthians." In Karris, *The Collegeville Bible Commentary*, 1100–1104 (NT).

———. "2 Corinthians." In Karris, *The Collegeville Bible Commentary*, 1100–1133 (NT).

Gibson, J. C. L. *Language and Imagery in the Old Testament*. Peabody, Mass.: Hendrickson, 1998.

Ginzberg, Louis. *The Legends of the Jews*. 7 vols. Baltimore: Johns Hopkins University Press, 1998.

Godolpin, F. R. B., ed. *Great Classical Myths*. New York: Random House, 1964.

Gollwitzer, Helmut. *Song of Love: A Biblical Understanding of Sex*. Philadelphia: Fortress Press, 1979.

Gordon, Cyrus H. *Ugaritic Literature: A Comprehensive Translation of the Poetic and Prose Texts*. Rome: Pontificiom Institutum Biblicum, 1949.

Gunkel, Hermann. *Genesis*. Macon, Ga.: Mercer University Press, 1997.

Habel, Norman. *The Book of Job: A Commentary*. London: Cambridge University Press, 1975.

Hanson, Paul D. *Isaiah 40–66*. Interpretation. Louisville, Ky.: John Knox, 1989.

Harrelson, Walter. *The New Interpreter's Study Bible: New Revised Standard Version with the Apocrypha*. Nashville, Tenn.: Abingdon Press, 2003.

———. *Understanding the Bible*, 6th ed. Boston: McGraw-Hill, 2003.

Harrington, Wilfrid J. *Understanding the Apocalypse*. Washington, D.C.: Corpus Books, 1969.

Harris, Stephen L. *The New Testament: A Student's Introduction*. 2nd ed. Mountain View, Calif.: Mayfield, 1995.

Hartley, John E. *The Book of Job*. Grand Rapids, Mich.: Eerdmans, 1988.

Havener, Ivan. "1 Thessalonians." In Karris, *The Collegeville Bible Commentary*, 1156 (NT).

Hillel, Daniel. *The Natural History of the Bible: An Environmental Exploration of the Hebrew Scriptures*. New York: Columbia University Press, 2005.

Huesman, John E. "Exodus." In Brown et al., *The Jerome Biblical Commentary*, 50–51 (OT)

Jameson, Fredric. *The Political Unconscious: Narrative as a Socially Symbolic Act*. Ithaca, N.Y.: Cornell University Press, 1981.

Janzen, Gerald J. *Job*. Interpretation. Atlanta, Ga.: John Knox, 1985.

Josephus, Flavius. *The Complete Works of Josephus*. Translated by W. Whiston. Grand Rapids, Mich.: Kregel, 1981.

Kaiser, Walter C., Jr., and Duane Garrett, eds. *NIV Archaeological Study Bible: An Illustrated Walk through Biblical History and Culture*. Grand Rapids, Mich.: Zondervan, 2006.

Karris, Robert J., ed. *The Collegeville Bible Commentary*. Collegeville, Minn.: Liturgical Press, 1988.

Keck, Leander E. *Paul and His Letters*. Philadelphia: Fortress, 1988.

Kee, Howard Clark. *The Beginnings of Christianity: An Introduction to the New Testament*. New York: T & T Clark International, 2005.

Keel, O. *The Song of Songs*. Minneapolis, Minn.: Fortress, 1994.

Keller, Werner. *The Bible as History*. New York: William Morrow and Co., 1981.

Kensky, Tikva Frymer. *Reading the Women of the Bible: A New Interpretation of Their Stories*. New York: Schocken Books, 2002.

Klüger, Rivkah Schärf. *Satan in the Old Testament*. Evanston, Ill.: Northwestern University Press, 1967.

Knight, George A. F. *Deutero-Isaiah: A Theological Commentary on Isaiah 40–55*. New York: Abingdon Press, 1965.

Kodell, Jerome. "Luke." In Karris, *The Collegeville Bible Commentary*, 944–45 (NT).

Kreeft, Peter. *Three Philosophies of Life: Ecclesiastes, Life as Vanity; Job, Life as Suffering; Song of Songs, Life as Love.* San Francisco: Ignatius Press, 1989.

Kugel, James L. *The Bible as It Was.* Cambridge, Mass.: Belknap Press, 1997.

Kurz, William S. *Reading Luke–Acts: Dynamics of Biblical Narrative.* Louisville, Ky.: Westminster John Knox, 1993.

Kushner, Harold S. *When Bad Things Happen to Good People.* New York: Avon Books, 1981.

Kysar, Robert. *John.* Augsburg Commentary on the New Testament. Minneapolis, Minn.: Augsburg, 1986.

Lattimore, Richard. *Hesiod: The Works and Days, Theogony, The Shield of Herakles.* Ann Arbor, Mich.: University of Michigan Press, 1965.

Lavey, Anton Szandor. *The Satanic Bible.* New York: Avon Books, 1986.

Leeming, David Adams. *Mythology: The Voyage of the Hero.* 3rd ed. Oxford: Oxford University Press, 1998.

Lemche, Niels Peter. *Prelude to Israel's Past: Background and Beginnings of Israelite History and Identity.* Translated by E. F. Maniscalco. Peabody, Mass.: Hendrickson, 1998.

Lemke, Werner E. "Hell." In *Harper Collins Bible Dictionary.* Paul Achtemeir, ed. San Francisco: Harper & Row, 1996.

Lesko, Leonard H. "Death and the Afterlife in Ancient Egyptian Thought." *Civilizations of the Ancient Near East.* Edited by Jack Sasson. 2 vols. Peabody, Mass.: Hendrickson, 2000. pp. 1763–74.

Levenson, Jon D. *Creation and the Persistence of Evil: The Jewish Drama of Divine Omnipotence.* San Francisco: Harper & Row, 1988.

———, *The Death and Resurrection of the Beloved Son: The Transformation of Child Sacrifice in Judaism and Christianity.* New Haven, Conn.: Yale University Press, 1993.

Littleton, C. Scott, ed. *Mythology: The Illustrated Anthology of World Myth and Storytelling.* London: Duncan Baird, 2002.

MacQueen, James G. *Babylon.* New York: Frederick A. Praeger, 1964.

Mally, Edward J. "The Gospel According to Mark." In Brown et al., *The Jerome Biblical Commentary*, 25 (NT).

Mason, Rex. *The Books of Haggai, Zechariah, and Malachi.* Cambridge Bible Commentary. Cambridge: Cambridge University Press, 1977.

McCann, J. Clinton, Jr. "The Book of Psalms." In *The New Interpreter's Bible.* Vol. 4. Nashville, Tenn.: Abingdon, 1996.

McKenzie, John. "The Gospel According to Matthew." In Brown et al., *The Jerome Biblical Commentary*, 68–69 (NT).

Meier, S. A. "Destroyer." In van der Toorn et al., *Dictionary of Deities and Demons in the Bible*, 240–44.

Metzger, Bruce M., and Roland Murphy, eds. *The New Oxford Annotated Bible: With Apocryphal/Deuterocanonical Books.* New York: Oxford University Press, 1994.

Meyers, Carol, Toni Craven, and Ross S. Kraemer, eds. *Women in Scripture: A Dictionary of Named and Unnamed Women in the Hebrew Bible, The Apocryphal/ Deuteroncanonical Books, and The New Testament.* New York: Houghton Mifflin Co., 2000.

Miles, Jack. *God: A Biography*. New York: Vintage, 1995.

Milgrom, Jacob. *Numbers*. JPS Torah Commentary. Philadelphia: JPS, 1990.

Milton, John, Stephen Orgel, and Jonathan Goldberg, eds. *Paradise Lost*. New York: Oxford University Press, 2004.

Mitchell, Stephen. *The Book of Job*. New York: Harper Perennial, 1987.

Mobley, Gregory, "The Wild Man in the Bible and the Ancient Near East." *Journal of Biblical Literature* 116 (1997): 217–33.

Moriarty, Frederick L. "Numbers." In Brown et al., *The Jerome Biblical Commentary*, 95 (OT).

Mounce, Robert H. *The Book of Revelation*. Grand Rapids, Mich.: Eerdmans, 1977.

Moynahan, Brian. *God's Bestseller: William Tyndale, Thomas More, and the Writing of the English Bible—a Story of Martyrdom and Betrayal*. New York: St. Martin's Press, 2002.

Nagel, Myra B. *Deliver Us from Evil: What the Bible Says about Satan*. Cleveland, Ohio: United Church Press, 1999.

Newsom, Carol A. "The Book of Job." In *The New Interpreter's Bible*. Vol. 4. Nashville, Tenn.: Abingdon, 1996.

Newsom, Carol A., and Sharon H. Ringe, eds. *The Women's Bible Commentary*. Louisville, Ky.: Westminster John Knox, 1992.

Nielsen, Kirsten. *Ruth: A Commentary*, translated by E. Broadbridge. Old Testament Library. Louisville, Ky.: Westminster/ John Knox Press, 1997.

O'Rourke, John J. "The Second Letter to the Corinthians." In Brown et al., *The Jerome Biblical Commentary*, 289 (NT).

Pagels, Elaine. *The Origin of Satan*. New York: Vintage Books, 1996.

Perkins, Pheme. *Reading the New Testament: An Introduction*. 2nd ed. New York: Paulist Press, 1988.

———. "Revelation." In Karris, *The Collegeville Bible Commentary*, 1267 (NT).

Pregeant, Russell. *Engaging the New Testament: Interdisciplinary Introduction*. Minneapolis, Minn.: Fortress, 1995.

Pritchard, James B. *Ancient Near Eastern Texts Relating to the Old Testament*. 3rd ed. Princeton, N.J.: Princeton University Press, 1969.

Puskas, Charles B., Jr. *The Letters of Paul: An Introduction*. Collegeville, Minn.: Liturgical Press, 1979.

Rawls, John. *Justice as Fairness: A Restatement*. Cambridge, Mass.: Belknap Press, 2001.

Russell, Jeffery Burton. *The Devil: Perceptions of Evil from Antiquity to Primitive Christianity*. Ithaca, N.Y.: Cornell University Press, 1977.

———. *Satan: The Early Christian Tradition*. Ithaca, N.Y.: Cornell University Press, 1981.

———. *Lucifer: The Devil in the Middle Ages*. Ithaca, N.Y.: Cornell University Press, 1984.

———. *Mephistopheles: The Devil in the Modern World*. Ithaca, N.Y.: Cornell University Press, 1986.

———. *The Prince of Darkness: Radical Evil and the Power of Good in History*. Ithaca, N.Y.: Cornell University Press, 1988.

Salzman, Todd A., and Michael G. Lawler. *The Sexual Person: Toward a Renewed Catholic Anthropology*. Washington, D.C.: Georgetown University Press, 2008.

Segal, Alan F. *Life after Death: A History of the Afterlife in Western Tradition*. New York: Doubleday, 2004.

Senior, Donald, ed. *The Catholic Study Bible*. New York: Oxford University Press, 2006.

Seow, Choon-Leong. *Ecclesiastes*. Anchor Bible 18C. New York: Doubleday, 1997.

Smelik, Klaas A. D. *Writings from Ancient Israel: A Handbook of Historical and Religious Documents*. Louisville, Ky.: Westminster John Knox, 1991.

Smith, Mark. *The Early History of God: Yahweh and the Other Deities in Ancient Israel*. 2nd ed. Grand Rapids, Mich.: Eerdmans, 2002.

Soards, Marion L. *The Apostle Paul: An Introduction to His Writings and Teaching*. New York: Paulist Press, 1987.

Speiser, E. A. *The Anchor Bible: Genesis*. New York: Doubleday & Co., Inc., 1964.

Steinberg, Naomi A. *Kinship and Marriage in Genesis: A Household Economics Perspective*. Minneapolis, Minn.: Fortress Press, 1993.

Strong, James. *New Strong's Expanded Exhaustive Concordance of the Bible*. Nashville, Tenn.: Thomas Nelson Publishers, 2010.

Stuhlmueller, Carroll. "Deutro-Isaiah." In Brown et al., *The Jerome Biblical Commentary*, 373 (OT).

———. "The Gospel According to Luke." In Brown et al., *The Jerome Biblical Commentary*, 130 (NT).

van der Toorn, Karel, Bob Becking, and Peter W. van der Horst, eds. *Dictionary of Deities and Demons in the Bible*. Rev. ed. Grand Rapids, Mich.: Eerdmans, 1999.

von Rad, Gerhard. *The Message of the Prophets*. San Francisco: Harper Collins, 1967.

Westermann, Claus. *Isaiah 40–66: A Commentary*. Philadelphia: Westminster Press, 1969.

———. *Prophetic Oracles of Salvation in the Old Testament*. Louisville: Westminster John Knox Press, 1999.

Whybray, R. N. *Isaiah 40–66*. New Century Bible Commentary. Grand Rapids, Mich.: Eerdmans, 1975.

Wilson, A. N. *Paul: The Mind of the Apostle*. New York: W. W. Norton & Co., 1997.

Woods, William. *The History of the Devil*. New York: G. P. Putnam's Sons, 1973.

Wray, T. J. *Good Girls, Bad Girls: The Enduring Lessons of Twelve Women of the Old Testament*. Lanham, Md.: Rowman & Littlefield, 2008.

Wray, T. J., and Gregory Mobley. *The Birth of Satan: Tracing the Devil's Biblical Roots*. New York: Palgrave Macmillan, 2005.

Wright, N. T. *Romans and the Theology of Paul*. Pauline Theology. Vol. III. Minneapolis, Minn.: Fortress Press, 1995.

Yee, Gale A., ed. *Judges and Method: New Approaches in Biblical Studies*. Minneapolis, Minn.: Fortress Press, 1995.

Electronic Resources

Benner, Jeff A. "Question of the Month—Subdue?" *Ancient Hebrew Research Center Biblical E-Magazine*, issue #027, May, 2006. www.ancient-hebrew .org/emagazine/

Bible History online (maps): www.bible-history.com/maps/

Newport, Frank. "One-Third of All Americans Believe the Bible Is Literally True." *The Gallup Organization.* May 25, 2007. www.gallup.com/poll/27682/ onethird-americans-believe-bible-literally-true.aspx

Index

Note to index: A *t* following a page number indicates a table on that page.

About the Author

T. J. Wray is an associate professor of religious studies at Salve Regina University in Newport, Rhode Island, where she teaches courses in biblical studies and world religions. The author of several books, including *The Birth of Satan: Tracing the Devil's Biblical Roots* (2005) and *Good Girls, Bad Girls: The Enduring Lessons of Twelve Women of the Old Testament* (2008), Dr. Wray has appeared on National Public Radio, several television documentaries on the History Channel, and various other television and radio programs across the country.